乡 村 教 师 教 育
4ACCESS模式特色教材

U0866972

YINGYU YUEDU YANJIU
XUNGUI ZIRAN DE XIANGCUN QINGHUAI

英语阅读研究：寻归自然的乡村情怀

冉力　谌艳　周榕 /主编
范丽娜　常丽 /副主编

北京师范大学出版集团
BEIJING NORMAL UNIVERSITY PUBLISHING GROUP
北京师范大学出版社

图书在版编目(CIP)数据

英语阅读研究：寻归自然的乡村情怀 / 冉力，谌艳，周榕主编．—北京：北京师范大学出版社，2021.12
乡村教师教育 4ACCESS 模式特色教材
ISBN 978-7-303-26761-3

Ⅰ.①英… Ⅱ.①冉…②谌…③周… Ⅲ.①英语—阅读教学—教学研究—中学 Ⅳ.①G633.412

中国版本图书馆 CIP 数据核字(2021)第 016543 号

营　销　中　心　电　话　010-57654738　57654736
北师大出版社高等教育与学术著作分社　http://xueda.bnup.com

YINGYU YUEDU YANJIU
出版发行：北京师范大学出版社　www.bnup.com
北京市西城区新街口外大街 12-3 号
邮政编码：100088
印　　刷：保定市中画美凯印刷有限公司
经　　销：全国新华书店
开　　本：710 mm×1 000 mm　1/16
印　　张：13
字　　数：330 千字
版　　次：2021 年 12 月第 1 版
印　　次：2021 年 12 月第 1 次印刷
定　　价：48.00 元

策划编辑：郭兴举　　责任编辑：陈　倩
美术编辑：李向昕　　装帧设计：李向昕
责任校对：康　悦　　责任印制：赵　龙

版权所有　侵权必究
反盗版、侵权举报电话：010—58800697
北京读者服务部电话：010—58808104
外埠邮购电话：010—58808083
本书如有印装质量问题，请与印制管理部联系调换。
印制管理部电话：010—58800825

前 言

根据师范生“来自乡土，回归乡土，扎根乡村教育事业”的特点，以自然文学为切入点，我们编写了《英语阅读研究：寻归自然的乡村情怀》这本教材，供高等学校师范生尤其是公费定向师范生的英语阅读课程教学使用。

《英语阅读研究：寻归自然的乡村情怀》的特点突出表现为语言与文化的结合、阅读与文学的融合、“精”与“泛”的相得益彰。本教材共分五章，每一章由 Part A、Part B、Part C、Part D 四部分构成。Part A 为与自然文学相关的经典文学选段，内容涵盖湖泊、山脉、家庭、生命与庄园，旨在通过英文原版文学作品扩大学生的词汇量，通过疑难长句提高学生的英语阅读能力，通过自然文学作品提升学生对自然的热爱之情，使其更加关注人与自然的关系。Part B 选自当下更新的三篇新闻，内容包括人类的发展与环境的保护，旨在拓展相关话题的讨论，让学生了解世界的变化与发展。Part C 为文化部分，主要介绍英美两国的文化习俗、教育体制和人文地理等。Part D 为优秀的中文文学作品选段及其权威翻译，内容涉及自然风光、乡土人文以及人在其中的成长。因此，本教材通过相对完备的系统配置，可以全面考查和系统提升学生的综合阅读能力和自然文学素养。

学生可以通过使用本教材提高英语阅读能力，增强对英语的感知力，扩大词汇量，加深对英语民族文化和社会背景知识的认识，最重要的是通过对美国自然文学选段的阅读，加深对人与自然关系的认识，升华对大自然尤其是对乡土自然的热爱之情，从而提升作为预备教师的责任感和使命感，把自己培养成符合新时代需要的应用型人才。

本教材由湖南文理学院经验丰富的一线优秀教师合作编写。由于时间匆促，加之水平有限，谬误难免，望各位读者不吝赐教并斧正。

冉 力

2020 年 5 月

目 录

Chapter 1 The Pond

Part A

《瓦尔登湖》是美国作家亨利·戴维·梭罗所著的一本著名散文集。

该书出版于 1854 年。梭罗在书中详尽地描述了他在瓦尔登湖畔一片再生林中度过的两年又两月的生活以及其间他的许多思考。瓦尔登湖地处美国马萨诸塞州东部的康科德城，离梭罗家不远。梭罗把这次经历称为简朴隐居生活的一次尝试。他在小木屋旁开荒种地，春种秋收，自给自足。他是一个自然之子，他崇尚自然，与自然交朋友，与湖水、森林和飞鸟对话，在林中观察动物和植物，在船上吹笛，在湖边钓鱼，晚上，在小木屋中记下自己的观察和思考。他追求精神生活，关注灵魂的成长。他骄傲地宣称："每个人都是自己王国的国王，与这个王国相比，沙皇帝国也不过是一个卑微小国，犹如冰天雪地中的小雪团。"梭罗以他的实际行动告诉我们：人们所追求的大部分奢侈品、所谓生活的舒适，非但没有必要，而且对人类进步大有妨碍。

美国的 19 世纪是一个辉煌的时代，一大批作家都深受超验主义的影响，生活在这一时代的梭罗也不例外。作为这个时代的代表人物，梭罗对超验主义更是身体力行。《瓦尔登湖》就是他这一思想的体现，它是一部蕴含了深刻哲理的散文。细细读过《瓦尔登湖》的人都有体会，他是在探求怎样实实在在地生活，怎样体验与经历有意义的生活，为自己，也为他的市民同胞，还有当时与后来的读者们。

本书以春天开始，历经了夏天、秋天和冬天，又以春天结束。这正是一个生命的轮回，终点又是起点，生命开始复苏。

这是一本宁静、恬淡、充满智慧的书，其中分析生活、批判习俗处，语语惊人，字字闪光，见解独特，耐人寻味。许多篇页的描绘形象、优美、细致，像湖水的纯洁透明，像山林的茂密翠绿，也有一些篇页说理透彻，十分精辟，给人启迪。

这是一本清新、健康、引人向上的书，对春天，对黎明，都有极其动人的描写。这里有大自然给人的澄净的空气，而无工业社会带来的环境污染。读着它，读者自然会感受到心灵的净化、精神的升华。

《瓦尔登湖》的伟大之处就在于梭罗能够通过艺术来实现自己决意要做的事业。通过创造一个有机的形式，他使自己的决定获得了新生；通过有意识的努力，他重新获得了一种成熟的恬静，如果说那不是黄金年龄的清纯狂喜的话。

整个《瓦尔登湖》记录着自我在微观宇宙历程中的经历。

如果梭罗仅仅记载了一个男人在林中的生活，或者说他仅仅是退隐到森林之中，在那儿记载着他对社会的抱怨，甚至说，如果他把这两者都合到一本书里，那么《瓦尔登湖》就不会有这一百多年的生命。

梭罗记下了人与自然的关系、人在社会中的困境和人希望提高自我精神的习性，连他自己恐怕也没有意识到自己在做什么。他一会儿为自己辩护，一会儿充满了喜悦、自由、奔放之情，一会儿又创造出一个独特的煎蛋卷，让人们在饥饿的一天中不断从中汲取营养。

Where I Lived, and What I Lived For

题注：对于新建房屋的地点，梭罗考虑过瓦尔登湖之外的其他地方。根据威廉·埃勒里·钱宁(William Ellery Channing)所言，除了下一段中提到的位于萨德伯里河(Sudbury River)西岸、哈伯德桥(Hubbard's Bridge)下的霍洛维尔(Hollowell)以外，梭罗还考虑过奇异戴尔(Weird Dell)、费尔黑文山(Fairhaven Hill)的一边(有果园的那一边)以及悬崖山(The Cliff Hill)和贝克农场(Baker Farm)。梭罗可能还考虑过弗林特湖(Flint's Pond)。

At a certain season of our life we are accustomed to consider every spot as the possible site of a house. I have thus surveyed the country on every side within a dozen miles of where I live. In imagination I have bought all the farms in succession, for all were to be bought, and I knew their price. I walked over each farmer's **premises**, tasted his wild apples, discoursed on **husbandry** with him, took his farm at his price, at any price, **mortgaging** it to him in my mind; even put a higher price on it, —took everything but a **deed** of it, —

took his word for his deed, for I dearly love to talk, —cultivated it, and him too to some extent, I trust, and withdrew when I had enjoyed it long enough, leaving him to carry it on. This experience entitled me to be regarded as a sort of **real-estate broker** by my friends. Wherever I sat, there I might live, and the landscape **radiated** from me accordingly. What is a house but a seat? —better if a country seat.[①] I discovered many a site for a house not likely to be soon improved, which some might have thought too far from the village, but to my eyes the village was too far from it. Well, there I might live, I said; and there I did live, for an hour, a summer and a winter life; saw how I could let the years run off, **buffet** the winter **through**, and see the spring come in. The future inhabitants of this region, wherever they may place their houses, may be sure that they have been anticipated. An afternoon **sufficed** to lay out the land into orchard woodlot and pasture, and to decide what fine oaks or pines should be left to stand before the door, and **whence** each **blasted tree**[②] could be seen to the best advantage; and then I let it lie, **fallow perchance**, for a man is rich in proportion to the number of things which he can afford to let alone.

premises[ˈpremɪsɪz]: *n.* 房屋建筑及附属场地
husbandry[ˈhʌzbəndri]: *n.* 农事;耕作
mortgage[ˈmɔːɡɪdʒ]: *v.* 抵押
deed[diːd]: *n.* 契约
real-estate broker: 房地产经纪人
radiate[ˈreɪdieɪt]: *v.* 辐射;发散
buffet through: 熬过
suffice[səˈfaɪs]: *v.* 足够
whence[wens]: *adv.* 从哪里
blasted tree: 枯萎了或枯死了的树
fallow[ˈfæləʊ]: *adj.* 休耕的
perchance[pəˈtʃɑːns]: *adv.* 或许;可能

My imagination carried me so far that I even had the refusal of several farms, —the refusal was all I wanted, —but I never got my fingers burned by actual possession. The nearest that I came to actual possession was when I bought the **Hollowell Place**, and had begun to sort my seeds, and collected materials with which to make a **wheelbarrow** to carry it on or off with; but before the owner gave me a deed of it, his wife—every man has such a wife—changed her mind and wished to keep it, and he offered me ten dollars to release him. Now, to speak the truth, I had but ten cents in the world, and it **surpassed** my arithmetic to tell, if I was that man who had ten cents, or who had a farm, or ten dollars, or all together. However, I let him keep the ten dollars and the farm too, for I had **carried it** far enough; or rather, to be generous, I sold him the farm for just what I gave for it, and, as he was not a rich man, made him a present of ten dollars, and still had my ten cents, and seeds, and materials for a wheelbarrow left. I found thus that I had been a rich man without any damage to my poverty. But I retained the landscape, and I have since annually carried off what it **yielded** without a wheelbarrow. With respect to landscapes, —

"I am **monarch** of all I survey. My right there is none to dispute. "③

Hollowell Place：霍洛维尔农场

wheelbarrow[ˈwiːlbærəʊ]：*n.* 手推车

surpass[səˈpɑːs]：*v.* 超出

carried it：此处为双关语，一是指继续开(买农场的)玩笑，二是指从经济上承受农场的负担。

yield[jiːld]：*v.* 产出

monarch[ˈmɒnək]：*n.* 君主

I have frequently seen a poet④ **withdraw**, having enjoyed the most valuable part of a farm⑤, while the **crusty** farmer supposed that he had got a few wild apples only. Why, the owner does not know it for many years when a poet has put his farm in **rhyme**⑥, the most admirable kind of invisible fence, has fairly **impounded** it, milked it, skimmed it, and got all the cream, and left the farmer only the skimmed milk.

withdraw[wɪðˈdrɔː]：*v.* 离去；走开

crusty[ˈkrʌsti]：*adj.* 粗俗的

rhyme[raɪm]：*n.* 押韵的短诗

impound[ɪmˈpaʊnd]：*v.* 围住

The real attractions of the Hollowell farm, to me, were: its complete retirement, being about two miles from the village, half a mile from the nearest neighbor, and separated from the highway by a broad field; its bounding on the river, which the owner said protected it by its fogs from **frosts** in the spring, though that was nothing to me; the gray color and **ruinous** state of the house and barn, and the **dilapidated** fences, which put such an interval between me and the last occupant; the hollow and **lichen**-covered apple trees,

gnawed by rabbits, showing what kind of neighbors I should have; but above all, the recollection I had of it from my earliest voyages up the river, when the house was concealed behind a dense **grove** of red maples, through which I heard the house-dog bark. I was **in haste** to buy it, before the **proprietor** finished getting out some rocks, cutting down the hollow apple trees, and **grubbing** up some young **birches** which had sprung up in the pasture, or, in short, had made any more of his improvements. To enjoy these advantages I was ready to carry it on; like **Atlas**, to take the world on my shoulders, —I never heard what compensation he received for that, —and do all those things which had no other motive or excuse but that I might pay for it and be **unmolested** in my possession of it; for I knew all the while that it would yield the most abundant crop of the kind I wanted if I could only afford to let it alone. But it turned out as I have said.

frost[frɒst]: *n.* 霜冻
ruinous[ˈruːɪnəs]: *adj.* 破败的
dilapidated[dɪˈlæpɪdeɪtɪd]: *adj.* 荒废的
lichen[ˈlaɪkən]: *n.* 青苔
gnaw[nɔː]: *v.* 啃; 咬
grove[grəʊv]: *n.* 小树林
in haste: 着急; 匆忙
proprietor[prəˈpraɪətə(r)]: *n.* 所有人; 业主; 农场主人
grub[grʌb]: *v.* 挖掘
birch[bɜːtʃ]: *n.* 白桦树
Atlas: 在希腊神话中, 阿特拉斯将世界扛在他的肩膀上。
unmolested[ˌʌnməˈlestɪd]: *adj.* 不受干扰的

All that I could say, then, **with respect to** farming on a large scale, (I have always cultivated a garden⑦,) was, that I had had my seeds ready.⑧ Many think that seeds improve with age. I have no doubt that time discriminates between the good and the bad; and when at last I shall plant, I shall be less likely to be disappointed. But I would say to my fellows, once for all, as long as possible live free and **uncommitted.** It makes but little difference whether you are committed to a farm or the county jail.

Old Cato, whose "**De Re Rusticâ**" is my "Cultivator", says, "When you think of getting a farm, turn it thus in your mind, not to buy greedily; nor spare your pains to look at it, and do not think it enough to go round it once. The oftener you go there the more it will please you, if it is good." I think I shall not buy greedily, but go round and round it as long as I live, and be buried in it first, that it may please me the more at last.

with respect to：关于

uncommitted[ˌʌnkəˈmɪtɪd]：*adj.* 毫无牵挂的

Old Cato：老加图[马尔库斯·波尔基乌斯·加图(Marcus Porcius Cato)]

De Re Rusticâ：《农业志》是公元前二世纪到四世纪四位罗马农业作家作品集的名称。1851年，梭罗阅读的是加图所著的《农业志》部分。

The present was my next experiment of this kind, which I purpose to describe more at length; for convenience⑨, putting the experience of two years into one. As I have said, I do not propose to write an ode to **dejection**⑩, but to **brag** as lustily as **chanticleer**⑪ in the morning, standing on his **roost**, if only to wake my neighbors up.

dejection[dɪˈdʒekʃn]：*n.* 沮丧

brag[bræg]：*v.* 自夸；引吭高歌

chanticleer[ˈtʃɑːntɪˌkliə]：*n.* 雄鸡

roost[rust]：*n.* 鸡棚

When first I took up my **abode** in the woods, that is, began to spend my nights as well as days there, which, by accident, was on Independence Day, or the fourth of July, 1845, my house was not finished for winter, but was merely a defence against the rain, without **plastering** or chimney, the walls being of rough **weather-stained** boards, with wide **chinks**, which made it cool at night. The upright white **hewn studs** and freshly **planed** door and window casings gave it a clean and airy look, especially in the morning, when its timbers were **saturated** with dew, so that I fancied that by noon some **sweet gum** would **exude** from them. To my imagination it retained throughout the day more or less of this **auroral** character, reminding me of a certain house⑫ on a mountain which I had visited the year before. This was an airy and unplastered cabin, fit to entertain a travelling god⑬, and where a goddess might trail her **garments**⑭. The winds which passed over my dwelling were such as sweep over the ridges of mountains, bearing the broken strains, or **celestial** parts only, of **terrestrial** music. The morning wind forever blows, the poem of creation is uninterrupted; but few are the ears that hear it. **Olympus** is but the outside of the earth everywhere.

abode[əˈbəʊd]：*n.* 住处；住所

plastering[ˈplæstərɪŋ]：*n.* 粉刷
weather-stained[ˈweðəsteɪnd]：*adj.* 因日晒雨淋而变色的
chink[tʃɪŋk]：*n.* 裂缝
hewn[hjuːn]：*adj.* 砍的
stud[stʌd]：*n.* 立柱
planed[pleɪnd]：*adj.* 磨平的；刨平的
saturate[ˈsætʃəreɪt]：*v.* 使浸透；使浸染
sweet gum：甜蜜的汁液
exude[ɪgˈzud]：*v.* 流出；渗出
auroral[ɔːˈrɔːrəl]：*adj.* 如曙光般迷人的
garment[ˈgɑrmənt]：*n.* 长袍
celestial[səˈlestiəl]：*adj.* 天上的；非凡的
terrestrial[təˈrestriəl]：*adj.* 地球的；陆生的
Olympus：奥林匹斯山，希腊神话中众神居住之地。

The only house I had been the owner of before, if I except a boat⑮, was a tent, which I used occasionally when making excursions in the summer, and this is still rolled up in my **garret**; but the boat, after passing from hand to hand, has gone down the stream of time⑯. With this more substantial shelter about me, I had made some progress toward settling in the world. This frame, so slightly **clad**, was a sort of **crystallization** around me, and reacted on the builder. It was suggestive somewhat as a picture in outlines. I did not need to go out doors to take the air, for the atmosphere within had lost none of its freshness. It was not so much within doors as behind a door where I sat, even in the rainiest weather. The ***Harivansa*** says, "An abode without birds is like a meat without **seasoning**." Such was not my abode, for I found myself suddenly neighbor to the birds; not by having imprisoned one, but having caged myself near them. I was not only nearer to some of those which commonly frequent the garden and the orchard, but to those wilder and more thrilling **songster**s of the forest which never, or rarely, **serenade** a villager, —the **wood-thrush**, the **veery**, the **scarlet tanager**, the **field-sparrow**, the **whippoorwill**, and many others.

garret[ˈgærət]：*n.* 阁楼
clad[klæd]：*adj.* 穿……衣服的；……覆盖的
crystallization[ˌkreɪstəlaɪˈzeɪʃn]：*n.* 晶体结构
Harivansa：《诃利世系》，印度大约五世纪关于奎师那神（Krishna）的

史诗。

seasoning[ˈsiːznɪŋ]：*n.* 作料；调味品

songster[ˈsɒŋstə(r)]：*n.* 鸣禽

serenade[ˌserəˈneɪd]：*v.* 为……弹奏或歌唱小夜曲

wood-thrush[ˈwʊdθrʌʃ]：*n.* 画眉

veery[ˈviəri]：*n.* 鸫鸟

scarlet tanager：猩红丽唐纳雀

field-sparrow[ˈfiːldspærəʊ]：*n.* 田麻雀

whippoorwill[ˈwɪpəwɪl]：*n.* 夜鹰

I was seated by the shore of a small pond, about a mile and a half south of the village of Concord and somewhat higher than it, in the midst of an extensive wood between that town and Lincoln, and about two miles south of that our only field known to fame, **Concord Battle Ground**; but I was so low in the woods that the opposite shore, half a mile off, like the rest, covered with wood, was my most distant horizon. For the first week, whenever I looked out on the pond it impressed me like a **tarn**⑰ high up on the side of a mountain, its bottom far above the surface of other lakes, and, as the sun arose, I saw it throwing off its nightly clothing of mist, and here and there, by degrees, its soft **ripples** or its smooth reflecting surface was revealed, while the mists, like ghosts, were **stealthily** withdrawing in every direction into the woods, as at the breaking up of some **nocturnal conventicle.** The very dew seemed to hang upon the trees later into the day than usual, as on the sides of mountains.

Concord Battle Ground：康科德战场，标志着美国革命开始的 1775 年 4 月 19 日的战争爆发之地。

tarn[tɑːn]：*n.* 天池

ripple[ˈrɪpl]：*n.* 波纹

stealthily[ˈstelθɪli]：*adv.* 暗地里；悄悄地

nocturnal[nɒkˈtɜːnl]：*adj.* 夜间的

conventicle[kənˈventɪkl]：*n.* 秘密会议；秘密或非法的宗教聚会

This small lake was of most value as a neighbor in the intervals of a gentle rain storm in August, when, both air and water being perfectly still, but the sky **overcast**, mid-afternoon had all the **serenity** of evening, and the woodthrush sang around, and was heard from shore to shore. A lake like this is never smoother than at such a time; and the clear portion of the air above it being shallow and darkened by clouds, the water, full of light and reflections, becomes a lower heaven itself so much the more important. From a hill top near by, where the wood had been recently cut off, there was a pleasing **vista** southward across the pond, through a wide **indentation** in the hills which form the shore there, where their opposite sides sloping toward each other suggested a stream flowing out in that direction through a wooded valley, but stream there was none. That way I looked between and over the near green hills to some distant and higher ones in the horizon, **tinged** with blue. Indeed, by standing on **tiptoe** I could catch a glimpse of some of the peaks of the still bluer and more distant mountain ranges in the north-west, those true-blue coins from heaven's own **mint**, and also of some portion of the village. But in other directions, even from this point, I could not see over or beyond the woods which surrounded me. It is well to have some water in your neighborhood, to give **buoyancy** to and float the earth. One value even of the smallest well is, that when you look into it you see that earth is not continent but **insular**. This is as important as that it keeps butter cool. ⑱ When I looked across the pond from this peak toward the **Sudbury Meadows**, which in time of flood I distinguished elevated perhaps by a **mirage** in their **seething** valley, like a coin in a basin, all the earth beyond the pond appeared like a thin **crust insulated** and floated even by this small sheet of **intervening** water, and I was reminded that this on which I dwelt was but dry land.

overcast[ˈəʊvəkɑːst]：*adj.* 灰蒙蒙的
serenity[səˈrenəti]：*n.* 宁静
vista[ˈvɪstə]：*n.* 景色
indentation[ˌɪndenˈteɪʃn]：*n.* 豁口；凹进处
tinged[tɪndʒd]：*adj.* 略带有……色的
tiptoe[ˈtɪptəʊ]：*n.* 脚尖
mint[mɪnt]：*n.* 造币厂
buoyancy[ˈbɔɪənsi]：*n.* 浮力
insular[ˈɪnsjələ]：*n.* 岛屿
Sudbury Meadows：萨德伯里草原
mirage[məˈrɑːʒ]：*n.* 海市蜃楼；幻景
seething[ˈsiːðɪŋ]：*adj.* 沸腾的；剧烈的
crust[krʌst]：*n.* 坚硬的外壳
insulate[ˈɪnsjuleɪt]：*v.* 隔离
intervening[ˌɪntəˈviːnɪŋ]：*adj.* 介于中间的

Though the view from my door was still more contracted, I did not feel crowded or **confined** in the least. There was pasture enough for my imagination. The **low shrub-oak plateau** to which the opposite shore arose, stretched away toward the prairies of the West and the steppes of **Tartary**, affording **ample** room for all the **roving** families of men. "There are none happy in the world but beings who enjoy freely a vast horizon," —said **Damodara**, when his herds required new and larger pastures.

confined[kən'faɪnd]：*adj.* 被限制的；封闭的

low shrub-oak：矮栎

plateau['plætəʊ]：*n.* 高地

Tartary['tɑːtəri]：*n.* 鞑靼式的草原

ample['æmpl]：*adj.* 充足的

roving['rəʊvɪŋ]：*adj.* 漫游的；不固定的；流浪的

Damodara：达摩达拉，奎师那神的别名。

Both place and time were changed, and I dwelt nearer to those parts of the universe and to those eras in history which had most attracted me. Where I lived was as far off as many a region viewed nightly by **astronomers.** We are **wont** to imagine rare and **delectable** places in some remote and more celestial corner of the system, behind the **constellation** of **Cassiopeia's Chair**, far from noise and disturbance. I discovered that my house actually had its site in such a withdrawn, but forever new and **unprofaned**, part of the universe. If it were worth the while to settle in those parts near to the **Pleiades** or the **Hyades**, to **Aldebaran** or **Altair**, then I was really there, or at an equal remoteness from the life which I had left behind, **dwindled** and twinkling with as fine a ray to my nearest neighbor, and to be seen only in moonless nights by him. Such was that part of creation where I had **squatted**; —

"There was a shepherd that did live,
And held his thoughts as high
As were the mounts whereon his flocks
Did hourly feed him by."[19]

What should we think of the shepherd's life if his flocks always wandered to higher pastures than his thoughts?

astronomer[ə'strɒnəmə]：*n.* 天文学家

wont[wəʊnt]：*adj.* 习惯的

delectable[dɪ'lektəbl]：*adj.* 美丽的

constellation[ˌkɒnstəˈleɪʃn]：*n.* 星座

Cassiopeia's Chair：仙后座，仙后星座中连在一起的五颗星，形状像 W。

unprofaned[ˌʌnprəˈfeɪnd]：*adj.* 不着尘埃的

Pleiades[ˈplaɪədiːz]：*n.* 昴宿星团

Hyades[ˈhaɪədiːz]：*n.* 毕宿星团

Aldebaran[ælˈdebərən]：*n.* 毕宿五

Altair[ˈælteə(r)]：*n.* 牵牛星

dwindle[ˈdwɪndl]：*v.* 减少

squat[skwɒt]：*v.* 偷住；擅自占用(房子或地方)

Every morning was a cheerful invitation to make my life of equal **simplicity**, and I may say **innocence**, with Nature herself. I have been as sincere a worshipper of **Aurora** as the Greeks. I got up early and bathed in the pond; that was a religious exercise, and one of the best things which I did. They say that characters were **engraven** on the bathing tub of king **Tching-thang** to this effect: "Renew thyself completely each day; do it again, and again, and forever again." I can understand that. Morning brings back the heroic ages. I was as much affected by the faint **hum** of a mosquito making its invisible and unimaginable tour through my apartment at earliest dawn, when I was sitting with door and windows open, as I could be by any **trumpet** that ever sang of fame. It was **Homer's requiem**; itself an ***Iliad*** and ***Odyssey*** in the air, singing its own **wrath** and wanderings. There was something **cosmical** about it; a standing advertisement, till forbidden, of the everlasting vigor and **fertility** of the world. The morning, which is the most memorable season of the day, is the awakening hour. Then there is least **somnolence** in us; and for an hour, at least, some part of us awakes which **slumbers** all the rest of the day and night. Little is to be expected of that day, if it can be called a day, to which we are not awakened by our Genius, but by the mechanical **nudging** of some **servitors**, are not awakened by our own newly-acquired force and aspirations from within, accompanied by the **undulations** of celestial music, instead of factory bells, and a fragrance filling the air—to a higher life than we fell asleep from; and thus the darkness bear its fruit, and prove itself to be good, no less than the light. That man who does not believe that each day contains an earlier, more sacred, and auroral hour than he has yet profaned, has despaired of life, and is pursuing a descending and darkening way. After a partial **cessation** of his **sensuous** life, the soul of man, or its organs rather, are reinvigorated each day, and his Genius tries again what noble life it can make. All memorable events, I should say, **transpire** in morning time and in a morning atmosphere. ***The Vedas***[20] say, "All intelligences awake with the morning." Poetry and art, and the fairest and most memorable of the actions of men, date from such an hour. All poets and heroes, like **Memnon**, are the children of Aurora, and emit their music at sunrise. To him whose elastic and vigorous thought keeps pace with the sun, the day is a **perpetual** morning. It matters not what the clocks say or the attitudes and labors of men. Morning is when I am awake and there is a dawn in me. Moral reform is the effort to throw off sleep. Why is it that men give so poor an account of their day if they have not been slumbering? They are not such poor calculators. If they had not been overcome with **drowsiness** they would have performed something. The millions are awake enough for physical labor; but only one in a million is awake enough for effective intellectual **exertion**, only one in a hundred millions to a poetic or divine life. To be awake is to be alive. I have never yet met a man who was quite awake. How could I have looked him in the face?

simplicity[sɪmˈplɪsəti]：*n.* 简单

innocence[ˈɪnəsəns]：*n.* 纯洁

Aurora：欧若拉，罗马神话中的黎明女神。她在希腊神话中的名字是厄俄斯(Eos)。

engrave[ɪnˈgreɪv]：*v.* 雕刻

Tching-thang：成汤，商朝(公元前1600—前1046)的建立者。

hum[hʌm]：*n.* 嗡嗡声

trumpet[ˈtrʌmpɪt]：*n.* 喇叭

Homer's requiem：荷马的安魂曲，可能指的是荷马称赞"一只蚊子不折不挠的勇敢，尽管被从人的皮肤上赶走，为了品尝人的鲜血，还是坚持要叮他"。

Iliad：《伊利亚特》，以阿喀琉斯的愤怒开篇。

Odyssey：《奥德赛》，希腊史诗。

wrath[ræθ]：*n.* 愤怒

cosmical[ˈkɒzmɪkl]：*n.* 宇宙的

fertility[fəˈtɪlətɪ]：*n.* 繁殖力

somnolence[ˈsɒmnələns]：*n.* 睡意

slumber[ˈslʌmbə(r)]：*v.* 睡眠；休止

nudge[nʌdʒ]：*v.* 轻推

servitor[ˈsɜːvɪtə(r)]：*n.* 男仆

undulation[ˌʌndju'leɪʃn]：*n.* 波动；起伏

cessation[se'seɪʃn]：*n.* 中断

sensuous['sensjuəs]：*adj.* 感官的；感觉上的

transpire[træn'spaɪə]：*v.* 发生；出现

The Vedas：《吠陀经》，印度教最古老和最神圣的经典，分四集传下来：《梨俱吠陀》《雅育尔吠陀》《萨马吠陀》《阿塔发吠陀》。

Memnon：门农，欧若拉的儿子，在特洛伊战争中被阿喀琉斯杀死。在底比斯附近修建的几座门农的大型雕像中，其中一座，当被太阳照暖时，会奏出音乐。

perpetual[pə'petʃuəl]：*adj.* 永恒的

drowsiness['draʊzɪnəs]：*n.* 昏昏欲睡

exertion[ɪg'zɜːʃn]：*n.* 劳动

We must learn to reawaken and keep ourselves awake, not by mechanical aids, but by an infinite expectation of the dawn, which does not **forsake** us in our soundest sleep. I know of no more encouraging fact than the unquestionable ability of man to elevate his life by a conscious **endeavor**. It is something to be able to paint a particular picture, or to carve a statue, and so to make a few objects beautiful; but it is far more glorious to carve and paint the very atmosphere and medium through which we look, which morally we can do. To affect the quality of the day, that is the highest of arts. Every man is tasked to make his life, even in its details, worthy of the **contemplation** of his most elevated and critical hour. If we refused, or rather used up, such **paltry** information as we get, the **oracles** would distinctly inform us how this might be done.

forsake[fə'seɪk]：*v.* 抛弃

endeavor[ɪn'devə(r)]：*n.* 努力

contemplation[ˌkɒntəm'pleɪʃn]：*n.* 审视

paltry['pɔːltri]：*adj.* 微不足道的

oracle['ɒrəkl]：*n.* 神谕

I went to the woods because I wished to live deliberately, to front only the essential facts of life, and see if I could not learn what it had to teach, and not, when I came to die, discover that I had not lived. I did not wish to live what was not life, living is so dear; nor did I wish to practise **resignation**, unless it was quite necessary. I wanted to live deep and suck out all the **marrow** of life, to live so **sturdily** and **Spartan**-like as to put to **rout** all that was not life, to cut a broad **swath** and shave close, to drive life into a corner, and reduce it to its lowest terms, and, if it proved to be **mean**, why then to get the whole and genuine meanness of it, and publish its meanness to the world; or if it were **sublime**, to know it by experience, and be able to give a true account of it in my next excursion. For most men, it appears to me, are in a strange uncertainty about it, whether it is of the devil or of God, and have somewhat hastily concluded that it is the chief end of man here to "glorify God and enjoy him forever".

resignation[rezɪɡˈneɪʃn]: *n.* 隐居

marrow[ˈmærəʊ]: *n.* 精髓

sturdily[ˈstəːdɪli]: *adv.* 坚强地

Spartan：斯巴达人。古希腊的斯巴达人以他们严明的纪律、简朴以及勇气和军事组织而著称于世。

rout[raʊt]: *v.* 摒弃

swath[swɒθ]: *n.* 长而宽的一条

mean[miːn]: *adj.* 卑劣的

sublime[səˈblaɪm]: *adj.* 高尚的

Still we live meanly, like ants; though the fable tells us that we were long ago changed into men[21]; like **pygmies** we fight with cranes[22]; it is error upon error, and **clout** upon clout, and our best virtue has for its occasion a **superfluous** and evitable **wretchedness.** Our life is **frittered** away by detail. An honest man has hardly need to count more than his ten fingers, or in extreme cases he may add his ten toes, and **lump** the rest. Simplicity, simplicity, simplicity! I say, let your affairs be as two or three, and not a hundred or a thousand; instead of a million count half a dozen, and keep your accounts on your thumb nail. In the midst of this chopping sea of civilized life, such are the clouds and storms and quick-sands and thousand-and-one items to be allowed for, that a man has to live, if he would not **founder** and go to the bottom and not make his port at all, by **dead reckoning**[23], and he must be a great calculator indeed who succeeds. Simplify, simplify. Instead of three meals a day, if it be necessary eat but one; instead of a hundred dishes, five; and reduce other things in proportion. Our life is like a German Confederacy[24], made up of petty states, with its boundary forever fluctuating, so that even a German cannot tell you how it is bounded at any moment. The nation itself, with all its so called internal improvements, which, by the way, are all external and superficial, is just such an **unwieldy** and overgrown establishment, **cluttered** with furniture and tripped up by its own traps, ruined by luxury and **heedless** expense, by want of calculation and a worthy aim, as the million households in the land; and the only cure for it as for them is in a rigid economy, a stern and more than Spartan simplicity of life and elevation of purpose. It lives too fast. Men think that it is essential that the Nation have commerce, and export ice, and talk through a telegraph, and ride thirty miles an hour, without a doubt, whether they do or not; but whether we should live like **baboons** or like men, is a little uncertain. If we do not get out **sleepers**, and forge rails, and devote days and nights to the work, but go to **tinker** upon our lives to improve them, who will build railroads? And if railroads are not built, how shall we get to heaven **in season**? But if we stay at home and mind our business, who will want railroads? We do not ride on the railroad; it rides upon us. Did you ever think what those sleepers are that underlie the railroad? Each one is a man, an Irishman, or a **Yankee man**. The rails are laid on them, and they are covered with sand, and the cars run smoothly over them. They are sound sleepers, I assure you. And every few years a new lot is laid down and run over; so that, if some have the pleasure of riding on a rail[25], others have the misfortune to be ridden upon. And when they run over a man that is walking in his sleep, a **supernumerary** sleeper in the wrong position, and wake him up, they suddenly stop the cars, and make a **hue** and cry about it, as if this were an exception. I am glad to know that it takes a gang of men for every five miles to keep the sleepers down and level in their beds as it is, for this is a sign that they may sometime get up again.

pygmy[ˈpɪgmi]: *n.* 侏儒
clout[klaʊt]: *n.* 打击
superfluous[suːˈpɜːfluəs]: *adj.* 多余的
wretchedness[ˈretʃɪdnəs]: *n.* 卑鄙；可怜
fritter[ˈfrɪtə(r)]: *v.* 浪费
lump[lʌmp]: *v.* 归并；加上
founder[ˈfaʊndə(r)]: *v.* 沉没
dead reckoning: 靠航位推算求生
unwieldy[ʌnˈwiːldi]: *adj.* 笨拙的；庞大的
clutter[ˈklʌtə(r)]: *v.* 弄乱；使……混乱
heedless[ˈhiːdləs]: *adj.* 不留心的；不注意的

baboon[bə'buːn]：*n.* 狒狒

sleeper['sliːpə(r)]：*n.* 枕木

tinker['tɪŋkə(r)]：*v.* 调整；改进

in season：及时

Yankee man：(美国)北方诸州的人；北方佬

supernumerary[ˌsuːpə'njuːmərəri]：*adj.* 超出的；多余的

hue[hjuː]：*n.* 喊叫

Why should we live with such hurry and waste of life? We are determined to be starved before we are hungry. Men say that a **stitch** in time saves nine, and so they take a thousand stitches today to save nine tomorrow. As for work, we haven't any of any consequence. We have the **Saint Vitus' dance**, and cannot possibly keep our heads still. If I should only give a few pulls at the **parish** bell-rope, as for a fire, that is, without setting the bell[26], there is hardly a man on his farm in the outskirts of Concord, **notwithstanding** that press of engagements which was his excuse so many times this morning, nor a boy, nor a woman, I might almost say, but would forsake all and follow that sound, not mainly to save property from the flames, but, if we will confess the truth, much more to see it burn, since burn it must, and we, be it known, did not set it on fire[27], —or to see it put out, and have a hand in it, if that is done as handsomely; yes, even if it were the parish church itself. Hardly a man takes a half hour's nap after dinner, but when he wakes he holds up his head and asks, "What's the news?" as if the rest of mankind had stood his **sentinels.** Some give directions to be waked every half hour, doubtless for no other purpose; and then, to pay for it, they tell what they have dreamed. After a night's sleep the news is as indispensable as the breakfast. "Pray tell me anything new that has happened to a man anywhere on this globe," —and he reads it over his coffee and rolls, that a man has had his eyes **gouged** out this morning on the **Wachito River**[28]; never dreaming the while that he lives in the dark **unfathomed Mammoth Cave** of this world, and has but the **rudiment** of an eye himself[29].

stitch[stɪtʃ]：*n.* 一针

Saint Vitus' dance：舞蹈病，一种影响神经系统的病，会引起痉挛性的运动、抑郁和情绪不稳定。

parish['pærɪʃ]：*n.* 教区

notwithstanding[ˌnɒtwɪð'stændɪŋ]：*prep.* 尽管

sentinel['sentɪnl]：*n.* 哨兵

gouge[gaʊdʒ]：*v.* 挖出

Wachito River：沃希托河，位于阿肯色南部。

unfathomed[ʌn'fæð(ə)md]：*adj.* 深不可测的

Mammoth Cave：猛犸洞窟，位于肯塔基州。

rudiment['ruːdɪmənt]：*n.* 发育不全的器官

For my part, I could easily do without the post-office. [30] I think that there are very few important communications made through it. To speak critically, I never received more than one or two letters in my life—I wrote this some years ago—that were worth the postage. The penny-post is, commonly, an institution through which you seriously offer a man that penny for his thoughts[31] which is so often safely offered in **jest**. And I am sure that I never read any memorable news in a newspaper. If we read of one man robbed, or murdered, or killed by accident, or one house burned, or one vessel wrecked, or one steamboat blown up, or one cow run over on the Western Railroad, or one mad dog killed, or one lot of **grasshoppers** in the winter, —we never need read of another. One is enough. If you are acquainted with the principle, what do you care for **myriad** instances and applications? To a philosopher all news, as it is called, is gossip, and they who edit and read it are old women over their tea. Yet not a few are greedy after this gossip.

jest[dʒest]：*n.* 玩笑

grasshopper['grɑːshɒpə(r)]：*n.* 蝗虫

myriad['mɪriəd]：*adj.* 无数的；五花八门的

Let us spend one day as deliberately as Nature, and not be thrown off the track[32] by every nutshell and mosquito's wing that falls on the rails. Let us rise early and fast, or breakfast, gently and without **perturbation**; let company come and let company go, let the bells ring and the children cry, —determined to make a day of it. Why should we **knock under** and go with the stream? With unrelaxed nerves, with morning vigor, sail by it, looking another way, tied to the **mast** like Ulysses[33]. If the engine whistles, let it whistle till it is hoarse for its pains. If the bell rings, why should we run? We will consider what kind of music they are like. Let us settle ourselves, and work and **wedge** our feet downward through the mud and **slush** of opinion, and prejudice, and tradition, and delusion, and **appearance**, that **alluvion** which covers the globe, through Paris and London, through New York and Boston and Concord, through church and state, through poetry and philosophy and religion, till we come to a hard bottom and rocks in place, which we can call reality, and say, this is, and no mistake; and then begin, having a **point d'appui**, below **freshet** and frost and fire, a place where you might found a wall or a state, or set a lamp-post safely, or perhaps a **gauge**, not a **Nilometer**, but a **Realometer**, that future ages might know how deep a freshet of shams and appearances had gathered from time to time. If you stand right fronting and face to face to a fact, you will see the sun glimmer on both its surfaces, as if it were a **cimeter**, and feel its sweet edge dividing you through the heart and marrow, and so you will happily conclude your mortal career. Be it life or death, we crave only reality. If we are really dying, let us hear the rattle in our throats and feel cold in the extremities; if we are alive, let us go about our business.

perturbation[ˌpɜːtəˈbeɪʃn]：*n.* 扰动；大张旗鼓

knock under：屈服

mast[mɑːst]：*n.* 桅杆

wedge[wedʒ]：*v.* 挤进

slush[slʌʃ]：*n.* 软泥

appearance[əˈpɪərəns]：*n.* 面子

alluvion[əˈl(j)uːvɪən]：*n.* 沙洲；泥沼

point d'appui：法语，即 a point of support，支撑点。

freshet[ˈfreʃɪt]：*n.* 山洪

gauge[ɡeɪdʒ]：*n.* 测量仪器

Nilometer：尼罗河仪，古埃及用来记录尼罗河(Nile)的水位，以便向城市发出洪水警告的仪器。

Realometer：现实计量器，此词为梭罗所造。

cimeter[ˈsɪmɪtə]：*n.* 短弯刀[一种有弧度的薄刃刀，因其锐度而著名，与下一段中的 cleaver(比较笨重的刀)正好相反]

Time is but the stream I go a-fishing in. ㉞ I drink at it; but while I drink I see the sandy bottom and detect how shallow it is. Its thin current slides away, but eternity remains. I would drink deeper; fish in the sky, whose bottom is **pebbly** with stars. ㉟ I cannot count one. I know not the first letter of the **alphabet**. I have always been regretting that I was not as wise as the day I was born. The intellect is a **cleaver**; it **discerns** and **rifts** its way into the secret of things. ㊱ I do not wish to be any more busy with my hands than is necessary. My head is hands and feet. I feel all my best faculties concentrated in it. My instinct tells me that my head is an organ for **burrowing**，as some creatures use their **snout** and fore-paws，and with it I would mine and burrow my way through these hills. I think that the richest **vein** is somewhere **hereabouts**；so by the **divining rod** and thin rising **vapors** I judge；and here I will begin to mine.

pebbly[ˈpebli]：*adj*. 鹅卵石的

alphabet[ˈælfəbet]：*n*. 字母表

cleaver[ˈkliːvə(r)]：*n*. 宽刃刀

discern[dɪˈsɜːn]：*v*. 辨别

rift[rɪft]：*v*. 割开

burrow[ˈbʌrəʊ]：*v*. 挖洞

snout[snaʊt]：*n*.（猪等动物的）口鼻部

vein[veɪn]：*n*. 矿脉

hereabouts[ˌhɪərəˈbaʊts]：*adv*. 附近

divining rod：探测棒

vapor[ˈveɪpə(r)]：*n*. 蒸汽

[选自：Henry David Thoreau. *Walden*. London：Oxford University Press，2008.]

Notes

①梭罗第一次谈到房子和座位的关系是在 1840 年 8 月的一则日记中："富人的房子是一个座位——一个坐着的地方；穷人的房子是屋顶——遮身之处。因此，在英语里，我们称绅士的房子为住宅（seat）或住所（residence），而称穷人的房子为住房（house）或房顶（roof）。"1841 年 4 月 5 日，梭罗写道："我不过是想要一个干净的座位。我会在某座山的南面修建我的住所，然后在那里享受神灵们送给我的生命。"

②威廉·吉尔平（William Gilpin）在《漫谈森林风景和其他树林风景》（*Remarks on Forest Scenery and Other Woodland Views*，1794）中写道："枯树常常在自然和人工风景设计方面有良好的效果。在某些风景中，它基本上是不可或缺的。当沉闷的树丛在眼前延伸开来，需要野生和荒凉的意境时，除了枯萎的橡树，粗糙、伤痕累累、枝叶落尽、树皮脱落的白色枝丫伸向暴风雨来临之前的乌云，还能有更合适的陪伴吗？"

③出自威廉·考珀（William Cowper）的《可能是亚历山大·塞尔柯克独居在胡安·费尔南德斯岛上时写的诗句》（"Verses Supposed to be Written by

Alexander Selkirk During His Solitary Abode in the Island of Juan Fernandez", 1909)。译文：我是我勘察过的所有土地的君主，我在那里的权力不容置疑。

④这里的诗人是指钱宁，在"动物邻居"一章中被称为诗人。他在有生之年发表了七本诗集，他也是梭罗第一部传记的作者，于1873年发表了《梭罗，诗人兼自然学家》(*Thoreau, the Poet-Naturalist*)。

⑤可能是回应爱默生的《论自然》："在地平线上有一种资产，只有一种人，亦即诗人的眼睛能够综合所有的部分。这是这些人的农场最好的一部分，虽然他们的保证契约没有给它一个名字。"

⑥钱宁在他的《贝克农场》("Baker Farm")中将贝克农场"入诗"，发表在《樵夫和其他诗歌》(*The Woodman and Other Poems*, 1849)中，梭罗在"贝克农场"一章中引用了一部分。

⑦梭罗在他每年举行的瓜宴上庆祝他种的瓜。

⑧梭罗在《种子的信仰》(*Faith in a Seed*, 1993)中写道："我不相信，没有种子，植物也能发芽，我心中有对种子的信仰。让我相信你有一颗种子，我等待着奇迹。"梭罗说，一个人只有准备好了才能成功。他在《瓦尔登湖》成书以后的日记中写道："我认为，我们会发现，在我们做出每一项发现之前，都有某种准备和朦胧的期望。"

⑨这个"方便"是一种文学方式，使梭罗不必遵从以夏天开始的季节顺序，使他能够用一种春天复苏的感觉结束全书。梭罗也用类似的手法，把他和哥哥约翰在河上为期两周的漂流经历压缩成一周并写了《在康科德河和梅里马克河上的一周》(*A Week on the Concord and Merrimack Rivers*)一书。它也提醒我们，《瓦尔登湖》是一种文学创作，而不是事实报道。

⑩对沮丧的歌颂。这一典故来自萨姆尔·泰勒·柯勒律治(Samuel Taylor Coleridge)的《沮丧颂》(*Ode to Dejection*, 1802)。柯勒律治的《朋友》(*The Friend*, 1810)和《协助反思》(*Aids to Reflection*, 1825)等哲学著作，对超验主义者们产生了重大影响。

⑪公鸡：尚特克勒(Chanticleer)，来自杰弗雷·乔叟(Geoffrey Chaucer)的《修女的教士的故事》("The Nun's Priest's Tale")中的雄鸡的名字。乔叟在故事中写道："在广袤的大地上，它的啼鸣，无人匹敌。"

⑫指艾拉·斯克里布纳(Ira Scribner)的家。梭罗和钱宁于1844年8月拜访过他。梭罗在1845年7月5日的日记中记录道："我去年夏天在一个锯木磨坊主的家里住过。他的家在卡茨基尔山(Catskill Mountains)上，跟松树果园一样高，在蓝莓和覆盆子地带。在那里，安宁、洁净和凉爽似乎都合而为一——都带着它们的芬芳的特质。他是卡茨基尔瀑布的磨坊主。他们一家人里里外外都干净健康，像他们的房子一样。"

⑬在希腊罗马神话中，神仙常来到大地上，对凡人生活产生一些影响。

⑭译文：女神或许会在这里挥洒她们的翩翩衣袂。

⑮指梭罗和他哥哥约翰为他们1839年的河上探险所造的那艘船。该船依康科德河的印第安名称“马斯克塔奎德”(Musketaquid)而命名，梭罗在《在康科德河和梅里马克河上的一周》中描述过它。

⑯纳撒尼尔·霍桑(Nathaniel Hawthorne)于1842年9月1日在笔记本里记下一条，说梭罗“因为缺钱，这个可怜的人想把船卖了，而他确是这条船最合适的舵手，这条船还是他亲手制造的；于是我同意出他要的价钱(只有七美元)，成了这条船的所有人”。船后来传给了钱宁。

⑰梭罗在日记中也写过类似的段落：“如果我们的精神没有升华，湖就不会像天池那样高高升起，而是会像一个低洼的水池、一片沉默浑浊的水塘、一个渔民光顾的地方。”

⑱译文：这个事实很重要，就像用井水浸泡能让黄油保持凉爽一样。

夏天时将黄油浸在井里，是一种冷藏黄油的办法。

⑲译文：曾经有一个牧羊人
他的思绪飞扬
像山一样高昂
每个时辰哺育着他的，是他的羔羊

出自《牧羊人对菲丽黛的爱》(*The Shepherd's Love for Philiday*)。这首诗歌由无名氏作词，罗伯特·琼斯(Robert Jones)作曲，并于1610年发表在《缪斯的快乐花园》(*The Muses Gardin of Delights*)中。

⑳梭罗在日记和其他作品中几次提到《吠陀经》，这表明了阅读《吠陀经》对他产生的影响之大。他在1850年的一则日记里写道：“我读过的《吠陀经》摘录像一束更高更纯洁的光芒照在我身上，它通过更纯洁的中介描绘着更高尚的过程，——不拘泥于细节，简洁，普遍。它在我身上升起，就像星星们都出来以后满月冉冉升起，穿行在夏日天空里某个遥远的层面。”

㉑在希腊神话中，奥诺皮亚(Oenopia)的国王埃阿科斯(Aeacus)，在他的子民被瘟疫毁灭之后，恳求宙斯通过将一株老橡树上的所有蚂蚁都变成人来重新填充他的王国。梭罗在他的《在康科德河和梅里马克河上的一周》中提到了这个神话：“根据寓言，当埃依纳因为疾病而变得无人居住的时候，在埃阿科斯这里，朱庇特将蚂蚁变成了人，亦即，在有些人看来，他将某些像蚂蚁那样卑鄙地生活着的生物变成了人。”

㉒在荷马的《伊利亚特》第三部中，特洛伊人被比作与侏儒作战的仙鹤。梭罗在他1846年4月17日的日记中将这一段翻译成：

特洛伊人像鸟儿一样高叫；

就像天上有仙鹤的铿锵
逃逸着冬天和无法言及的暴雨，
他们嘶叫着飞向大海的洪流
将屠杀和宿命带给矮小的人。

㉓航海术语，指根据一艘船的航线、速度和最后一次的已知位置而不是直接通过星星的位置来判断船的位置。

㉔是指在奥托·冯·俾斯麦王子统一德国之前，1815年至1866年德国大公国和小王国的松散联邦。

㉕本意指乘客，但也指一种除掉一个不受欢迎的人的习惯：强迫他跨越一道抬起来的木杆，通常是将他驱逐出城的方式。

㉖猛力拉钟绳，每一次拉的力量大到让钟口全部朝上，这被称为高敲，是呼唤人们上教堂的信号。低敲，钟敲得快一些，用作火警信号。

㉗梭罗曾帮着扑灭过很多次火，但这一次可能指的是1844年4月30日的那一次，他和同伴爱德华·霍尔不小心把树林点着了。篝火中的火星点着了附近非常干燥的草，三百英亩(1英亩≈4047平方米)的树林被烧掉了。《康科德自由人》于1844年5月3日报道："我们认为，火灾是由两个粗心大意的村民引起的，他们在瓦尔登湖附近的一棵松树墩上点着了火，目的是烧杂烩。由于他们周围的一切都像一只草船一样易燃，火焰很快蔓延开来，花了几小时才得到控制。我们希望，那些将来可能会去林中娱乐的人能够记住这种纯粹粗心的不幸后果。"很多年，梭罗都得忍受着人们在背后称他为"森林纵火犯"的窃窃私语。很长时间他都感到非常惭愧，这促使他于六年后的1850年6月写了一篇关于这次事故的长日记。

㉘在密西西比边疆，在不带武器的打斗中，人们通常通过大拇指的特殊一扭挖出对手的眼睛。"我看见不止一个人缺了一只眼睛，我敢肯定我现在到了'挖眼睛'地区。"蒂莫西·弗林特(Timothy Flint)于1816年这样描写了他在路易斯安那的传教活动。

㉙肯塔基州的猛犸洞窟中的鱼是瞎的，因而它有"极不发达的眼睛"(rudiment of an eye)。

㉚这可能更多的是愿望而不是事实。根据富兰克林·桑伯恩(Franklin Sanborn)，"康科德没有谁比他更准时地来邮局的了"。梭罗在《没有原则的生活》(*Life Without Principle*)中写道："按照比例，当我们的内在生活失败的时候，我们就去邮局。你可以肯定，那个带着最多邮件离开邮局、对他广泛的交流十分自豪的人，很长时间都没有收到自己的来信了。"

㉛人们所知的最早提到这个短语的地方是在约翰·赫伍德(John Heywood)的《谚语》中："(好人说)为你的思想付一分钱。"

㉜铁路早期，货车很容易脱轨。1853 年 7 月 16 日的《科学美国人》引用了《铁路杂志》上的这个话题："一列火车的引擎和前面的车厢经常会越过段轨、一头牛或者一块石头，而不会脱轨，而后面的车厢，因为没有什么东西把它拉进铁路线，很容易离开铁轨。"

㉝尤利西斯，罗马神话中的英雄，即希腊神话中的奥德修斯(Odysseus)。荷马史诗《奥德赛》中叙述了他在特洛伊战争后回国途中历尽艰辛，终于与妻儿团聚的故事。这里的典故是他为了抵制海上女妖塞壬(Siren)致命歌声的诱惑，让人把自己绑在桅杆上。

㉞参考译文：时间只不过是我垂钓的小溪。

㉟参考译文：我愿意痛饮更深之处的水；在天空钓鱼，天底点缀着星星。

㊱参考译文：智力是一把宽刃刀，它看准了，就一路切下去，直切到事物的秘密所在。

Remarks

《瓦尔登湖》于 1854 年 8 月 9 日出版，在梭罗搬到瓦尔登湖九年之后。该书经历了七次修改。"《瓦尔登湖》终于出版。"这是梭罗在那一天的日记里写下的唯一一句话。梭罗搬到瓦尔登湖那一天，在他的日记里也是一笔带过："7 月 5 日。星期六。瓦尔登湖。——我昨天搬到这儿来住了。"这个地方本身可能并不重要，重要的是，他自己独立出来了，而他自己尚未意识到这会对他产生什么影响。"瓦尔登"这个名字，不管是地名还是书名，一百五十年后，无论是在学术层面还是在个人层面都对成千上万人充满了象征意义，但梭罗当时在寻找居住地时，其实还考虑过其他几个地方。直到爱默生买下了面积为 62 英亩、深达 103 英尺(1 英尺≈0.3 米)的冰川深湖瓦尔登湖北面的十几英亩土地，并且允许梭罗在那里居住之后，梭罗才真正考虑去那里居住。这其实是在响应爱默生在《美国学者》(*The American Scholar*，1837)里提倡的精神：

> 年轻人，充满着最美好的希望，他们的生活在我们的海滩上开始，山间的风吹拂着他们，上帝的所有星星把他们照耀得熠熠闪光，他们发现下面地球上的一切和这些并不协调，下面管理烦琐俗事的原则令他们感到厌恶，他们因为这种厌恶而无所作为，因而转向无足轻重的事务，或者死于厌恶，其中有些人还会自杀。怎么解决这个问题呢？他们还没有认识到，那些成千上万同样有希望却碰到了职业障碍的年轻人还没有认识到，如果独立的个人不受任何控制地完全将自己的本能作为自我的根基，整个庞大的世界就会环绕到他的周围来。耐心——耐心；唯一的慰藉是，你自己的生命有可能是无限的；你的任务是对原则进行研究和交流，使这些本能流传开来，从而改变整个世界。世界上最严重的问题，就是不能成为一个独

立的个体单位；——不能被人当作一个独有的特殊个体；——不能结出每一个人生来就应当结出的独特的果实……我们将用自己的双脚行走，我们将用自己的双手劳作，我们会说出我们自己的心声。

激励梭罗搬到瓦尔登湖的一个主要动机是他需要空间来独立完成他的一本书，这本书后来题为《在康科德河和梅里马克河上的一周》。1842 年，他的哥哥约翰突然去世，令人震惊万分。梭罗自此开始写作，纪念二人在 1839 年 8 月至 9 月进行的为期两周的航行中的兄弟情谊。在瓦尔登湖，梭罗重新修改了这份手稿。通过这次航行，梭罗开始思考友谊、精神、社会和自然，并把这些主题融入了书中。

《瓦尔登湖》共有 18 章："简朴生活""生活在何处、生活的目的""阅读""声籁""独处""访客""豆圃""村庄""湖泊""贝克农场""更高的法则""动物邻居""室内取暖""从前的居民、冬天的访客""冬天的动物""冬天的瓦尔登湖""春天""结语"。以上阅读选篇来自第二章——"生活在何处、生活的目的"。

参考译文

生活在何处、生活的目的

到达我们生命的某个时期，我们就习惯于把可以安家落户的地方，一个个地加以考察了。正是这样我把住所周围一二十英里(1 英里≈1.6 千米)内的田园统统考察到了。我在想象中已经接二连三地买下了那儿的所有田园，因为所有的田园都得要买下来，而且我都已经知道它们的价格了。我步行到各个农民的田地上，尝尝他的野苹果，和他谈谈庄稼，再请他随便开出什么价钱，就照他开的价把它买下来，心里却想着再以任何价钱把它押给他；甚至付给他一个更高的价钱，——把什么都买下来，只不过没有立契约，——而是把他的闲谈当作他的契约，我这个人原来就很爱闲谈，——我耕耘了那片田地，而且在某种程度上，我想，耕耘了他的心田，如是尝够了乐趣以后，我就扬长而去，好让他继续耕耘下去。这种经营，竟使我的朋友们当我是一个地产掮客。其实我是无论坐在哪里，都能够生活的，哪里的风景都能相应地为我而发光。家宅者，不过是一个座位，——如果这个座位是在乡间就更好些。我发现许多家宅的位置，似乎都是不容易很快加以改进的，有人会觉得它离村镇太远，但我觉得倒是村镇离它太远了点。我总说，很好，我可以在这里住下；我就在那里过一小时夏天的和冬天的生活，我看到那些岁月如何地奔驰，挨过了冬季，便迎来了新春。这一区域的未来居民，不管他们将要把房子造在哪里，都可以肯定那儿过去就有人住过了。只要一个下午就足够把田地化为果园、树林和牧场，并且决定门前应该留着哪些优美的橡树或松树，甚至于砍伐了的树也都派上了最好的用场了；然后，我就由它去啦，好比休耕了一样，一个人越是有许多事情能够放得下，他越是富有。

我的想象却跑得太远了些，我甚至想到有几处田园会拒绝我，不肯出售给我，——被拒绝正合我的心愿呢，——我从来不肯让实际地占有这类事情灼伤过我的手指头。几乎已实际地占有田园那一次，是我购置霍乐威尔那个地方的时候，都已经开始选好种子，找出了木料来，打算造一架手推车，来推动这事，或载之而他往了；可是在原来的主人正要给我一纸契约之前，他的妻子——每一个男人都有一个妻子的——变卦了，她要保留她的田产了，他就提出赔我十元钱，解除约定。现在说句老实话，我在这个世界上只有一角钱，假设我真的有一角钱的话，或者有了田园，有了十元，或有了所有的这一切，那我这点数学知识可就无法计算清楚了。不管怎样，我退回了那十元钱，退还了那田园，因为这一次我已经做过头了；应该说，我是很慷慨的啊，我按照我买进的价格，按原价又卖给了他，更因为他并不见得富有，还送了他十元，但保留了我的一角钱和种子，以及备而未用的独轮车的木料。如此，我觉得我手面已很阔绰，而且这样做无损于我的贫困。至于那地方的风景，我却也保留住了，后来我每年都得到丰收，却不需要独轮车来载走。关于风景，——

“我勘察一切，像一个皇帝，

谁也不能够否认我的权力。”

我时常看到一个诗人，在欣赏了一片田园风景中的最珍贵部分之后，就扬长而去，那些固执的农夫还以为他拿走的仅仅是几枚野苹果。诗人却把他的田园押上了韵脚，而且多少年之后，农夫还不知道这回事，这么一道最可羡慕的、肉眼不能见的篱笆已经把它圈了起来，还挤出了它的牛乳，去掉了奶油，把所有的奶油都拿走了，他只把去掉了奶油的奶水留给了农夫。

霍乐威尔田园的真正迷人之处，在我看是，它的遁隐之深，离开村子有两英里，离开最近的邻居有半英里，并且有一大片地把它和公路隔开了；它傍着河流，据它的主人说，由于这条河，而升起了雾，春天里就不会再下霜了，这却不在我心坎上；而且，它的田舍和棚屋带有灰暗而残败的神色，加上零落的篱笆，好似在我和先前的居民之间，隔并了多少岁月；还有那苹果树，树身已空，苔藓满布，兔子咬过，可见得我将会有什么样的一些邻舍了；但最主要的还是那一度回忆，我早年就曾经溯河而上，那时节，这些屋宇藏在密密的红色枫叶丛中，还记得我曾听到过一头家犬的吠声。我急于将它购买下来，等不及那产业主搬走那些岩石，砍伐掉那些树身已空的苹果树，铲除那些牧场中新近跃起的赤杨幼树，一句话，等不及它的任何收拾了。为了享受前述的那些优点，我决定干一下了，像那阿特拉斯一样，把世界放在我肩膀上好啦，——我从没听到过他得了哪样报酬，——我愿意做一切事：简直没有别的动机或任何推托之辞，只等付清了钱款，便占有这个田园，再不受他人侵犯就行了；因为我知道我只要让这片田园自生自展，它将要生产出我所企求的最丰美的收获。但后来的结果已见上述。

所以，我所说的关于大规模的农事(至今我一直在培育着一座园林)，仅仅是我已经预备好了种子。许多人认为年代越久的种子越好。我不怀疑时间是能分别好和坏的，但到最后我真正播种了，我想我大约更不像是会失望的。可是我要告诉我的伙伴们，只说这一次，以后永远不再说了：你们要尽可能长久地生活得自由，生活得并不执着才好。执迷于一座田园，和关在县政府的监狱中，简直没有分别。

老加图——他的《农业志》是我的“启蒙者”，曾经说过——可惜我见到的那本唯一的译本把这一段话译得一塌糊涂，——“当你想要买下一个田园的时候，你可以在脑中多多地想着它，可绝不要贪得无厌地买下它，更不要嫌麻烦而再不去看望它，也别以为绕着它兜了一个圈子就够了。如果这是一个好田园，你去的次数越多你就越喜欢它。”我想我是不会贪得无厌地购买它的，我活多久，就去兜多久的圈子，死了之后，也先要葬在那里。这样才能使我终于更加喜欢它。

目前要写的，是我的这一类实验中接下来的一个，我打算更详细地描写描写，而为了便利起见，且把这两年的经验归并为一年。我已经说过，我不预备写一首沮丧的颂歌，可是我要像黎明时站在栖木上的金鸡一样，放声啼叫，即使我这样做只不过是为了唤醒我的邻人罢了。

我第一天住在森林里，就是说，白天在那里，晚上也在那里过夜的那一天，凑巧得很，是一八四五年七月四日，独立日，我的房子没有盖好，过冬还不行，只能勉强避避风雨，没有粉刷，没有烟囱，墙壁用的是饱经风雨的粗木板，缝隙很大，所以到晚上很是凉爽。笔直的、砍伐得来的、白色的间柱，新近才刨得平坦的门户和窗框，使屋子具有清洁和通风的景象，特别是在早晨，木料里饱含着露水的时候，总使我幻想到午间大约会有一些甜蜜的树胶从中渗出。这房间在我的想象中，一整天里还将多少保持这个早晨的情调，不禁使我想起上一年我曾游览过的一个山顶上的一所房屋。这是一所空气好的、不涂灰泥的房屋，适宜于旅行的神仙途中居住，那里还适宜于仙女移动，曳裙而过。吹过我的屋脊的风，正如那扫荡山脊而过的风，唱出断断续续的调子来，也许是天上人间的音乐片段。晨风永远在吹，创世纪的诗篇至今还没有中断；可惜听得到它的耳朵太少了。灵山只在大地的外部，处处都是。

除了一条小船之外，从前我曾经拥有的唯一屋宇，不过是一顶帐篷，夏天里，我偶或带了它出去郊游，这顶帐篷现在还被卷了起来，放在我的阁楼里；只是那条小船，辗转经过了几个人的手，已经消隐于时间的溪流里。如今我却有了这更实际的避风雨的房屋，看来我活在这世间，已大有进步。这座屋宇虽然很单薄，却是围绕我的一种结晶了的东西，这一点立刻在建筑者心上发生了作用。它富有暗示的作用，好像绘画中的一幅素描。我不必跑出门去换空气，因为屋子里面的气氛一点也没有失去新鲜。坐在一扇门背后，几乎和不坐在门里面一样，便是下大雨的天气，亦如此。《诃利世系》中说过："并无鸟雀巢居的房屋像未曾调味的烧肉。"寒舍却并不如此，因为我发现我自己突然跟鸟雀做起邻居来了；但不是我捕到了一只鸟把它关起来，而是我把我自己关进了它们邻近的一只笼子里。我不仅跟那些时常飞到花园和果树园里来的鸟雀弥形亲近，而且跟那些更野性、更逗人惊诧的森林中的鸟雀亲近了起来，它们从来没有，就是有也很难得，向村镇上的人民唱出良宵的雅歌，——它们是画眉、鸫鸟、猩红丽唐纳雀、田麻雀、夜鹰和许多别的鸣禽。

我坐在一个小湖的湖岸上，离开康科德村子南面约一英里半，较康科德高出些，就在市镇与林肯乡之间那片浩瀚的森林中央，也在我们唯一的著名地区，康科德战场之南的两英里地；但因为我是低伏在森林下面的，而其余的一切地区，都被森林掩盖了，所以半英里之外的湖的对岸便成了我最遥远的地平线。在第一个星期内，无论什么时候我凝望着湖水，湖给我的印象都好像山里的一泓龙潭，高高在山的一边，它的底还比别的湖沼的水平面高了不少，以至日出的时候，我看到它脱去了夜晚的雾衣，它轻柔的鳞波，或它波平如镜的湖面，都渐渐地在这里那里呈现了，这时的雾，像幽灵偷偷地从每一个方向，退隐入森林中，又好像是一个夜间的秘密宗教集会散会了一样。露水后来要悬挂在林梢，悬挂在山侧，到第二天还一直不消失。

八月里，在轻柔的斜风细雨暂停的时候，这小小的湖做我的邻居，最为珍贵，那时水和空气都完全平静了，天空中却密布着乌云，下午才过了一半，却已具备了一切黄昏的肃穆，而画眉在四周唱歌，隔岸相闻。这样的湖，再没有比这时候更平静的了；湖上的明净的空气自然很稀薄，而且被乌云映得很黯淡了，湖水却充满了光明和倒影，成为一个下界的天空，更加值得珍视。从最近被伐木的附近一个峰顶上向南看，穿过小山间的巨大凹处，看得见隔湖的一幅愉快的图景，那凹处正好形成湖岸，那儿的两座小山坡相倾斜而下，使人感觉到似有一条溪涧从山林谷中流下，但是，却没有溪涧。我是这样从近处的绿色山峰之间和之上，远望一些蔚蓝的地平线上的远山或更高的山峰的。真的，踮起了足尖来，我可以望见西北角上更远、更蓝的山脉，这种蓝颜色是天空的染料制造厂中最真实的出品，我还可以望见村镇的一角。但是要换一个方向看的话，虽然我站得如此高，却被郁茂的树木围住，什么也看不透，看不到了。在邻近，有一些流水真好，水有浮力，地就浮在上面了。即便是最小的井也有这一点值得推荐，当你窥望井底的时候，你发现大地并不是连绵的大陆，而是隔绝的孤岛。这是很重要的，正如井水之能冷藏牛油。当我的目光从这一个山顶越过湖向萨德伯里草原望过去的时候，在发大水的季节里，我觉得草原升高了，大约是蒸腾的山谷中显示出海市蜃楼的效果，它好像沉在水盆底下的一个天然铸成的铜币，湖之外的大地都好像薄薄的表皮，成了孤岛，给小小一片横亘的水波浮载着，我才被提醒，我居住的地方只不过是干燥的土地。

虽然从我的门口望出去，风景范围更狭隘，我却一点不觉得它拥挤，更无被囚禁的感觉，尽够我的想象力在那里游牧的了。矮橡树丛生的高原升起在对岸，一直向西去的大平原和鞑靼式的草原伸展开去，给所有的流浪人家一个广阔的天地。当达摩达拉的牛羊群需要更大的新牧场时，他说过："再没有比自由地欣赏广阔的地平线的人更快活的人了。"

时间和地点都已变换，我生活在了更靠近宇宙的这些部分，更挨紧了历史中最吸引我的那些时代。我生活的地方遥远得跟天文学家每晚观察的太空一样。我们惯于幻想，在天体的更远更僻的一角，有着更稀罕、更愉快的地方，在仙后星座的椅子形状的后面，远远地离了喧闹和骚扰。我发现我的房屋位置正是这样一个遁隐之处，它是终古常新的没有受到污染的宇宙的一部分。如果说居住在更靠近昴宿星团或毕宿星团、牵牛星或毕宿五的地方更加值得的话，那么我真正是住在那些地方的，至少，就跟那些星座一样远离我抛在后面的人世，那些闪闪的小光，那些柔美的光线，传给我最近的邻居，只有在没有月亮的夜间才能够看得到。我所居住的便是创造物中那部分；——

"曾有个收羊人活在世上，
他的思想像高山那样
崇高，在那里他的羊群
每小时都给予他营养。"

如果牧羊人的羊群老是走到比他的思想还要高的牧场上，我们会觉得他的生活是怎样的呢？

每一个早晨都是一个愉快的邀请，使得我的生活跟大自然同样地简单，也许我可以说，同样地纯洁无瑕。我向曙光顶礼，忠诚如同希腊人。我起身很早，在湖中洗澡；这是个宗教意味的运动，我所做到的最好的一件事。据说在成汤王的浴盆上就刻着这样的字："苟日新，日日新，又日新。"我懂得这个道理。黎明带来了英雄时代。在最早的黎明中，我坐着，门窗大开，一只看不到也想象不到的蚊虫在我的房中飞，它那微弱的吟声都能感动我，就像我听到了宣扬美名的金属喇叭声一样。这是荷马的一首安魂曲；空中的《伊利亚特》和《奥德赛》，歌唱着它的愤怒与漂泊。此中大有宇宙本体之感；宣告着世界的无穷精力与生生不息，直到它被禁。黎明啊，一天之中最值得纪念的时节，是觉醒的时辰。那时候，我们的昏沉欲睡的感觉是最少的了，至少可有一小时之久，整日夜神魂颠倒的官能大都要清醒起来。但是，如果我们并不是被我们自己的禀赋所唤醒的，而是被什么仆人机械地用肘子推醒的；如果并不是我们内心的新生力量和内心的要求唤醒了我们，既没有那空中的芬芳，也没有回荡的天籁的音乐，而是工厂的汽笛声唤醒了我们，——如果我们醒时，并没有比睡前有了更崇高的生命，那么这样的白天，即便能被称为白天，也不会有什么希望可言；要知道，黑暗可以产生这样的好果子，黑暗是可以证明它自己的功能并不亚于白昼的。一个人如果不能相信每一天都有一个比他亵渎过的更早、更神圣的曙光时辰，他一定是已经对生命失望了，正在摸索着一条降入黑暗去的道路。感官的生活在休息了一夜之后，人的灵魂，或者就说是人的官能吧，每天都重新精力弥漫一次，而他的禀赋又可以去试探他能完成何等崇高的生活了。可以纪念的一切事，我敢说，都在黎明时间的氛围中发生。《吠陀经》说："一切知，俱于黎明中醒。"诗歌与艺术，人类行为中最美丽最值得纪念的事都出发于这一时刻。所有的诗人和英雄都像门农，那曙光之神的儿子，在日出时他播送竖琴音乐。以富有弹性的和精力充沛的思想追随着太阳步伐的人，白昼对于他而言便是一个永恒的黎明。这和时钟的鸣声不相干，也不用管人们是什么态度，在从事什么劳动。早晨是我醒来时内心有黎明感觉的一个时候。改良德行是为了把昏沉的睡眠抛弃。人们如果不是在浑浑噩噩地睡觉，那为什么他们在回顾每一天的时候要说得这么可怜呢？他们都是精明人嘛。如果他们没有被昏睡所征服，他们是可以干成一些事的。几百万人清醒得足以从事体力劳动，但是一百万人中，只有一个人才清醒得足以有效地服役于智慧，一亿人中，才能有一个人，生活得诗意而神圣。清醒就是生活。我还没有遇到过一个非常清醒的人。要是见到了他，我怎敢凝视他呢？

我们必须学会再苏醒，更须学会保持清醒而不再昏睡，但不能用机械的方法，而应寄托无穷的期望于黎明，就在最沉的沉睡中，黎明也不会抛弃我们的。我没有看到过更使人振奋的事实了，人类无疑是有能力来有意识地提高他自己的生命的。能画出某一幅画，雕塑出某一个肖像，美化某几个对象，是很了不起的；但更加荣耀的事是能够塑造或画出那种氛围与媒介来，从而能使我们发现，而且能使我们正当地有所为。能影响当代的本质的，是最高的艺术。每个人都应该把最崇高的和紧急时刻内他所考虑到的做到，使他的生命配得上他所想的，甚至在小节上也配得上。如果我们拒绝了，或者说虚耗了我们得到的这一点微不足道的思想，神谕自会清清楚楚地把如何做到这一点告诉我们。

我到林中去，因为我希望谨慎地生活，只面对生活的基本事实，看看我是否学得到生活要教育我的东西，免得到了临死的时候，才发现我根本就没有生活过。我不希望度过非生活的生活，生活是这样的可爱；我却也不愿意去修行过隐逸的生活，除非是万不得已。我要深深地把生命的精髓都吸到，我要生活得稳稳当当，我要生活得像个斯巴达人，以便根除一切非生活的东西，划出一块刈割的面积来，细细地刈割或修剪，把生活压缩到一个角隅里去，把它缩小到最低的条件中，如果它被证明是卑微的，那么就把那真正的卑微全部认识到，并把它的卑微之处公布于世；如果它是崇高的，就用切身的经历来体会它，在我下一次远游时，也可以做出一个真实的报道。因为，我看，大多数人还确定不了他们的生活是属于魔鬼的，还是属于上帝的呢，然而又多少有点轻率地下了判断，认为人生的主要目标是“归荣耀于神，并永远从神那里得到喜悦”。

然而我们依然生活得卑微，像蚂蚁；虽然神话告诉我们说，我们早已经变成人了，像小人国里的人，我们和长脖子仙鹤作战；这真是错误之上加错误，脏抹布之上更抹脏；我们最优美的德行在这里成了多余的本可避免的劫数。我们的生活在琐碎之中被消耗掉了。一个老实的人除十指之外，使用不着更大的数字了，在特殊情况下也顶多加上十个脚趾，其余不妨笼而统之。简单化，简单化，简单化！我说，最好你的事只有两件或三件，不要有一百件或一千件；不必计算一百万，半打不是够计算了吗，总之，账目可以记在拇指指甲上就好了。在这波浪滔天的文明生活的海洋中；一个人要生活，得经历这样的风云和流沙以及一千零一种事变，除非他纵身一跃，直下海底，不要靠船位推算去安抵目的港了，那些事业成功的人，真是伟大的计算家啊。简单化，简单化！不必一日三餐，如果必要，一顿也够了，不要百道菜，五道够多了；至于别的，就在同样的比例下来减少好了。我们的生活像德意志联邦，全是由小邦组成的。联邦的边界永在变动，甚至一个德国人也不可能在任何时候都能把边界告诉你。国家是有所谓内政改进的，实际上它全是些外表的，甚至肤浅的事务，它是这样一种不易运用的生长得臃肿庞大的机构，拥塞着家具，掉进自己设置的陷阱，被奢侈和挥霍毁坏完了，因为它没有计算，也没有崇高的目标，好比地面上的一百万户人家一样；对于这种情况，和对于他们一样，唯一的医疗办法是一种严峻的经济学，一种严峻得更甚于斯巴达人的简单的生活，并提高生活的目标。生活现在是太放荡了。人们以为国家必须有商业，必须把冰块出口，还要用电报来说话，还要一小时奔驰三十英里，毫不怀疑它们有没有用处；但是我们应该生活得像狒狒，还是像人呢，这一点倒又确定不了。如果我们不做出枕木来，不轧制钢轨，不日夜工作，而只是笨手笨脚地对付我们的生活，来改善它们，那么谁还想修筑铁路呢？如果不造铁路，我们如何能准时赶到天堂去呢？可是，我们只要住在家里，管我们的私事，谁还需要铁路呢？我们没有乘坐铁路，铁路倒乘坐了我们。你难道没有想过，铁路底下躺着的枕木是什么？每一根都是一个人，爱尔兰人，或北方佬。铁轨就铺在他们身上，他们身上又铺起了黄沙，而列车平滑地驰过他们。我告诉你，他们真是睡得熟呵。每隔几年，就换上了一批新的枕木，车辆还在上面奔驰着，如果一批人能在铁轨之上愉快地乘车经过，必然有另一批不幸的人是在下面被乘坐或被压过去的。当他们撞倒一个梦中行路的人，一根出轨的多余的枕木，他们只得唤醒他，突然停下车子，吼叫不已，好像这是一个例外。我听到了真觉得有趣，他们每隔五英里就派定一队人，要那些枕木长眠不起，并保持应有的高低，因为这标志着他们有时候还是要站起来的。

为什么我们要生活得这样匆忙，这样浪费生命呢？我们下定决心，要在饥饿以前就饿死。人们时常说，及时缝一针，可以将来少缝九针，所以现在他们缝了一千针，只是为了明天少缝九千针。说到工作，任何结果也没有。我们患了舞蹈病，连脑袋都无法保持静止。如果在寺院的钟楼下，我刚拉了几下绳子，使钟声发出火警的信号来，钟声还没大响起来，在康科德附近的田园里的人，尽管今天早晨说了多少次他如何如何地忙，没有一个男人，或孩子，或女人，我敢说是会不放下工作而朝着那声音跑来的，主要不是要从火里救出财产来，如果我们说老实话，更多的还是来看火烧的，因为已经烧着了，而且这火，要知道，不是我们放的；或者是来看这场火是怎么被救灭的，要是不费什么劲，也还可以帮忙救救火；就是这样，即使教堂本身着了火也是这样。一个人吃了午饭，还只睡了半小时的午觉，一醒来就抬起了头，问，“有什么新闻？”好像全人类在为他放哨。有人还下命令，每隔半小时唤醒他一次，无疑的是并不为什么特别的原因，然后，为报答人家起见，他谈了谈他的梦。睡了一夜之后，新闻之不可缺少，正如早饭一样重要。“请告诉我发生在这个星球之上的任何地方的任何人的新闻，”——于是他一边喝咖啡，吃面包卷，一边读报纸，知道了这天早晨的瓦奇多河上，有一个人的眼睛被挖掉了；一点不在乎他自己就生活在这个世界的深不可测的大黑洞里，自己的眼睛里早就是没有瞳仁的了。

拿我来说，我觉得有没有邮局都无所谓。我想，只有很少的重要消息是需要邮递的。我一生之中，确切地说，至多只收到过一两封信是值得花费那邮资的——这还是我几年之前写过的一句话。通常，一便士邮资的制度，其目的是给一个人一便士，你就可以得到他的思想了，但结果你得到的常常只是一个玩笑。我也敢说，我从来没有从报纸上读到过什么值得纪念的新闻。如果我们读到某某人被抢了，或被谋杀或者死于非命了，或一幢房子被烧了，或一只船沉了，或一只轮船被炸了，或一头母牛在西部铁路上被撞死了，或一只疯狗死了，或冬天有了一大群蚱蜢，——我们不用再读别的了。有这么一条新闻就够了。如果你掌握了原则，何必去关心那亿万的例证及其应用呢？对于一个哲学家来说，这些被称为新闻的，不过是瞎扯，编辑的人和读者就只不过是在喝茶的长舌妇。然而不少人都贪婪地听着这种瞎扯。

我们如大自然一般谨慎地过一天吧，不要因硬壳果或掉在轨道上的蚊虫的一只翅膀而出了轨。让我们黎明即起，用或不用早餐，平静得并无不安之感；让人去人来，让钟响吧，让孩子哭吧，——下个决心，好好地过一天。为什么我们要投降，何至于随波逐流呢？让我们不要卷入在子午线浅滩上的所谓午宴之类的可怕急流与旋涡中。熬过了这种危险，你就平安了，以后便是下山的路了。神经不要松弛，利用那黎明似的魄力，向另一个方向航行，像尤利西斯那样拴在桅杆上过活。如果汽笛鸣叫了，就让它叫到沙哑吧。钟声响起，我们为什么要奔跑呢？我们还要研究它算什么音乐呢。让我们定下心来工作，并用我们的脚跋涉在那些污泥似的意见、偏见、传统、谬见与表面中间，这蒙蔽全地球的淤土啊，让我们越过巴黎、伦敦、纽约、波士顿、康科德，教会与国家，诗歌，哲学与宗教，直到我们到达一个坚硬的底层，在那里的岩盘上，我们称之为现实，然后说，这就是了，不错的了，然后你可以在这个支点之上，在洪水、冰霜和火焰下面，开始在这地方建立一道城墙或一片国土，也许能安全地立起一个灯柱，或一个测量仪器，不是尼罗河水测量器，而是测量现实的仪器，让未来的时代能知道，谎骗与虚有其表曾洪水似的积了又积，积得多么深呀。如果你直立且面对着事实，你就会看到太阳闪耀在它的两面，它好像一柄东方的短弯刀，你能感受到它的甘美的锋镝正剖开你的心和骨髓，你也欢乐地愿意结束你的人间事业了。生也好，死也好，我们仅仅追求现实。如果我们真要死了，让我们听到我们喉咙中的咯咯声，感到四肢上的寒冷好了，如果我们活着，让我们干我们的事业。

时间只是我垂钓的溪。我喝着它；喝水时候我看到，那河的底层多么浅啊。它的汩汩的流水逝去了，可是永恒留了下来。我愿饮得更深；在天空中打鱼，天空的底层里有着石子似的星星。我不能数出“一”来。我不知道字母表上的第一个字母。我常常后悔，我不像初生时聪明了。智力是一把刀子；它看准了，就一路切开事物的秘密。我不希望我的手比所必需的忙得更多些。我的头脑是手和足。我觉得我最好的官能都集中在那里。我的本能告诉我，我的头可以挖洞，像一些动物，有的用鼻子，有的用前爪，我要用它挖掘我的洞，在这些山峰中挖掘出我的道路来。我想那最富有的矿脉就在这里的什么地方；用探寻藏金的魔杖，根据那升腾的薄雾，我要判断；在这里我要起始开矿。

［选自：亨利·戴维·梭罗．瓦尔登湖．杜先菊，译．上海：华东师范大学出版社，2015.］

Questions for discussion

1. According to Thoreau, how can a person become wealthy?
2. What did Thoreau live for? Do you agree with him or not?

3. Is your hometown similar with (to) the place in which Thoreau lived? Describe your hometown in your own words.

After-class reading

Read the book *Nature* written by Ralph Waldo Emerson.

Part B

(1) Stopping the Use of Animal Fur

Michael Kors has announced that they will no longer use animal fur in their products. The new policy will also apply to Jimmy Choo, which Michael Kors Holdings acquired in July for a multimillion pound deal. The **initiative** comes just a few months after Gucci announced that they would also abolish fur from their products. Kors decided to go fur-free after executive chief officer John Idol had a meeting with Dan Matthews of PETA. The US luxury label has since revealed that any fur products currently in production will be **phased out** by December 2018 and that they will introduce a new **faux alternative** in their forthcoming collections.

initiative[ɪ'nɪʃətɪv]: *n.* 倡议

phase out: 逐步淘汰

faux[fəʊ]: *adj.* 假的；人造的

alternative[ɔːl'tɜːnətɪv]: *n.* 供替代的选择

"This decision marks a new chapter as our company continues to evolve its use of innovative materials," explained Idol. "We now have the ability to create a luxe aesthetic using non-animal fur," he added.

Kors has previously been a **perennial** target for animal rights activists. In June, a group of PETA demonstrators disrupted a live interview with the American designer at the Metropolitan Museum of Art in New York by chanting: "Michael Kors has blood on his hands."

perennial[pə'reniəl]: *adj.* 永久的

It is reported that the brand showcased their new faux fur alternatives as early as February 2018, where the designer presented his autumn/winter 2018 collection at New York Fashion Week.

The announcement has been welcomed by animal rights activists. Wayne

Pacelle, president of The Humane Society of the United States, noted: "With the advances in faux fur and the introduction of other innovative materials, it's becoming clear that there is simply no reason to continue using a product that causes so much pain and suffering."

参考译文

停用皮毛

迈克·高仕(Michael Kors，美国轻奢品牌设计师)宣布他们在产品中将不再使用动物皮毛。这项新政策也将适用于周仰杰品牌(Jimmy Choo，女士鞋包品牌)。迈克·高仕公司曾于7月以数百万英镑收购了该品牌。先前古驰也宣布他们的产品将不再使用皮毛，而就在几个月之后，迈克·高仕也宣布了这项计划。迈克·高仕的首席执行官约翰·伊多尔与"善待动物组织"的丹·马修会谈之后，就决定不再使用皮毛。之后该美国奢侈品牌就表示，截至2018年12月，他们目前正在生产的所有皮毛产品将逐步被淘汰，而且他们将在新产品中引入一种新的人造替代材料。

"我们公司一直在研究创新材料的应用，而这一决定也标志着我们的研究进入了新篇章，"伊多尔解释道。"如今我们已经有能力用非动物皮毛造出奢华且有美感的面料，"他补充道。

先前迈克·高仕一直是动物权利活动家们的目标。6月，"善待动物组织"的一群示威者在纽约大都会艺术博物馆反复呼喊着"迈克·高仕手上沾满了鲜血"，扰乱了这位美国设计师在这里的一次现场采访。

据报道，该品牌最早将于2018年2月展示他们的新式人造皮毛替代材料，届时这位设计师将在纽约时装周推出他的2018年秋冬新款服饰。

迈克·高仕的这项公告受到了动物权利活动家们的欢迎。美国人道主义协会主席韦恩·帕瑟勒表示："随着人造皮毛的发展和其他创新材料的引进，显然我们没有理由继续使用一种会引起诸多伤痛的产品。"

(2) Recycling Coffee Cups

The UK's largest coffee retailer, Costa Coffee, has committed to recycling half a billion coffee cups a year by 2020 in a **landmark** act to tackle plastic waste. The pledge, which amounts to recycling the same volume of cups it puts onto the market, would take a significant **chunk** out of the 2.5 billion takeaway cups thrown away across the country every year. Despite often being marked as recyclable, the vast majority of paper coffee cups end up on landfill or being **incinerated** due to the plastic lining used to make them waterproof.

landmark[ˈlændmɑːk]：*n.* 里程碑

chunk[tʃʌŋk]：*n.* 相当大的量

incinerate[ɪnˈsɪnəreɪt]：*v.* 焚化；把……烧成灰

By paying waste collectors to take coffee cups to specialist facilities, Costa hopes to massively increase the rate at which cups are recycled. Ultimately, all a customer will need to do to ensure their cup avoids landfill is throwing it into a standard recycling bin.

The move is the most ambitious so far by a major coffee chain since the start of *The Independent*'s Cut the Cup Waste campaign. Launched following the Environmental Audit Committee's report recommending ministers take drastic action to tackle coffee cup waste, the campaign has pushed for action from governments and businesses and promoted potential solutions. "*The Independent*'s campaign has highlighted the importance of finding a solution to this issue," Costa managing director Dominic Paul told *The Independent*.

Starbucks has pledged £7m to develop a "fully recyclable cup" following pressure from campaigners, while Waitrose has pledged to phase out disposable coffee cups from its stores by autumn.

The company has entered into a partnership with five national waste collectors—Veolia, Biffa, Suez, Grundon and First Mile—that between them cover public spaces across the UK including hospitals, universities and transport **hubs**. The coffee giant is also working with paper mills to ensure their products are recycled effectively. James Cropper, for example, has planned to "upcycle" 500 million cups a year to create plastic-free packaging. By building more partnerships with waste contractors in every region, Costa intends to hit its half a billion mark within two years.

hub[hʌb]：*n.* 枢纽；中心

With one report predicting the number of takeaway drink cups thrown away in the UK is set to rise by a third by 2030, and the government recently failing to back a "latte **levy**" to discourage cup use, it falls to businesses to act on the huge amount of waste from their products. Commenting on the announcement, Environment Minister Therese Coffey said, "Congratulate Costa on taking this significant step to help coffee lovers do the right thing and increase recycling. We all have a responsibility to our environment and this is a significant step by a British business which should dramatically increase the number of disposable coffee cups we recycle in this country. We want to help companies become plastic-free and through our '25-Year Environment Plan' we are putting in place the ambitions to encourage all of us to play our part in ending the **scourge** of plastic waste in our natural environment."

levy['levi]：*n.* 征税；召集

scourge[skɜːdʒ]：*n.* 灾难；祸患

参考译文

回收咖啡杯

英国最大的咖啡零售商科斯塔咖啡承诺将在2020年之前，每年回收5亿个咖啡杯，以此应对塑料浪费问题。这个承诺相当于回收科斯塔每年投入市场的所有杯子。英国每年有25亿杯子用于外带，最后被丢弃在英国各个角落，5亿占了相当大的比例。虽然咖啡纸杯有可回收的美誉，但是大部分还是被丢弃在垃圾场，或者因为上面的防水塑料被焚烧。

科斯塔会给环保工人付费，请他们把咖啡杯带到指定场所，希望能以此提高回收率。消费者需要做的就是避免杯子进入垃圾场，只要把它们扔进可回收垃圾箱就好。

这场运动是继《独立报》"减少纸杯浪费"运动后规模最大的咖啡产业环保行动。环境审查委员会发布了报告，建议各部门部长采取大规模行动，遏制咖啡杯浪费，由此发起了这场运动，从政界到商界，人们都在行动，各种办法纷纷涌现。科斯塔的管理总监多米科·保罗告诉《独立报》："你们的运动使寻找解决方法的重要性更加突出。"

星巴克碍于运动参与者的压力，也承诺会投入700万英镑研发"可回收咖啡杯"，维特罗斯超市表示会在秋季前清除所有一次性咖啡杯。

科斯塔也和五个国家级垃圾回收站进行了合作(分别是威立雅、比法、苏伊士、润东、"最初一英里")。这五个回收站覆盖了英国的公共场所，其中有医院、大学和交通枢纽。科斯塔也和纸厂有所联系，确保产品能有效回收。詹姆斯·克罗珀纸厂就计划每年"废弃"5亿杯子，用来做无塑料包装盒。科斯塔正在和各个地区多个垃圾承包商建立合作关系，意在于两年内达成5亿的目标。

有报告预测，英国外带咖啡杯的废弃量将在2030年增加三分之一。近日，英国政府的"拿铁税"征收失败，其本意在于不鼓励大家使用咖啡杯，现在只能靠商界行动，限制产品浪费量了。环境署署长特锐斯·科菲在声明中说："恭喜科斯塔做出这项重大决定，帮助咖啡爱好者矫正行为，也提高了回收率。环境保护，人人有责，这也是英国商界迈出的一大步，一次性纸杯的回收量将大大增加。我们希望能帮助企业逐渐消灭塑料，通过'25年环境计划’，激励大家终结大自然中的塑料污染。”

(3) Amazon’s Newest Headquarters Building

From the fourth floor of a striking rainforest-like conservatory built of glass and white steel in downtown Seattle, Amazon. com boss Jeff Bezos turned toward the top of his newest headquarters building to summon his favorite assistant. In a proud little show on Monday for the media and **dignitaries**—which also doubled as product placement for Amazon’s voice assistant—the world’s richest man ordered out loud, symbolically: “Alexa, open The **Spheres.**”

dignitary[ˈdɪgnɪtəri]: *n.* 官方

sphere[sfɪə(r)]: *n.* 球体

The **domed** structure is only steps away from the executive office tower where Bezos leads the online retail **behemoth.** It’s part of the company’s urban campus near downtown Seattle that is largely made up of unmarked office buildings where more than 40000 people report to work. The four-story Spheres’ structure from the outside looks like three connected glass orbs planted into the ground in a caterpillar shape. Lighting **mimics** a position near the **equator**, with 12 hours of shade and sun. During the day, the interior is maintained at 22 degrees with 60 percent **humidity**, to **emulate** a cloud forest ecosystem. Amazon’s Amazonesque rainforest-like conservatory is now home to more than 40000 plants from 50 countries on five continents. Its centerpiece is a 50-foot (15. 2-meter) fig tree. Most plants will flower and some can yield fruit, though visitors must keep their hands off all plant life. About 90 percent of the plants were grown and tended to in a suburban greenhouse for years in anticipation for their permanent home in The Spheres.

domed[dəʊmd]: *adj.* 有圆顶的；圆顶状的

behemoth[bɪˈhiːmɒθ]: *n.* 超级公司

mimic[ˈmɪmɪk]: *v.* 模仿；模拟

equator[ɪˈkweɪtə(r)]: *n.* 赤道

humidity[hjuːˈmɪdəti]: *n.* 湿度

emulate[ˈemjuleɪt]: *v.* 效仿

Though masked by nature, the **sleek** and **minimalist** “alternative work space” is also designed to make you forget you’re at work, in a startup environment that is rumored to be aggressively demanding. “The idea is that we connect them with nature. We get them away from their normal desk environment so you don't see any desks or cubicles around," said Ron Gagliardo, Amazon's leading **horticulturist**. The corporate office space, however **selfie**-worthy, is already such a hit that the company had to create a reservation system to contain the flow of traffic for the time being. Employees will have to **snag** a reservation to get in but it's currently already booked out until April. The building has capacity for about 1000 people but is more comfortable with about 800 at a time. Once inside, workers can use **nooks** with tables and chairs that can serve as a casual meeting space. Coffee breaks can be taken in a cafe and "picnic" area offering an interior **reprieve** from Seattle's unrelenting rainy season.

sleek[sliːk]：*adj*. 光滑的；圆滑的

minimalist[ˈmɪnɪməlɪst]：*adj*. 极简抽象风格的

horticulturist[ˌhɔːtɪˈkʌltʃərɪst]：*n*. 园艺家

selfie[ˈselfɪ]：*n*. 自拍

snag[snæg]：*v*. 抓住

nook[nʊk]：*n*. 角落

reprieve[rɪˈpriːv]：*n*. 缓解

Critics have called The Spheres a vanity project, illustrating Seattle's sometimes strained relationship with its largest employer. The company's presence has changed the local economy and raised its cost of living—but none of that was on show at the unveiling of The Spheres. Instead, Bezos received glowing praise from the governor, mayor and county officials for his recent commitments to the city's homelessness crisis plus a personal donation of $33 million to a scholarship foundation that helps immigrant youth in the country illegally. Bezos was **coy** when asked by The Associated Press whether the company's much-anticipated second headquarters to be built in an undetermined U. S. city will have another statement building space like The Spheres, saying: "We'll see."

coy[kɔɪ]：*adj*. 不肯作答的；含糊其词的

参考译文

亚马逊的新办公楼

亚马逊最新总部坐落在西雅图商业区，高达四层，是座热带雨林般的温室建筑，由玻璃和白色钢筋建造而成，老板杰夫·贝佐斯站在顶楼召唤他最喜欢的助手。周一，贝佐斯为媒体和官方开启了一场微型秀，也是为亚马逊的产品语音助手打宣传。贝佐斯大声地说："Alexa，开启苍穹。"

这座圆顶状的建筑离贝佐斯的办公室只有几步远，是亚马逊公司靠近西雅图商区的一部分，办公楼特征并不显著，但是有超过 4 万人在此工作。这座四层的圆形建筑远看像拔地而起的三个草堆做的毛毛虫。光线像是从赤道发出来的，12 小时光影太阳不停歇。白天，建筑内部 22 度，湿度 60%，仿照云雾笼罩的密林生态系统。亚马逊雨林式的温室办公楼有来自五大洲 50 个国家超过 4 万株的植物。中心是一棵高达 15.2 米的无花果树。大多数植物都开花，有一些甚至会结果，但是游客禁止触碰植物。90%的植物都在郊区温室被养护多年，就是为了能在亚马逊的苍穹落户。

亚马逊办公楼以自然做装饰，非常平整而简约，这样另类的工作空间就是为了让人忘记工作，毕竟在要求严苛的创业公司亚马逊，这样的设计别有用意。亚马逊首席园艺师罗·戈里亚多说："我们把工作环境和自然联系起来，让大家远离普通办公桌，在这里看不到办公桌和小隔间。"不管公司办公区域的拍照价值有多大，都得建立预约系统，以确保当前不会发生人员堵塞。员工要抢预约名额，眼下 4 月之前的都已经预约完了。这栋建筑能容纳 1000 名员工，人数维持在 800 是最合适的。在建筑内部，员工可以用桌椅的边角组成会议区域，在咖啡时段可以去咖啡厅，也可以去"野餐区"，以避开西雅图连绵不绝的雨季。

评论人士说"苍穹"毫无价值，西雅图与其最大的雇佣商——亚马逊的关系时有紧张。亚马逊改变了当地经济，使消费水平提高，这些在"苍穹"的开幕式上都没有被提及。但是西雅图州长、市长和郡县官员都对贝佐斯赞赏有加，因为贝佐斯刚对西雅图流浪汉危机做出了一番馈赠，也以个人名义向某奖学金项目捐赠 330 万美元，帮助非法移民西雅图的年轻人。美联社问贝佐斯，万众期待的亚马逊第二总部是否会成为其他城市的苍穹，贝佐斯说："可以期待一下。"

Part C

Brief Introduction to the United Kingdom

The full name of the country we are studying is the United Kingdom of Great Britain and Northern Ireland. It is a **complicated** name for what is in many ways a complicated country. Most people know something about it because its huge overseas **empire** gave it an important international role which only came to an end in the years following the Second World War. However, the things that people know about the UK (which they will probably call simply Britain or, wrongly, England) may have little to do with how most real British people live their lives today.

complicated ['kɒmplɪkeɪtɪd]: *adj.* 复杂的

empire['empaɪə(r)]: *n.* 帝国

For one thing, the days of empire are now long enough ago that only old people remember it as anything of any importance in their lives. ① Britain is no longer an **imperial** country, though the effects of its imperial past may be often **encountered** in all sorts of ways; not least in the close relationships which exist with the fifty or more countries which used to be a part of that empire, and which maintain links through a loose (and **voluntary**) organization called the Commonwealth of Nations②. But more important today in Britain's international relations is the European Union③, of which the UK has been a member since 1973, and it is more useful when considering modern Britain to **emphasize** its role as a European nation, rather than its membership of the Commonwealth. It remains a relatively wealthy country, a member of the Group of Seven (made up of seven large developed economies).

imperial [ɪm'pɪəriəl]: *adj.* 帝国的

encounter[ɪn'kaʊntə(r)]: *v.* 遇到；受到

voluntary['vɒləntri]: *adj.* 自愿的；自发的

emphasize['emfəsaɪz]: *v.* 强调

One other obvious effect of that old imperial role lies in the make-up of the British population itself. **Immigration** from some of those Commonwealth countries, which was encouraged in the 1950s and 1960s, has produced a population of which 1 in 20 are of non-European **ethnicity**. They themselves, or their parents or grandparents, were born in India or **Pakistan**, the countries of **the Caribbean**, to name only the most common④.

immigration[ˌɪmɪ'greɪʃn]: *n.* 移民

ethnicity[eθ'nɪsəti]: *n.* 种族渊源

Pakistan:（国家名）巴基斯坦

the Caribbean: 加勒比海地区

As is the case for most, or all, countries, it is not possible to sum up the British people with a few simple phrases. Many people who think of Britain think of the English gentleman. But this is just a **stereotype** which never applied to the majority of the British people, and really has little **validity** today. The UK is one nation, with a single passport, and a single government having **sovereignty** over it all, but as the full name of the nation suggests, it is made up of different elements. It includes 4 parts: the island of Great Britain is made up of England, Scotland and Wales, and Northern Ireland, a province on the neighboring island of Ireland, completes the set⑤. So when discussing Britain and the British some consideration has to be made of these differences, for example, a woman from Scotland would not be pleased if we were to call her an "English gentleman"! She is Scottish and female, and sees her identity as different from that of men and separate from the English.

stereotype['steriətaɪp]: *n.* 陈规

validity[və'lɪdəti]: *n.* 有效

sovereignty['sɒvrənti]: *n.* 主权

But this **distinction** between the 4 **constituent** parts is only one, and perhaps the simplest, of the differences which divide the United Kingdom. It has been already pointed out that the UK is now a **multiracial** society, and these quite recent groups of immigrants have brought aspects of their own cultures with them which sit side by side with more traditionally British ways of life, for example, many are **Muslims**, while most British people (in name at least) are **Christians.** And clearly involved in the above example of the Scottish woman is the fact that men and women do not have the same experience of life in Britain. Also Britain is divided economically: it is a society with a class-structure. ⑥ It is possible to exaggerate the importance of this class structure, because of course most countries have some kind of class system, but it is true to say that the class structure of UK society is relatively obvious. The culture of a factory worker whose father was a factory worker may be quite different from that of a **stockbroker** whose father as a stockbroker: they will tend to read different newspapers, watch different television programs, speak with a different accent, do different things in their free-time, and have different **expectations** for their children.

distinction[dɪ'stɪŋkʃn]: *n.* 差别

constituent[kən'stɪtjuənt]: *adj.* 组成的；构成的

multiracial[ˌmʌlti'reɪʃl]: *adj.* 多种族的

Muslim['mʊzlɪm]: *n.* 伊斯兰教信徒

Christian['krɪstʃən]: *n.* 基督教徒

stockbroker[ˈstɒkbrəʊkə(r)]：*n.* 股票(证券)经纪人

expectation[ˌekspekˈteɪʃn]：*n.* 期待

Another difference which marks British society is that of regions. Even within each of the four parts there are different regions. The difference between the "highland" and "lowland" Scots has a long historical significance. North and south England are also considered to be culturally distinct, though the boundary between them is not marked on any map, and exists only as a rather unclear mental attitude.⑦ Further more there is distinction in economic terms as the south is on average wealthier than the north.

Part of the reason for that economic difference between north and south is found in another distinction which marks British society, a distinction which can be seen in many societies but is perhaps particularly obvious in the UK, that is, the difference between the capital and the provinces. London is in the south of the country, and is dominant in the United Kingdom in all sorts of ways. It is by far the largest city in the country, with about one seventh of the nation's population; it is the **seat** of government⑧; it is the cultural center, home to all the major newspapers, TV stations, and with far and away the widest selection of galleries, theatres and museums. Also it is the business center, headquarters of the vast majority of Britain's big companies; it is the financial center of the nation, and one of the three major international financial centers in the world. As such it combines the functions of Beijing, Shanghai and Guangzhou, or New York, Washington and Los Angeles, in one city. And given its long-standing historical role in the UK, perhaps Xi'an, too! London is a huge weight in Britain's economic and cultural life, and to some extent the rest of the country lives in its shadow.

seat[siːt]：*n.* 所在地

Notes

①For one thing, the days of empire are… as anything of any importance in their lives：首先，大英帝国的时代已经过去很久了，只有老人们视其为生活中有意义的一件事并留在记忆里。

②the Commonwealth of Nations：英联邦国家，包括英国及其前殖民地，它们在第一次世界大战前曾被称为大英帝国。女王是这些国家的最高权力象征，她每年举行定期会议，但并无实际控制权力。英国目前与这些国家仍保持着经常性的往来和交流。

③the European Union：欧洲联盟，简称欧盟，前身为欧洲共同体。

④to name only the most common：仅列举出几个最具代表性的国家和地区。指前面所提到的印度、巴基斯坦和加勒比海国家。

⑤ … and Northern Ireland，a province on the neighboring island of Ireland，completes the set：北爱尔兰是与大不列颠岛临近的爱尔兰岛上的一个省，即前面提到的大不列颠岛上的三个区域再加上北爱尔兰，组成一个完整的国家。to complete the set：指 the set of the nation，即完整的国家。

⑥Also Britain is divided economically：it is a society with a class-structure：而且英国社会是根据经济状况来划分的，即它是有阶级结构的社会。

⑦North and south England are also considered … a rather unclear mental attitude：尽管英格兰北部和南部的分界线在任何地图上都没有标出，而且它只是一条模糊的、存在于人们心理上的纬线，但这两个地区的文化迥然不同。

⑧it is the seat of government：伦敦是(英国)政府所在地。

Questions

1. What was the British Empire? What do you know about it? In what way is the Empire still felt in Britain and in the international field?

2. Why does the author say that it is not possible to sum up the British people with a few simple phrases?

3. “British history has been a history of invasion.” Please illustrate this point with the examples from the text. How did each of the invasions influence English culture?

Part D

Pre-reading activities

1. Draw a picture of the Lotus Pond based on your memory of this literary work.

2. Where would you go when you feel happy or unhappy?

荷塘月色

这几天心里颇不宁静。今晚在院子里坐着乘凉，忽然想起日日走过的荷塘，在这满月的光里，总该另有一番样子吧。月亮渐渐地升高了，墙外马路上孩子们的欢笑，已经听不见了；妻在屋里拍着闰儿，迷迷糊糊地哼着眠歌。我悄悄地披了大衫，带上门出去。

沿着荷塘，是一条曲折的小煤屑路。这是一条幽僻的路；白天也少人走，夜晚更加寂寞。荷塘四面，长着许多树，蓊蓊郁郁的。路的一旁，是些杨柳，和一些不知道名字的树。没有月光的晚上，这路上阴森森的，有些怕人。今晚却很好，虽然月光也还是淡淡的。

路上只我一个人，背着手踱着。这一片天地好像是我的；我也像超出了平常的自己，到了另一世界里。我爱热闹，也爱冷静；爱群居，也爱独处。像今晚上，一个人在这苍茫的月下，什么都可以想，什么都可以不想，便觉是个自由的人。白天里一定要做的事，一定要说的话，现在都可不理。这是独处的妙处，我且受用这无边的荷香月色好了。

曲曲折折的荷塘上面，弥望的是田田的叶子。叶子出水很高，像亭亭的舞女的裙。层层的叶子中间，零星地点缀着些白花，有袅娜地开着的，有羞涩地打着朵儿的；正如一粒粒的明珠，又如碧天里的星星，又如刚出浴的美人。微风过处，送来缕缕清香，仿佛远处高楼上渺茫的歌声似的。这时候叶子与花也有一丝的颤动，像闪电般，霎时传过荷塘的那边去了。叶子本是肩并肩密密地挨着，这便宛然有了一道凝碧的波痕。叶子底下是脉脉的流水，遮住了，不能见一些颜色；而叶子却更见风致了。

月光如流水一般，静静地泻在这一片叶子和花上。薄薄的青雾浮起在荷塘里。叶子和花仿佛在牛乳中洗过一样；又像笼着轻纱的梦。虽然是满月，天上却有一层淡淡的云，所以不能朗照；但我以为这恰是到了好处——酣眠固不可少，小睡也别有风味的。月光是隔了树照过来的，高处丛生的灌木，落下参差的斑驳的黑影，峭楞楞如鬼一般；弯弯的杨柳的稀疏的倩影，却又像是画在荷叶上。塘中的月色并不均匀；但光与影有着和谐的旋律，如梵婀玲上奏着的名曲。

荷塘的四面，远远近近，高高低低都是树，而杨柳最多。这些树将一片荷塘重重围住；只在小路一旁，漏着几段空隙，像是特为月光留下的。树色一例是阴阴的，乍看像一团烟雾；但杨柳的丰姿，便在烟雾里也辨得出。树梢上隐隐约约的是一带远山，只有些大意罢了。树缝里也漏着一两点路灯光，没精打采的，是渴睡人的眼。这时候最热闹的，要数树上的蝉声与水里的蛙声；但热闹是它们的，我什么也没有。

忽然想起采莲的事情来了。采莲是江南的旧俗，似乎很早就有，而六朝时为盛；从诗歌里可以约略知道。采莲的是少年的女子，她们是荡着小船，唱着艳歌去的。采莲人不用说很多，还有看采莲的人。那是一个热闹的季节，也是一个风流的季节。梁元帝《采莲赋》里说得好：

> 于是妖童媛女，荡舟心许；鹢首徐回，兼传羽杯；棹将移而藻挂，船欲动而萍开。尔其纤腰束素，迁延顾步；夏始春余，叶嫩花初，恐沾裳而

浅笑，畏倾船而敛裾。

可见当时嬉游的光景了。这真是有趣的事，可惜我们现在早已无福消受了。

于是又记起，《西洲曲》里的句子：

采莲南塘秋，莲花过人头；低头弄莲子，莲子清如水。

今晚若有采莲人，这儿的莲花也算得“过人头”了；只不见一些流水的影子，是不行的。这令我到底惦着江南了。——这样想着，猛一抬头，不觉已是自己的门前；轻轻地推门进去，什么声息也没有，妻已睡熟好久了。

一九二七年七月，北京清华园

参考译文

Moonlight over the Lotus Pond

I have felt quiet upset recentiy. Tonight, when I was sitting in the **yard** enjoying the **cool**, it **occurred** to me that the **Lotus Pond**, which I pass by every day, must **assume** quite a different look in such **moonlit** night. A full moon was rising high in the sky; the laughter of children playing outside had **died away**; in the room, my wife was **patting** the son, Run-er, **sleepily humming** a **cradle** song. **Shrugging** on an overcoat, quietly, I made my way out, closing the door behind me.

yard[jɑːd]: *n.* 院子
cool[kuːl]: *n.* 凉爽
occur[əˈkɜː(r)]: *v.* 闪现
lotus[ˈləʊtəs]: *n.* 莲花；荷花
pond[pɒnd]: *n.* 池塘
assume[əˈsjuːm]: *v.* 呈现
moonlit[ˈmuːnlɪt]: *adj.* 月光照耀的
die away:（尤指声音、光、风）逐渐消失
pat[pæt]: *v.* 轻拍；爱抚
sleepily[ˈsliːpɪli]: *adv.* 困倦地
hum[hʌm]: *v.* 哼唱
cradle[ˈkreɪdl]: *n.* 摇篮
shrug[ʃrʌg]: *v.* 提高肩膀

Alongside the Lotus Pond runs a small **cinder footpath**. It is peaceful and **secluded** here, a place not frequented by **pedestrians** even in the daytime; now at night, it looks more **solitary**, in a **lush**, **shady ambience** of trees all around the pond. On the side where the path is, there are **willows**, **interlaced** with some others whose names I do not know. The **foliage**, which, in a **moonless** night, would **loom somewhat frighteningly** dark, looks very nice tonight, although the moonlight is not more than a thin, **grayish veil**.

alongside[əˌlɒŋˈsaɪd]：*prep.* 在……旁边

cinder[ˈsɪndə(r)]：*n.* 煤渣；炭渣

footpath[ˈfʊtpɑːθ]：*n.* 小路；小径

secluded[sɪˈkluːdɪd]：*adj.* 僻静的；清静的

pedestrian[pəˈdestriən]：*n.* 行人；步行者

solitary[ˈsɒlətri]：*adj.* 孤独的

lush[lʌʃ]：*adj.* 葱翠的

shady[ˈʃeɪdi]：*adj.* 背阴的

ambience[ˈæmbiəns]：*n.* 周围环境（"ambiance"的变体）

willow[ˈwɪləʊ]：*n.* 柳树

interlace[ˌɪntəˈleɪs]：*v.* 使交错；使交织

foliage[ˈfəʊliɪdʒ]：*n.* 树叶

moonless[ˈmuːnləs]：*adj.* 无月光的

loom[luːm]：*v.* 令人惊恐地隐现

somewhat[ˈsʌmwɒt]：*adv.* 稍微；有点

frighteningly[ˈfraɪtnɪŋli]：*adv.* 吓人地

grayish[ˈgreɪɪʃ]：*adj.* 浅灰色的

veil[veɪl]：*n.* 面纱

I am on my own, **strolling**, hands behind my back. This **bit** of the universe seems in my **possession** now; and I myself seem to have been **uplifted** from my **ordinary** self into another world. I like a **serene** and peaceful life, as much as a busy and active one; I like being in solitude, as much as in **company**. As it is tonight, **basking** in a **misty moonshine** all by myself, I feel I am a free man, free to think of anything, or of nothing. All that one **is obliged to** do, or to say, in the daytime, can be very well **cast aside** now. That is the beauty of being alone. For the moment, just let me **indulge in** this **profusion** of moonlight and lotus **fragrance**.

stroll[strəʊl]：*v.* 散步

bit[bɪt]：*n.* 一块

possession[pəˈzeʃn]：*n.* 拥有

uplift[ˈʌplɪft]：*v.* 举起；使上升
ordinary[ˈɔːdnri]：*adj.* 平庸的
serene[səˈriːn]：*adj.* 安宁的
company[ˈkʌmpəni]：*n.* 陪伴
bask[bɑːsk]：*v.* 享受乐趣
misty[ˈmɪsti]：*adj.* 被雾笼罩的
moonshine[ˈmuːnʃaɪn]：*n.* 月光
be obliged to：必须；不得不
cast aside：扔；抛
indulge in：任凭自己沉溺于……
profusion[prəˈfjuːʒn]：*n.* 丰富；充沛
fragrance[ˈfreɪgrəns]：*n.* 芳香；芬芳

All over this **winding stretch** of water，what meets the eye is a **silken** field of leaves，reaching rather high above the **surface**，like the skirts of dancing girls in all their **grace**. Here and there，**layers** of leaves are **dotted** with white lotus **blossoms**，some in **demure bloom**，others in shy **bud**，like **scattering** pearls，or **twinkling** stars，or beauties just out of the bath. A **breeze stirs**，sending over breaths of fragrance，like **faint** singing **drifting** from a distant building. At this moment，a tiny **thrill** shoots through the leaves and **lilies**，like，a **streak** of **lightning**，straight across the forest of lotuses. The leaves，which have been standing shoulder to shoulder，are caught **shimmering** in an **emerald heave** of the pond. **Underneath**，the **exquisite** water is covered from **view**，and none can tell its color；yet the leaves on top **project** themselves all the more **attractively**.

winding[waɪndɪŋ]：*adj.* 蜿蜒曲折的
stretch[stretʃ]：*n.* 一片
silken[ˈsɪlkən]：*adj.* 柔软的
surface[ˈsɜːfɪs]：*n.* 水面
grace[greɪs]：*n.* 优雅
layer[ˈleɪə(r)]：*n.* 层
dot[dɒt]：*v.* 点缀
blossom[ˈblɒsəm]：*n.* 花
demure[dɪˈmjʊə(r)]：*adj.* 娴静的；袅娜的
bloom[bluːm]：*n.*（常指供观赏的）花
bud[bʌd]：*n.* 花骨朵

scatter['skætə(r)]：*v.*（使）散开；（使）分散
twinkle['twɪŋkl]：*v.* 闪烁
breeze[briːz]：*n.* 微风
stir[stɜː(r)]：*v.*（使）微动
faint[feɪnt]：*adj.* 微弱的
drift[drɪft]：*v.* 漂流
thrill[θrɪl]：*n.* 震颤
lily['lɪli]：*n.* 百合花
streak[striːk]：*n.* 一道
lightning['laɪtnɪŋ]：*n.* 闪电
shimmer['ʃɪmə(r)]：*v.* 闪烁；发微光
emerald['emərəld]：*n.* 绿宝石；翡翠
heave[hiːv]：*n.* 起伏；波动
underneath[ˌʌndə'niːθ]：*prep.* 在……下面
exquisite[ɪk'skwɪzɪt]：*adj.* 细腻的；优美的
view[vjuː]：*n.* 视域
project['prɒdʒekt]：*v.* 放映；放射
attractively[ə'træktɪvli]：*adv.* 动人地；迷人地

The moon **sheds** her **liquid** light silently over the leaves and flowers, which, in the **floating transparency** of a **bluish haze** from the pond, look as if they had just been bathed in milk, or like a dream **wrapped** in a **gauzy hood**. Although it is a full moon, shining through a **film** of clouds, the light is not at its brightest; it is, however, just right for me—a **profound** sleep is **indispensable**, yet a **snatched doze** also has a **savor** of its own. The moonlight is **streaming down** through the foliage, casting **bushy** shadows on the ground from high above, **jagged** and **checkered**, as **grotesque** as a party of **spectres**; **whereas** the **benign** figures of the **drooping** willows, here and there, look like paintings on the lotus leaves. The moonlight is not spread **evenly** over the pond, but rather in a **harmonious rhythm** of light and shade, like a famous **melody** played on a violin.

shed[ʃed]：*v.* 流下
liquid['lɪkwɪd]：*n.* 液体
floating['fləʊtɪŋ]：*adj.* 流动的；浮动的
transparency[træns'pærənsi]：*n.* 透明；透明的东西
bluish['bluːɪʃ]：*adj.* 接近蓝色的；浅蓝的

haze[heɪz]：*n.* 烟雾

wrap[ræp]：*v.* 包；用……包裹

gauzy[ˈɡɔːzi]：*adj.* 纱似的；薄的

hood[hʊd]：*n.* 面罩

film[fɪlm]：*n.* 薄层

profound[prəˈfaʊnd]：*adj.* 深深的

indispensable[ˌɪndɪˈspensəbl]：*adj.* 不可缺少的；绝对必要的

snatch[snætʃ]：*v.* 抓紧时间做；乘机获得

doze[dəʊz]：*n.* 瞌睡

savor[ˈseɪvə(r)]：*n.* 味道；滋味

stream down：流下来

bushy[bʊʃi]：*adj.* 浓密的

jagged[dʒæɡɪd]：*adj.* 锯齿状的；参差的

checkered[ˈtʃekəd]：*adj.*（格子）花纹的；斑驳的

grotesque[ɡrəʊˈtesk]：*adj.* 怪诞的

spectre[ˈspektə(r)]：*n.* 幽灵；鬼怪

whereas[ˌweərˈæz]：*conj.* 然而

benign[bɪˈnaɪn]：*adj.* 温和的

droop[druːp]：*v.* 低垂；垂落

evenly[ˈiːvnli]：*adv.* 均匀地

harmonious[hɑːˈməʊniəs]：*adj.* 协调的；和谐的

rhythm[ˈrɪðəm]：*n.* 节奏；韵律

melody[ˈmelədi]：*n.* 旋律；曲调；美妙的音乐

Around the pond, far and near, high and low, are trees. Most of them are willows. Only on the path side, can two or three gaps be seen through the heavy **fringe**, as if specially **reserved** for the moon. The **shadowy** shapes of the **leafage** at first sight seem **diffused** into a **mass** of **mist**, against which, however, the **charm** of those willow trees is still **discernible.** Over the trees appear some distant mountains, but merely in **sketchy silhouette.** Through the branches are also a couple of **lamps**, as **listless** as sleepy eyes. The most lively **creatures** here, for the moment, must he the **cicadas** in the trees and the frogs in the pond. But the **liveliness** is theirs, I have nothing.

fringe[frɪndʒ]：*n.* 边缘

reserve[rɪˈzɜːv]：*v.* 保留

shadowy[ˈʃædəʊi]：*adj.* 影影绰绰的

leafage[ˈliːfɪdʒ]：*n.* 树叶
diffused[dɪˈfjuːzd]：*adj.* 扩散的
mass[mæs]：*n.* 大量
mist[mɪst]：*n.* 薄雾
charm[tʃɑːm]：*n.* 魅力
discernible[dɪˈsɜːnəbl]：*adj.* 可辨别的；可识别的
sketchy[ˈsketʃi]：*adj.* 概要的；粗略的
silhouette[ˌsɪluˈet]：*n.* 轮廓；剪影
lamp[læmp]：*n.* 灯
listless[ˈlɪstləs]：*adj.* 倦怠的；无精打采的
creature[ˈkriːtʃə(r)]：*n.* 生物
cicada[sɪˈkɑːdə]：*n.* 蝉
liveliness[ˈlaɪvlɪnəs]：*n.* 生气；热闹

Suddenly, something like lotus-**gathering** crosses my mind. It used to be **celebrated** as a **folk** festival in the South, **probably** dating very far back in history, most popular in the period of Six **Dynasties.** We can pick up some **outlines** of this activity in the **poetry.** It was young girls who went gathering lotuses, in **sampans** and singing love songs. **Needless** to say, there were a great number of them doing the gathering, **apart from** those who were watching. It was a **lively** season, **brimming** with **vitality**, and **romance.** A **brilliant description** can be found in *Lotus Gathering* written by the Yuan **Emperor** of the Liang Dynasty:

suddenly[ˈsʌdənli]：*adv.* 忽然
gather[ˈgæðə(r)]：*v.* 采集
celebrate[ˈselɪbreɪt]：*v.* 庆祝
folk[fəʊk]：*adj.* 民间的；民俗的
probably[ˈprɒbəbli]：*adv.* 大概；或许；很可能
dynasty[ˈdɪnəsti]：*n.* 王朝；朝代
outline[ˈaʊtlaɪn]：*n.* 梗概
poetry[ˈpəʊətri]：*n.* 诗歌
sampan[ˈsæmpæn]：*n.* 小船
needless[ˈniːdləs]：*adv.* 不需要地；不必要地
apart from：除了……以外
lively[ˈlaɪvli]：*adj.* 充满活力的
brim[brɪm]：*v.* 注满

vitality[vaɪˈtæləti]：*n.* 活力；生命力
romance[rəʊˈmæns]：*n.* 浪漫气氛
brilliant[ˈbrɪliənt]：*adj.* 美好的
description[dɪˈskrɪpʃn]：*n.* 描述
emperor[ˈempərə(r)]：*n.* 皇帝；君主

So those ***charming youngsters rowed*** *their sampans, heart* ***buoyant*** *with* ***tacit*** *loneliness, pass on to each other cups of* ***wire*** *while their bird-shaped* ***prows drift*** *around. Their* ***oars*** *are caught in* ***dangling alga***, *and* ***duckweed*** *flow apart the moment their boats are about to move on. Their* ***slender figures***, ***girdled*** *with* ***plain*** *silk,* ***tread watchfully*** *on board. This is the time when spring is into summer, the leaves a* ***tender*** *green and the flowers blooming—among which the girls are* ***giggling*** *when* ***evading*** *an out-reaching* ***stem***, *their skirts* ***tucked*** *in for* ***fear*** *that the sampan might* ***tilt***.

charming[ˈtʃɑːmɪŋ]：*adj.* 迷人的；可爱的；英俊的
youngster[ˈjʌŋstə(r)]：*n.* 少年
row[rəʊ]：*v.* 划船
buoyant[ˈbɔɪənt]：*adj.* 漂浮的
tacit[ˈtæsɪt]：*adj.* 心照不宣的；缄默的
wire[ˈwaɪə(r)]：*n.* 电线；金属丝
prow[praʊ]：*n.* 船首
drift[drɪft]：*v.* 漂流
oar[ɔː(r)]：*n.* 桨
dangle[ˈdæŋgl]：*v.* 使摇晃地挂着或摆荡
alga[ˈælgə]：*n.* 水藻
duckweed[ˈdʌkwiːd]：*n.* 浮萍
slender[ˈslendə(r)]：*adj.* 苗条的
figure[ˈfɪgə(r)]：*n.* 身材
girdle[ˈgɜːdl]：*v.* 包裹
plain[pleɪn]：*adj.* 朴素的
tread[tred]：*v.* 踏；行走
watchfully[ˈwɒtʃfəlɪ]：*adv.* 留心地
tender[ˈtendə(r)]：*adj.* 嫩的
giggle[ˈgɪgl]：*v.* 娇笑一下
evade[ɪˈveɪd]：*v.* 避开；躲避
stem[stem]：*n.*（花草的）茎

tuck[tʌk]：*v.* 把（衣服等的边缘）塞进……

fear[fɪə(r)]：*n.* 担心

tilt[tɪlt]：*v.* 倾斜

That is a **glimpse** of those **merrymaking scenes.** It must have been **fascinating**：but **unfortunately** we have long been **denied** such a **delight.**

glimpse[glɪmps]：*n.* 隐约的闪现

merrymaking[ˈmerimeɪkɪŋ]：*n.* 嬉笑玩乐；行乐

scene[siːn]：*n.* 场面

fascinating[ˈfæsɪneɪtɪŋ]：*adj.* 有趣的

unfortunately[ʌnˈfɔːtʃənətli]：*adv.* 可惜；遗憾地

deny[dɪˈnaɪ]：*v.* 拒绝占有……

delight[dɪˈlaɪt]：*n.* 使人高兴的事

Then I **recall** those **lines** in ***Ballad*** *of Xizhou Island*：

Gathering the lotus，I am in the South Pond. The lilies in autumn reach over my head. ***Lowering*** *my head I* ***toy with*** *the lotus seeds. Look，they are as fresh as the water underneath.*

recall[rɪˈkɔːl]：*v.* 回想起

line[laɪn]：*n.* 词句

ballad[ˈbæləd]：*n.* 民歌；民谣

lower[ˈləʊə(r)]：*v.* 降低

toy with：玩耍；摆弄

If there were somebody gathering lotuses tonight，she could tell that the lilies here are high enough to "reach over her head"；but，one would certainly miss the **sight** of the water. So my memories drift back to the South after all. Deep in my **thoughts**，I looked up，just to find myself at the door of my own house. Gently I pushed the door open and walked in. Not a sound inside，my wife had been fast asleep for quite a while.

Qinghua Campus，Beijing

July，1927

sight[saɪt]：*n.* 景象

thought[θɔːt]：*n.* 思想；想法

［选自：杨平．名作精译：汉译英．青岛：青岛出版社，2003.］

After-reading activities

1. Discuss with your classmates about writing techniques of description.

2. Name some rhetorical devices used in this work.

3. Describe a natural place you appreciate by employing the writing techniques you have learnt in this work.

作者简介

朱自清(1898—1948)，原名自华，字佩弦，号秋实。江苏扬州人。“文学研究会”的早期成员，现代著名的散文家、学者。原任清华大学教授，抗日战争爆发后转西南联合大学任教。在抗日民主运动的影响下，政治态度明显倾向进步。晚年积极参加抗日民主运动。他的散文结构严谨，笔触细致，不论写景还是抒情，均能通过细密观察或深入体味，委婉地表现出对自然景色的内心感受，抒发自己的真挚感情，充满诗情画意。主要作品有《毁灭》《踪迹》《背影》《欧游杂记》《伦敦杂记》等。

写作背景

《荷塘月色》作于1927年7月，正值大革命失败，白色恐怖笼罩中国大地。这时，蒋介石叛变革命，中国处于一片黑暗之中。朱自清作为“大时代中的一名小卒”，一直在呐喊和斗争，但是在“四一二”政变之后，却从斗争的“十字街头”，钻进古典文学的“象牙之塔”。作者既做不到投笔从戎，拿起枪来革命，又始终平息不了对黑暗现实产生的不满与憎恶，作者对生活感到惶惑矛盾，内心是抑郁的，是始终无法平静的，于是写下了这篇文章。这篇散文通过对冷清的月夜下荷塘景色的描写，流露出作者想寻找安宁但又不可得、幻想超脱现实但又无法超脱的复杂心情，这正是那个黑暗的时代在作者心灵上的折射。

作品鉴赏

全文可以分为四个部分。作者首先交代了去荷塘的时间和缘由。开头就说出这几天“颇不宁静”的内心状态。“颇”字是对不宁静心情的强调。下文中作者思绪翻飞，神驰万里，或行或止，或喜或愁，都和这“颇不宁静”的心情有着紧密的联系。这一句是作者进行艺术构思的焦点，也是《荷塘月色》这篇文章的文眼。它以强烈的直接抒情开始，将淡淡哀愁流露在字里行间，为全文定下了感情的基调。

第二部分从荷塘周遭的环境写起，向《荷塘月色》的主体进发。作者先写曲折幽僻的小煤屑路。通过“白天也少人走，夜晚更加寂寞”的叙述，暗写了在这种气氛环境中作者的一颗寂寞的心。继而实写荷塘四周的林木，虚写没有月光时的阴森气象，虚实相间地勾勒出此刻荷塘的环境和作者的心境。最后以赞美今夜的淡淡月光作结。平时无意于荷塘的月色，尽管今晚的月光只是淡淡的，仍然觉得很好。读者带着这种思索转入了下一段。这个结句完成了由写景到抒情之间的过渡。第三段紧承第二段，披露自己之所以中意于今夜荷塘的原委，抒发自己踏月寻幽的万端感慨。由“路上只我一个人”提起了下边关于踽踽独行于荷塘的一番妙论。“背着手踱着”这一细节，微妙地展示了作者此刻稍有宽解的心情。接下去是一段内心剖白：“这一片天地好像是我的；我也像超出了平常的自己，到了另一世界里。”一种喜悦之情溢于言表，但是都加了“好像”“像”这样的修饰语，说明这种喜悦之情是建立在虚幻的遐想上的自我慰藉。从以后的行文中可知这当然也只能是不堪现实一击的淡淡的喜悦。尽管如此，由于此时此地能使身心挣脱生活的种种羁绊，偷得片刻安宁，因而才有了“什么都可以想，什么都可以不想”“是个自由的人”的感觉。只是这样一种感觉的获得，就能使作者发出“且受用这无边的荷香月色”的自足的惬意的心声，足见这样一个小天地对于被现实局势困扰的作者来说，是多么难求的境界。这句话，细加品味，最能撩人心绪。从作者苦涩的微笑中，读者看到了一个痛楚的灵魂对现实的反抗。

第三部分开始正式地对荷塘和月色的景致进行详细的描写，最先映入眼帘的是满塘荷叶。“亭亭”一词表现了荷叶的风姿秀丽，“舞女的裙”的比喻，恰到好处地写出了荷叶临风摇曳的姿态。在纵观之后，凝神细审，视线移到万绿丛中的点点白花。盛开的袅娜喜人，含苞欲放地流露着勾人情思的娇羞，十分传神地写出了荷花的不同姿态。进而用“正如一粒粒的明珠，又如碧天里的星星”这样的比喻，写出荷花从光色上给人的感受。“明珠”是写近处荷花的玲珑剔透，“碧天里的星星”是写在满塘荷叶衬托和月光的辉映下，远处荷花的闪烁迷离。既看到宜人的花色，也就必然会嗅到沁人的花香。“缕缕清香”，能让读者真切地感受到是很难的，但作者以歌声设比，用时断时续、若有若无的远处的歌声，把听觉和嗅觉两种感觉联通起来，这种通感修辞手法的运用，实在可以传神。在这番静态描写之后，又把荷塘的动态捕捉进镜头里。清风徐徐，荷叶的一丝颤动，化为一道碧痕，荡向荷塘那边。这种细致的描摹，使人宛然若见。在一连串的比喻描写之后，作者又用“更见风致”概括地写出淡淡月色之下、脉脉流水之上的荷叶的美。第五段描绘荷塘的月色。月色是单调的，难以着笔，而作者把它和形态不一、色彩有别的景物结合在一起进行描写，就使月色有了光上的变化。作者继续展示出月光下荷塘四周的景象。“远远近近”“高高低低”等叠词的运用，造就了树木错落有致的层次感。

第四部分为文章的结尾，从单纯地写景写开来，进一步表现了作者不满现实、幻想超脱而不能得的复杂心理。

作品具有如下艺术特色。

构思特色：散文具有“文眼”，这是我国古代散文一条传统的艺术经验。唯有有“眼”，题旨才会有隐显意境，才会有虚实，剪裁才会有详略，结构才会有疏密。《荷塘月色》是十分注重“眼”的安设的，并且充分地使之成为构思的“焦点”，也使之成为将作品的思想与艺术辩证统一起来的“凝光点”。

《荷塘月色》一开篇就点出文章的“文眼”——“这几天心里颇不宁静”。接着写小路的“静”、月色朦胧的“静”，来反衬作者的“心里颇不宁静”。再接着以荷塘四周蝉声和蛙鸣的“闹”突出荷塘月色的“静”，又联想到江南采莲的旧俗。梁元帝的《采莲赋》和《西洲曲》中关于采莲的热闹、嬉戏的情景，进一步反衬此时此地“荷塘月色”的“静”。最后画龙点睛——“这令我到底惦着江南了”——含蓄地揭示出“心里颇不宁静”的原因所在。文章的结构严谨细密，脉络清晰，又不露人工斧凿的痕迹，达到了散文“形散神不散”的可贵境界。散文的艺术魅力，集中地体现在艺术构思方面。朱自清的散文在构思上是十分讲究的：缜密而严谨，新奇而精巧，营构合理，“设眼有致”。

画面感强：有学者评论朱自清的写景散文如同“工笔画”，景物描绘精雕细刻，细腻传神。此论于《荷塘月色》尤为确切。《荷塘月色》第四、第五自然段充分体现了朱自清散文“工笔画”的特点。

首先，朱自清把水乳交融、浑然一体的“荷塘月色”细分为“月色下的荷塘”与“荷塘上的月色”两部分。“曲曲折折的荷塘上面，弥望的是田田的叶子……而叶子却更见风致了。”这一段以月色为背景，重点描写荷塘的各样景。“月光如流水一般……如梵婀玲上奏着的名曲。”这一段以荷塘为背景，重点描写了月色的层次变化。这样划分，使景物描写得以细腻地进行。

其次，朱自清对剖开来的“月色下的荷塘”与“荷塘上的月色”两部分做进一步的“精耕细作”，从视觉（“弥望”“不能见”等）、听觉（“渺茫的歌声”“梵婀玲上奏着的名曲”等）、嗅觉（“清香”等）等角度去描写对象的形状、色彩、大小、数量、气味、声音，以及它们的运动变化。这样就把景物表现得非常细腻了。

最后，“月色下的荷塘”与“荷塘上的月色”两部分的描写表现出朱自清高超的修辞技巧。《荷塘月色》第四、第五自然段短短三百多字仅比喻就有十一处，另有拟人两处，通感两处以及排比、夸张等修辞手法，比喻、拟人、通感的运用巧妙而自然。这样就把“荷塘月色”描绘得细致入微、形象生动，让读者有身临其境之感。

语言隽永：朱自清散文的语言基调是朴素的，有一种清新、自然、典雅的美。

一是朴素美。朱自清的语言艺术是最为人称道的。他一向追求“谈话风”的语言境界，认为文学只有像“寻常谈话一般，读了才能亲切有味”。例如，朱自清开篇就说“这几天心里颇不宁静”，似乎把读者当作可以倾诉的朋友，让人觉得诚恳自然，一下子就把读者带入了那种情境中。又如，“我悄悄地披上大衣，带上门出去”，“这路上阴森森的，有些怕人”等，都平白如话，自然流畅，读之使人感觉分外亲切。

二是凝练美。朱自清具有很强的语言驾驭能力。他的语言看似普通，不做惊人之语，但实际上是经过精心锤炼的。例如，“月光如流水一般，静静地泻在这一片叶子和花上”，“泻”字紧扣“月光如流水一般”这个比喻，写月光照耀、一泻无余的景象，再加上“静静地”这个修饰语，就准确地写出了月光既像流水一般倾泻，但又绝无声响的幽静。又如，“薄薄的青雾浮起在荷塘里”，“浮”这个动词把水气和月色交织在一起、雾的轻柔以及自下而上逐渐扩散的特点准确地表达出来，给画面涂上一层素淡清雅的底色，月色朦胧，若有若无，给人以无穷的想象。一个“泻”字，一个“浮”字，用得绝妙之极。

三是音乐美。作者常常运用叠词叠句来深化物态情貌的形象感[在《荷塘月色》中，共运用了“日日”“渐渐”等叠词 25 个 26 次(“淡淡”重复了一次)]，使文章柔美、舒缓、流畅。同时“袅娜”“仿佛”“斑驳”“均匀”“到底”和“苍茫”“独处”“零星”“宛然”“酣眠”“一例”等双声叠韵词的运用也增强了语言的音乐美。

四是修辞美。生动形象的比喻、拟人、排比、对比等修辞手法的运用也是这篇文章语言的一大特点。经这些修辞手法装饰的语言更具艺术魅力。朱自清是一位善用比喻的高手。他的比喻，往往能出乎人的意料，发前人所未发，但又在情理之中，贴切自然。例如，“叶子出水很高，像亭亭的舞女的裙”。以“亭亭的舞女的裙”喻叶子自然舒展的形态，赋予荷叶动态的美，极为生动，又极为贴切。又如，“层层的叶子中间，零星地点缀着些白花，有袅娜地开着的，有羞涩地打着朵儿的；正如一粒粒的明珠，又如碧天里的星星”。作者用“一粒粒的明珠”和“碧天里的星星”两个喻体同时比喻“白花”，分别突出苍茫的月光下荷花的光亮和白花在绿叶丛中隐约闪烁的动态美。从色彩和光华上极写荷花之美，十分生动形象，又不落俗套，更能唤起读者的联想和想象。

另外，朱自清也善于运用通感手法来塑造形象美。例如，“微风过处，送来缕缕清香，仿佛远处高楼上渺茫的歌声似的”。清香是嗅觉感受，可闻而不可听，可嗅而不可见。作者把淡淡的清香比作渺茫的歌声，就让读者很形象地体会到这香气是缥缈不定、似有若无的，非常新颖而又贴切。又如，“塘中的月色并不均匀；但光与影有着和谐的旋律，如梵婀玲上奏着的名曲”。朱自清把树影与月光交织在一起时所构成的黑白相间的优美画面的视觉形象，转化为听觉形象，激起读者无限的遐想。这样写，不但可以促使读者进一步想象荷塘上和谐的画面、宁静的气氛，而且大大丰富了月下荷塘诗一般美的意境。

Chapter 2　The Mountain

Part A

约翰·缪尔(John Muir，1838—1914)，是美国自然文学的代表作家之一，也是美国自然保护运动的倡导者与实践者。多年来，缪尔一直被人们称为"康科德最后的信徒""心醉神迷的梭罗""大自然的推销者"以及"美国自然保护运动的圣人"。腊斯克(Ralph L. Nux)在《爱默生的一生》(*Ralph Waldo Emeron's Life*)中写道："爱默生生前曾列出一张'我敬佩的人'的名单，它以英国的托马斯·卡莱尔(Thomas Carlyle)为首，以约翰·缪尔为尾。"缪尔数十年来跋涉于美国西部的广袤山区，以山川、河流为伴，以动物、植物为友，亲近自然，对话生命，将其在旅行中的观察与体验物化为充满诗情画意的文字。一生中他共发表三百多篇文章，创作了 60 本记录自然生态的日记和十多部描写自然的生态散文，其代表性作品有《加利福尼亚的山脉》(*The Mountains of California*，1894)、《我们的国家公园》(*Our National Parks*，1901)、《夏日走过山间》(*My First Summer in the Sierra*，1911)、《优胜美地》(*The Yosemite*，1912)、《阿拉斯加游记》(*Travels in Alaska*，1915)等。

缪尔以敏锐开放的感官来感受自然之美，从视觉、听觉、嗅觉、味觉、触觉等方面感知自然，描绘自然，构建了一个有声有色、有形有味的散文世界。他采用色彩斑斓的话语去表现丰富多彩的自然生命之态，以拟人化的语言体现自然万物的亲和之感，以激情洋溢的话语去表达对自然的热爱之情，将科学家的严谨缜密与诗人的激情浪漫结合了起来。这使得他的作品有种特殊的吸引力，对推动美国生态文学的发展具有重要意义。

缪尔的作品描摹了自然生态景观，传达着敬畏自然、呵护生命以及希望自然万物和谐共生的思想。大自然是一个共同体，万物之间存在着密切的联系，包括人类在内的各个成员之间都相互依赖，相互支持。缪尔在其代表作《夏日走过山间》中感叹道："沉浸在这样的地方，你会越来越强烈地感受到我们自己正属于这野性的大自然，是她的一个组成部分，且与万物有着不能割舍的亲缘……""那些真正的石头似乎是健谈的、热情而亲切的，当我们想到我们共有同一个自然之父和自然之母时，这些石头就是我们的兄弟……"人类是自然万物中的一员，我们在利用自然资源的同时也要充分考虑在地球上生存的其他物种的利益，我们没有权利凌驾于其他生命之上。保护自然、热爱自然就是保护和热爱我们人类自己。缪尔是自然美的发现者和表现者，是自然环境保护的呐喊者与践行者。他的一生都在用生命和散文不断地呼吁和号召人们欣赏自然之美，以便人类能合理地利用自然，与自然万物和谐共生。缪尔曾说："如果神圣的人类能够变得真正富有人性，学会把动物当成朋友放在心里，而不是放在背上作衣服，或者放在餐桌上当食物，一个更好的时代肯定会到来。"缪尔的这种思想和观点即使放在当今社会也一点不过时。21 世纪是生态文明建设的世纪，关爱自然、爱护植物、保护动物，人与自然万物诗意地栖居于大地之上应当是人类的生态理想，我们期待约翰·缪尔的预言——"一个更好的时代肯定会到来"成为现实。

My First Summer in the Sierra (Excerpt)

题注：此选段是 6 月 4 日到 6 月 6 日的日记部分。作者主要对山中的松树进行了细致入微的观察并进行了诗情画意的描写，将树木的美丽以及与周围环境和谐共生的画面清晰而美好地展现在我们面前，让我们对大自然无与伦比的美充满着无尽想象。

June 4.

The **camp** was **astir at daybreak**; coffee, **bacon**, and beans formed the breakfast, followed by quick dish-washing and packing.① A general **bleating** began about sunrise. As soon as a mother **ewe** arose, her **lamb came bounding and bunting for** its breakfast, and after the thousand youngsters had been suckled the **flock** began to nibble and spread. The restless **wethers** with **ravenous appetites** were the first to move, but dared not go far from the main body. **Billy and the Indian and the Chinaman** kept them headed along the weary road, and allowed them to pick up what little they could find on a breadth of about a quarter of a mile. But as several flocks had already gone ahead of us, scarce a leaf, green or dry, was left; therefore the starving flock had to be hurried on over the bare, hot hills to the nearest of the green pastures, about twenty or thirty miles from here. ②

camp[kæmp]：*n.* 营地

astir[əˈstɜː(r)]：*adj.* 活跃的；骚动的

at daybreak：黎明时分；破晓时分

bacon[ˈbeɪkən]：*n.* 培根

bleating[bliːtɪŋ]：*n.*（小羊）咩咩叫

ewe[juː]：*n.* 母羊

lamb[læm]：*n.* 小羊羔

come bounding and bunting for：跌跌撞撞地冲过来。bounding and bunting 在这里使用了头韵(alliteration)的修辞手法。

flock[flɒk]：*n.* 羊群

wether[ˈweðə]：*n.* 阉羊

ravenous appetite：极强的食欲。ravenous 是指极度饥饿的，比 hungry 程度要高。

Billy and the Indian and the Chinaman：这里指的是三个牧羊人，比利、一个印第安人和一个中国人。

The pack-animals were led by **Don Quixote**, a heavy **rifle** over his shoulder **intended for** bears and wolves. This day has been as hot and dusty as the first, leading over gently sloping brown hills, with mostly the same **vegetation**, excepting the strange-looking **Sabine pine** (Pinus Sabiniana), which here forms small groves or is scattered among the blue **oaks**. The trunk divides at a height of fifteen or twenty feet into two or more stems, outleaning or nearly upright, with many straggling branches and long gray needles, casting but little shade. ③ In general appearance this tree looks more like a **palm** than a pine. The **cones** are about six or seven inches long, about five in diameter, very heavy, and last long after they fall, so that the ground beneath the trees is covered with them. They make fine **resiny**, light-giving camp-fires, next to ears of Indian corn the most beautiful fuel I've ever seen. The nuts, the Don tells me, are gathered in large quantities by the Digger Indians for food. They are about as large and hard-shelled as **hazelnuts**—food and fire fit for the gods from the same fruit.

Don Quixote：堂吉诃德，源自西班牙作家塞万提斯的骑士小说《堂吉诃德》。他一方面脱离现实，爱幻想，企图仿效游侠骑士的生活；另一方面又心地善良，立志铲除人间邪恶。此处指牧场主德莱尼先生。

rifle[ˈraɪfl]：*n.* 步枪
intend for：为……而准备
vegetation[ˌvedʒəˈteɪʃn]：*n.* 植物(总称)
Sabine pine：加州大子松
oak[əʊk]：*n.* 橡树
palm[pɑːm]：*n.* 棕榈树
cone[kəʊn]：*n.* 松树果
resiny[ˈrezənɪ]：*adj.* 树脂质的
hazelnut[ˈheɪzlnʌt]：*n.* 榛子

June 5.

This morning a few hours after setting out with the **crawling sheep-cloud**, we gained the **summit** of the first well-defined bench on the mountain-flank at **Pino Blanco**. The Sabine pines interest me greatly. They are so airy and strangely palm-like I **was eager to sketch** them, and was in **a fever of excitement** without accomplishing much. I managed to **halt** long enough, however, to make a tolerably fair sketch of Pino Blanco peak from the southwest side, where there is a small field and vineyard **irrigated** by a **stream** that makes a pretty **fall** on its way down a **gorge** by the roadside. ④

crawl[ˈkrɔːl]：*v.* 爬行
sheep-cloud[ˈʃɪpklaʊd]：*n.* 像云朵一样的羊群
summit[ˈsʌmɪt]：*n.* 顶点
Pino Blanco：皮诺布兰克山峰
be eager to：盼望；渴望
sketch[sketʃ]：*v.* 素描
a fever of excitement：极度兴奋
halt[hɔːlt]：*v.* 暂停；停留；中断
irrigate[ˈɪrɪgeɪt]：*v.* 灌溉
stream[striːm]：*n.* 河流；小溪
fall[fɔːl]：*n.* 瀑布
gorge[gɔːdʒ]：*n.* 峡谷

After gaining the open summit of this first bench, feeling the natural **exhilaration** due to the slight **elevation** of a thousand feet or so, and the hopes excited concerning the outlook to be obtained, a magnificent section of **the Merced Valley** at what is called **Horseshoe Bend** came full **in sight**—a glorious **wilderness** that seemed to be calling with a thousand songful voices. ⑤ Bold, down-sweeping **slopes**, feathered with pines and **clumps of manzanita** with sunny, open spaces between them, make up most of the foreground; the middle and background present **fold** beyond fold of finely modeled hills and ridges rising into mountain—like masses in the distance, all covered with a shaggy growth of **chaparral**, mostly adenostoma, planted so **marvelously** close and even that it looks like soft, rich **plush** without a single tree or bare spot. ⑥ As far as the eye can reach it extends, a heaving, swelling **sea of green** as regular and continuous as that produced by the heaths of Scotland. ⑦ The **sculpture** of the landscape is as **striking** in its main lines as in its lavish richness of detail; a grand **congregation** of massive heights with the river shining between, each carved into smooth, graceful folds without leaving a single rocky angle exposed, as if the delicate **fluting and ridging** fashioned out of metamorphic **slates** had been carefully **sandpapered.** The whole landscape showed design, like man's noblest sculptures. How wonderful the power of its beauty! Gazing awe-stricken, I might have left everything for it. Glad, endless work would then be mine tracing the forces that have brought forth its features, its rocks and plants and animals and glorious weather. Beauty beyond thought everywhere, beneath, above, made and being made forever. ⑧ I gazed and gazed and longed and admired until the dusty sheep and packs were far out of sight, made hurried notes and a sketch, though there was no need of either, for the colors and lines and expression of this **divine** landscape-**countenance** are so burned into mind and heart they surely can never grow dim.

exhilaration[ɪgˌzɪlə'reɪʃn]: *n.* 愉快的心情

elevation[ˌelɪ'veɪʃn]: *n.* 海拔

the Merced Valley: 默塞德山谷。位于美国加州地区，是美国著名的风景名胜地。

Horseshoe Bend: 马蹄湾

in sight: 在视线范围内；映入眼帘

wilderness['wɪldənəs]: *n.* 荒野；(草木丛生的)荒地

slope[sləʊp]: *n.* 斜坡

clumps of: (树、灌木、植物等的)丛、簇

manzanita[ˌmænzə'niːtə]: *n.* 石兰科常绿灌木

fold: 原意为"折叠"，此处指层层叠叠、高低不平的起伏地。

chaparral[ˌʃæpə'ræl]: *n.* (生长稠密的交缠在一起的)灌木丛

marvelously['mɑːvələsli]: *adv.* 令人惊讶地；不可思议地

plush[plʌʃ]：*n.* 长绒毯

sea of green：绿色的海洋，此处运用了比喻的修辞手法。

sculpture[ˈskʌlptʃə(r)]：*n.* 雕塑；塑像

striking[ˈstraɪkɪŋ]：*adj.* 引人注目的；显著的

congregation[ˌkɒŋgrɪˈgeɪʃn]：*n.* 集合

fluting and ridging：凹槽与隆脊

slate[sleɪt]：*n.* 岩石

sandpaper[ˈsændpeɪpə(r)]：*v.*（用砂纸）打磨

divine[dɪˈvaɪn]：*adj.* 神圣的；天赐的；极好的

countenance[ˈkaʊntənəns]：*n.* 表情

The evening of this charmed day is **cool**, **calm**, **cloudless**, and full of a kind of lightning I have never seen before—white glowing cloud-shaped masses down among the trees and bushes, like quick-throbbing fireflies in the Wisconsin **meadows** rather than the so-called "wild fire". The spreading hairs of the horses' tails and **sparks** from our **blankets** show how highly charged the air is.

cool, **calm**, **cloudless**：此处运用了头韵的修辞手法。

meadow[ˈmedəʊ]：*n.* 草地；牧场

spark[spɑːk]：*n.* 火花

blanket[ˈblæŋkɪt]：*n.* 毯子；毛毯

June 6.

We are now on what may be called the second bench or plateau of the Range, after making many small ups and downs over belts of hill-waves, with, of course, corresponding changes in the vegetation. In open spots many of the lowland **composite** are still to be found, and some of the Mariposa tulips and other conspicuous members of the lily family; but the characteristic blue oak of the foothills is left below, and its place is taken by a fine large **species** (*Quercus Californica*) with deeply **lobed** deciduous leaves, picturesquely divided trunk, and broad, massy, finely lobed and modeled head. Here also at a height of about twenty-five hundred feet we come to the edge of the great **coniferous** forest, made up mostly of **yellow pine** with just a few **sugar pines**. We are now in the mountains and they are in us, kindling enthusiasm, making every nerve quiver, filling every pore and cell of us. ⑨ Our **flesh-and-bone tabernacle** seems transparent as glass to the beauty about us, as if truly an inseparable part of it, thrilling with the air and trees, streams and rocks, in the waves of the sun, —a part of all nature, neither old nor young, sick nor well, but **immortal.** ⑩ Just now I can hardly **conceive** of any bodily condition dependent on food or breath any more than the ground or the sky. How glorious a conversion, so complete and wholesome it is, scarce memory enough of old bondage days left as a standpoint to view it from! In this newness of life we seem to have been so always.

composite[ˈkɒmpəzɪt]: *n.* 菊科植物

species[ˈspiːʃiːz]: *n.* 物种

lobed[ləʊbd]: *adj.* 浅裂的

coniferous[kəˈnɪfərəs]: *adj.* 针叶植物的；松类的

yellow pine: 西黄松

sugar pine: 兰伯氏松(俗称糖松)

flesh-and-bone tabernacle: 血肉躯壳

immortal[ɪˈmɔːtl]: *adj.* 永恒的；不朽的；流芳百世的

conceive[kənˈsiːv]: *v.* 想象

Through a meadow opening in the pine woods I see snowy peaks about the headwaters of the Merced above **Yosemite.** How near they seem and how clear their outlines on the blue air, or rather in the blue air; for they seem to be saturated with it. How consuming strong the invitation they extend! Shall I be allowed to go to them? Night and day I'll **pray** that I may, but it seems too good to be true. Someone worthy will go, able for the Godful work, yet as far as I can I must drift about these love-monument mountains, glad to be a servant of servants in so holy a wilderness. ⑪

Yosemite: 约塞米蒂地区。此地有著名的约塞米蒂国家公园(Yosemite National Park)，位于美国加利福尼亚州中部，跨地中海气候与高原山地气候，植被类型主要包括亚热带针叶林。

pray[preɪ]: *v.* 祈祷

Found a lovely lily (**Calochortus albus**) in a shady adenostoma **thicket** near **Coulterville, in company with Adiantum Chilense.** ⑫ It is white with a faint purplish **tinge** inside at the base of the **petals**, a most impressive plant, pure as a snow crystal, one of the plant saints that all must love and be made so much the purer by it every time it is seen. It puts the roughest mountaineer on his good behavior. With this plant the whole world would seem rich though none other existed. It is not easy to keep on with the camp cloud while such plant people are standing **preaching** by the wayside.

Calochortus albus：白花仙灯百合

thicket[ˈθɪkɪt]：*n.* 灌木丛；丛状物

Coulterville：(地名)科尔特维尔

in company with：伴随着

Adiantum Chilense：智利铁线蕨

tinge[tɪndʒ]：*n.* 色调

petal[petl]：*n.* 花瓣

preach[priːtʃ]：*v.* 说教；布道；宣传

During the afternoon we passed a fine meadow bounded by stately pines, mostly the **arrowy** yellow pine, with here and there a noble sugar pine, its feathery arms outspread above the **spires** of its companion species in marked contrast; a glorious tree, its cones fifteen to twenty inches long, swinging like **tassels** at the ends of the branches with superb ornamental effect. **Saw** some **logs** of this species at the Greeley Mill. They are round and regular as if turned in a **lathe**, excepting the butt cuts, which have a few buttressing **projections**. The fragrance of the **sugary sap** is delicious and scents the mill and lumber yard. How beautiful the ground beneath this pine thickly strewn with slender needles and grand cones, and the piles of cone-scales, seed-wings and shells around the instep of each tree where the **squirrels** have been feasting! They get the seeds by cutting off the scales at the base in regular order, following their spiral arrangement, and the two seeds at the base of each scale, a hundred or two in a cone, must make a good meal. The yellow pine cones and those of most other species and genera are held upside down on the ground by the Douglas squirrel, and turned around gradually until **stripped**, while he sits usually with his back to a tree, probably for safety. Strange to say, he never seems to get himself **smeared** with gum, not even his paws or whiskers—and how cleanly and beautiful in color the cone—litter kitchen-middens he makes.

arrowy[ˈærəʊɪ]：*adj.* 笔直的

spire[spaɪə(r)]：*n.* 尖顶

tassel[ˈtæsl]：*n.* 流苏

saw：see 的过去式，这句话省略了主语 I，应为“I saw…”。

log[lɒg]：*n.* 木材

lathe[leɪð]：*n.* 车床

projection[prəˈdʒekʃn]：*n.* 突起

sugary sap：树脂

squirrel[ˈskwɪrəl]：*n.* 松鼠

strip[strɪp]：*v.* 剥皮

smear[smɪə(r)]：*v.* 弄脏

We are now **approaching** the **region of clouds** and cool streams. Magnificent white **cumuli** appeared about noon above the Yosemite region，—floating **fountains** refreshing the glorious wilderness，—sky mountains in whose pearly hills and dales the streams take their rise，—blessing with cooling shadows and rain. ⑬ No rock landscape is more varied in sculpture，none more delicately modeled than these landscapes of the sky; domes and peaks rising，**swelling**，white as finest marble and firmly outlined，a most impressive **manifestation** of world building. ⑭ Every **rain-cloud**，however fleeting，leaves its mark，not only on trees and flowers whose pulses are quickened，and on the replenished streams and lakes，but also on the rocks are its marks engraved whether we can see them or not.

approach[əˈprəʊtʃ]：*v.* 接近；靠近

region of clouds：云中王国

cumuli[ˈkjuːmjʊlaɪ]：*n.* 积云

fountain[ˈfaʊntən]：*n.* 喷泉

swell[swel]：*v.* 膨胀

manifestation[ˌmænɪfeˈsteɪʃn]：*n.* 表示；显示

rain-cloud[ˈreɪnklaʊd]：*n.* 积雨云

I have been examining the curious and influential shrub Adenostoma fasciculata，first noticed about Horseshoe Bend. It is very abundant on the lower slopes of the second plateau near Coulterville，forming a dense，almost impenetrable growth that looks dark in the distance. It belongs to the rose family，is about six or eight feet high，has small white flowers in **racemes** eight to twelve inches long，round needle-like leaves，and reddish **bark** that becomes **shreddy** when old. It grows on sun-beaten slopes，and like grass is often swept away by running fires，but is quickly renewed from the roots. Any trees that may have established themselves in its midst are at length killed by these fires，and this no doubt is the secret of the unbroken character of its broad belts. A few manzanitas，which also rise again from the root after consuming fires，make out to dwell with it，also a few bush composite—**baccharis** and **linosyris**，and some **liliaceous plants**，mostly **calochortus** and

brodiaea, with deepset bulbs safe from fire. A multitude of birds and "wee, sleekit, cow'rin', tim'rous beasties" find good homes in its deepest thickets, and the open bays and lanes that fringe the margins of its main belts offer shelter and food to the deer when winter storms drive them down from their high mountain pastures. ⑮ A most admirable plant! It is now in bloom, and I like to wear its pretty fragrant racemes in my buttonhole.

raceme[rə'siːm]：*n.* 总状花序

bark[bɑːk]：*n.* 树皮

shreddy['ʃredɪ]：*adj.* 破皮的

baccharis：香根菊属，约有 500 种，主要分布在美洲。

linosyris：麻菀属，分布于欧洲和亚洲，我国有两种。

liliaceous plants：百合科植物

calochortus：蝴蝶百合属，广泛分布于北美洲西部的太平洋沿岸地区。

brodiaea：卜若地属，原产美国加利福尼亚北部，是南非共和国的国花。

Azalea occidentalis, another charming shrub, grows beside cool streams hereabouts and much higher in the Yosemite region. We found it this evening in bloom a few miles above **Greeley's Mill**, where we are camped for the night. It is closely related to the **rhododendrons**, is very **showy** and fragrant, and everybody must like it not only for itself but for the shady **alders** and willows, **ferny** meadows, and **living water** associated with it.

Azalea occidentali：西洋杜鹃

Greeley's Mill：格里利锯木场

rhododendrons[rəʊdə'dendrən]：*n.* 杜鹃花

showy[ʃəʊi]：*adj.* 艳丽的

alder['ɔːldə(r)]：*n.* 桤木

ferny ['fəːni]：*n.* 蕨类

living water：叮咚的流水

Another **conifer** was met today—**incense cedar**, a large tree with warm yellow-green foliage in **flat plumes** like those of **arborvitae**, bark cinnamon-colored, and as the boles of the old trees are without limbs they make striking **pillars** in the woods where the sun chances to shine on them—a worthy companion of the kingly sugar and yellow pines. I feel strangely attracted to this tree. The brown close-grained wood, as well as the small scale-like leaves, is fragrant, and the flat overlapping plumes make fine beds, and must shed the rain well. It would be **delightful** to be storm-bound beneath one of these

noble, **hospitable**, inviting old trees, its broad sheltering arms bent down like a tent, incense rising from the fire made from its dry fallen branches, and a hearty wind chanting overhead. But the weather is calm tonight, and our camp is only a sheep camp. We are near the North Fork of the Merced. The night wind is telling the wonders of the upper mountains, their snow fountains and gardens, forests and groves; even their **topography** is in its tones. And the stars, the everlasting sky lilies, how bright they are now that we have climbed above the lowland dust! The horizon is bounded and adorned by **a spiry wall of pines**, every tree harmoniously related to every other; definite symbols, divine **hieroglyphics** written with sunbeams. Would I could understand them! The stream flowing past the camp through ferns and lilies and alders makes sweet music to the ear, but the pines **marshaled** around the edge of the sky make a yet sweeter music to the eye. [16] **Divine** beauty all. Here I could stay tethered forever with just bread and water, nor would I be lonely; loved friends and neighbors, as love for everything increased, would seem all the nearer however many the miles and mountains between us.

conifer[kɒnɪfə(r)]：*n.* 针叶林；松柏科植物

incense cedar：香肖楠

flat[flæt]：*adj.* 扁平的

plume[pluːm]：*n.* 羽毛状物

arborvitae[ɑːˈbɔːviːtaɪ]：*n.* 侧柏(亦称扁柏)

pillar[ˈpɪlə(r)]：*n.* 柱子

delightful[dɪˈlaɪtfl]：*adj.* 令人愉快的

hospitable[hɒˈspɪtəbl]：*adj.* 好客的；热情友好的

topography[təˈpɒgrəfi]：*n.* 地貌

a spiry wall of pines：松树墙。这里运用了暗喻的修辞手法，指松树形成的墙。

hieroglyphics[ˌhaɪərəˈglɪfɪks]：*n.* 象形文字

marshal[ˈmɑːʃl]：*v.* 排列

divine[dɪˈvaɪn]：*adj.* 天赐的；极好的

[选自：John Muir. *My First Summer in the Sierra*. London：Mariner Books，1979.]

Notes

①译文：破晓时分，营地活跃了起来。早餐有咖啡、培根和豆子，餐后我

们很快地清洗好餐具并打包行李。formed：在句中是谓语动词，意为“组成；构成”。followed：在句中是过去分词作定语从句，表示早餐后紧接着是清洗餐具和打包行李。

②译文：但因为之前已经有好几拨羊群经过了这个地区，所以无论是绿叶还是干树叶都所剩无几，因此这群饥饿的羊必须赶紧穿过这片荒芜、炎热的山丘，尽快到达二十到三十英里外最近的绿色草场。scarce a leaf，green or dry：很少有树叶，无论是绿色的还是干枯的。green or dry，作后置定语，修饰leaf。

③译文：它的树干在十五到二十英尺高处分支成两根或更多，有的分支向外斜生，有的则笔直地朝天生长，杂乱生长的枝丫上是灰色的长针叶，但几乎无法形成树荫。trunk：树干。stem：分出的树干、枝丫。branch：较细的树枝。

④译文：不过我还是尽力驻留了一段时间，完成了一幅尚能入眼的皮诺布兰克峰的素描。我画的山峰西南侧有一片小小的农田和葡萄园，山上一条小溪成了天然的灌溉水源，形成了一条美丽的瀑布，此后又汇入路边的峡谷。manage to do sth.：试图，尽力去做某事。where there is…：地点状语，“在这儿有……”。

⑤译文：登上山顶平台之后，海拔上升了约一千英尺，即将呈现在眼前的美景让人抑制不住地兴奋。默塞德山谷中的壮丽的马蹄湾的美景在我们眼前铺开：美妙的山野景色仿佛是回荡在耳边的千千阙歌。

⑥译文：首先映入眼帘的前景是松树林、石兰灌木丛，以及在树丛间洒满阳光的开阔地。远处的背景则是层层叠叠、轮廓秀丽的山脊，绵延成一片被灌木丛覆盖的山脉。这些以丛状田下蓟为主的灌木生长得非常浓密，远看就像一条柔软的长绒毯，里面不见一棵树或一点空地。feathered with 作后置定语，修饰 slopes。all covered with 修饰 hills and ridges。planted 修饰 chaparral。

⑦译文：极目远眺，所见之处尽是浓密蓬松的绿色海洋，绵延不绝，仿佛是铺满了苏格兰杜鹃。as far as the eye can reach it extends：极目远眺；目之所及。

⑧译文：天上地下，这美景已经超越了人类的想象，浑然天成，又不断新生。

⑨译文：我们已经身在山间，大山的气息也充满了我们的每一个毛孔，让我们心神悸动。

⑩译文：我们的血肉躯壳在四周的美景中就像透明的一样，完全融入周遭环境中，与山间的空气、树木、溪流、岩石一起，在阳光的照射下颤抖。我们已然成为大自然的一部分，非老非少，非疾病非健康，却是不变的永恒。在这

里作者感到人与自然已经融为一体，抒发了对大自然的热爱之情。

⑪译文：真正的贤德之人必定能去到那里，完成神圣的使命，而我甘愿成为这圣洁大自然谦卑的奴仆，在这让人心生爱意的群山间流连忘返。able for the Godful work：能够完成这神圣的工作（使命）。drift about these love-monument mountains：流连于这些让人心生爱意的群山中。

⑫译文：在科尔特维尔附近一个庇荫处的丛状田下蓟灌木丛中，我发现了一株白花仙灯百合和智利铁线蕨。在此句中，主语“I”被省略。

⑬译文：中午时分，约塞米蒂地区的上空出现了壮丽的堆积云，就像悬浮的喷泉，洗净了广阔的荒野，又如云中山岳，有溪水流经珍珠般的山峰峡谷，有清凉雨水和阴凉庇佑的大地。

⑭译文：地上岩石雕琢的形象千变万化，却也丝毫不能与这空中的奇景相媲美。云朵形成的山峰与穹顶渐渐升高，慢慢膨胀，洁白如最纯净的大理石，而且棱角分明，可谓世间最宏伟壮观的建筑。no more … than …：没有……比这个更……

⑮译文：许多鸟类以及“身子小巧、毛色光滑、羞涩胆怯”的动物们都将家安在了灌木丛的深处。灌木丛地带边缘的空地和小径则是冬季在暴风雪中被迫离开高原草场的鹿群栖息和觅食的去处。offer shelter and food：提供栖息地和食物。

⑯译文：营地旁的小溪轻轻地流经蕨类、百合和桤树，流水声就像是美妙的音符，不断地流进我们的耳朵。天际矗立的松树，则是献给我们眼睛的甜美歌谣。

Remarks

《夏日走过山间》是约翰·缪尔的一本日记体散文集。它是作者于 1869 年夏天在内华达山间跟随一支牧羊队伍进行为期 4 个月的考察期间所记下的日记。在这 4 个月的行程中，缪尔除了参与牧羊之外，还考察了山脉、矿石、冰川痕迹、气候、植物、动物等，他所获得的成果不亚于任何一支科普考察队。

在文字中缪尔更是表现了大师级的文采。他表现出敏锐的观察力和超强的运笔能力。他文采飞扬，所写内容毫不枯燥。在他描写的对象中，不管是松树、冷杉、云彩、石头还是溪水，在每一天的笔下都绝不相同。他的考察充满了激情与勇敢的精神。在山中，缪尔经常会连续几日漫步于群峰、峡谷、草甸之中，只带着极少的面包。那种在荒野中的怡然自乐以及与自然和谐相处的态度，让人感叹，绝不是今天破坏荒野的“驴友”“背包族”们所能企及的。整本书中自始至终没有对荒野中的恶劣环境表达一句抱怨，因为荒野对于他来说就是天堂。每天他总是以极大的热情去迎接黎明的到来，然后去大自然中“朝圣”。

在书中，缪尔将人类对蛮荒自然的激情以及荒野的意义进行了最直率的文学表达，实现了科学观察与诗意想象的完美结合，传达着敬畏自然、呵护生命、自然万物和谐共生的生态思想。

参考译文

夏日走过山间(片段)

6 月 4 日

破晓时分，营地活跃了起来。早餐有咖啡、培根和豆子，餐后我们很快地清洗好餐具并打包行李。日出时刻，羊群已经开始咩咩叫唤了。有一只母羊醒过来，她的小羊跌跌撞撞地冲过去吃奶，一直到上千只羊羔都吃饱了，整个羊群才开始散开吃草。饥饿的阉羊往往冲在最前面，但是也不敢离开羊群太远。比利、印第安人和中国人赶着羊群沿着那条沉闷的路前进，容许羊群在四分之一英里的范围内寻找一点可怜的食物。但因为之前已经有好几拨羊群经过了这个地区，所以无论是绿叶还是干树叶都所剩无几，因此这群饥饿的羊必须赶紧穿过这片荒芜、炎热的山丘，尽快到达二十到三十英里外最近的绿色草场。

“堂吉诃德”仍然带领着驮行李的马走在最前面，他肩上沉重的来复枪是为熊和狼准备的。今天的天气和第一天一样炎热，路上仍然尘土飞扬。脚下是一片棕色的沙丘，斜坡上的植被也没有什么变化，除了长相很奇怪的加州大子松。这些松树有的聚成一片小树林，有的则散落在蓝橡树林里。它的树干在十五到二十英尺高处分支成两根或更多，有的分支向外斜生，有的则笔直地朝天生长，杂乱生长的枝丫上是灰色的长针叶，但几乎无法形成树荫。整体看来，这种树的外形更接近棕榈树而非松树。它结的球果很重，有六到七英寸(1 英寸≈2.5 厘米)长，直径约为五英寸，成熟落地后还能保存很长时间不腐，所以每棵树下几乎都堆满了松果。这种松果富含上乘的松脂，点燃后能发出极强的亮光，是除了玉蜀黍穗之外我见过的最好的篝火燃料。“堂吉诃德”告诉我，迪格尔印第安人喜欢大量收集这些加州大子松球果的松子来当食物。这种松子和榛子差不多大小，也有一样的硬壳。既是美食，也能点亮足以祭神的火焰，真是一物多用啊！

6 月 5 日

清早，和云朵一般的羊群一起出发几小时后，我们到达了皮诺布兰克峰侧面第一块轮廓清晰的平台。我被加州大子松深深地吸引了，它奇怪的外形像棕榈树，整体造型轻盈秀丽。我很想为它画一幅素描，但在兴奋之余，实际行动却滞后了。不过我还是驻留了一段时间，完成了一幅尚能入眼的皮诺布兰克峰的素描。我画的山峰西南侧有一片小小的农田和葡萄园，山上一条小溪成了天然的灌溉水源，形成了一条美丽的瀑布，此后又汇入路边的峡谷。

登上山顶平台之后，海拔上升了约一千英尺，即将呈现在眼前的美景让人抑制不住地兴奋。默塞德山谷中的壮丽的马蹄湾的美景在我们眼前铺开：美妙的山野景色仿佛是回荡在耳边的千千阙歌。首先映入眼帘的前景是松树林、石兰灌木丛，以及在树丛间洒满阳光的开阔地。远处的背景则是层层叠叠、轮廓秀丽的山脊，绵延成一片被灌木丛覆盖的山脉。这些以丛状田下蓟为主的灌木生长得非常浓密，远看就像一条柔软的长绒毯，里面不见一棵树或一点空地。极目远眺，所见之处尽是浓密蓬松的绿色海洋，绵延不绝，仿佛是铺满了苏格兰杜鹃。这片土地无论远观还是近看，都散发着令人惊叹的气质：高大的山峰簇拥在一处，其间有闪亮的河水流淌，河流流经处，留下优雅的弯道，在变质岩间勾勒出高低不平的起伏，却没有一处突兀的岩角，一切仿佛用砂纸细细打磨过一般顺滑。这片美景就像是精心设计过的圣洁雕塑一般，让人不禁对大自然的鬼匠神工叹为观止。我心怀敬畏地凝望着眼前的壮丽景色，恨不得用我的一生来与之交换。我心甘情愿穷尽毕生努力，来探索造就这地形、这岩石、这植物、这动物、这气候的大自然神力。天上地下，这美景已经超越了人类的想象，浑然天成，又不断新生。我出神地望着，心中充满敬畏和期望，蓦然回首，发现扬起尘土的羊群已经从视野中消失，我赶紧拿出本子做好笔记，并迅速完成了一幅素描——不过内心里我却觉得笔记、素描什么的都是多余的，因为这些色彩和线条、这美景的无限风情，已经深深铭刻在我的脑海里，再也无法抹去。

梦幻的一天在凉爽、平静的夜晚中结束。天空中没有一丝云彩，空气中却布满了一种我从未见过的光芒。像云一样的大片发光物质充满着树林和灌木丛的空隙，就像威斯康星草原上闪烁的萤火虫，而非传说中的“野火”。空气中有大量静电，导致马尾的鬃毛根根散开，我们的毛毯也时不时地擦出火星。

6月6日

在翻越了好多个有着不同植被的山丘之后，我们到达了山脉的第二个平原。开阔地里仍然生长着很多低地植物、一些蝴蝶百合和其他一些明显的百合属植物。不过低地代表的典型植物蓝橡树已经被大量的加州黑栎取代。这种落叶乔木长着巨大裂纹的叶片，拥有美丽如画的枝丫和宽大厚实、造型优美的树冠。在海拔两千五百英尺的这片地区，我们眼前已经出现一片巨大的针叶林，林子里以西黄松为主，也有小部分的兰伯氏松(别名“糖松”)。我们已经身在山间，大山的气息也充满了我们的每一个毛孔，让我们心神悸动。我们的血肉躯壳在四周的美景中就像透明的一样，完全融入周遭环境中，与山间的空气、树木、溪流、岩石一起，在阳光的照射下颤抖。我们已然成为大自然的一部分，非老非少，非疾病非健康，却是不变的永恒。在这一瞬间，我仿佛跟脚下的大地、头顶的天空一样，已经脱离了依靠食物、空气才能存活的肉身。这伟大的转变是如此地完美和圆满，让以前凡夫俗子的记忆淡到仅仅成为只供对比的凭借。在这崭新的生命里，我们仿佛已永垂不朽。

透过松树林间的一片草地，我能望见约塞米蒂上默塞德河源头附近的雪峰。在蓝天的背景下，雪峰的轮廓清晰得仿佛在眼前，它们甚至像是镶嵌在了蓝天里一样，被浸染上了天空之蓝。我强烈地感受到雪峰向我发出的邀请！我真的能靠近它们吗？我愿日夜祈祷达成心愿，但却不敢奢望美梦成真。真正的贤德之人必定能去到那里，完成神圣的使命，而我甘愿成为这圣洁大自然谦卑的奴仆，在这让人心生爱意的群山间流连忘返。

在科尔特维尔附近一个庇荫处的丛状田下蓟灌木丛中，我发现了一株白花仙灯百合和智利铁线蕨。这株百合通体洁白，仅仅在花瓣根部晕染了一丝淡淡的紫色，这如冰晶般纯洁的美丽花朵，就如人人爱慕的花中仙子一般，每次露面，她的圣洁便增添一分。即使最粗野的登山者，在她面前也会变得彬彬有礼；即使再空虚的世界，有了它也会显得丰富多彩。有这样一位花之仙子伫立在路边，我想要拔腿赶上那云朵般的羊群，可谓难之又难。

下午我们经过了一片被松林围绕的美好草坪，松林里主要是西黄松，也时不时地有挺拔的兰伯氏松出现。后者的树冠如羽翼般伸展开，比西黄松的塔状树冠高出一大截，它的松果有十五到二十英寸长，像流苏垂挂在身形壮美的树梢上，仿佛是特地定制的装饰。我在格里利锯木场见到了一些兰伯氏松的木材，就像从车床加工出来的一样，又圆又规则，只有底部有一些砍伐后留下的不规则突起。糖浆般的树脂散发出的香味弥漫在锯木场和伐木场的上空。松树下洒满了细长的松针和巨大的松果。附近松鼠在大餐之后，在树脚边留下一堆堆的松果鳞片、种翅和果壳。松鼠们总是从松果底部的鳞片处下口，吃到每个鳞片下的两颗松子，然后沿着天然的螺旋走向往上啃，直到把整个松果的一两百粒松子全都送到胃里，才结束这一顿饱餐。在啃食西黄松和其他同属松树的果实时，道格拉松鼠一般会背靠大树坐着——我想是出于安全考虑吧——然后把松果倒立，一边旋转松果一边往下啃。很神奇的是，这些松鼠啃松果时从来不会把自己的身上、爪子上和胡须上弄上黏稠的树脂，反而是留下一堆整洁而色彩靓丽的松果厨余垃圾。

现在我们在朝着流淌着清凉溪流的云中王国进发。中午时分，约塞米蒂地区的上空出现了壮丽的堆积云，就像悬浮的喷泉，洗净了广阔的荒野，又如云中山岳，有溪水流经珍珠般的山峰峡谷，有清凉雨水和阴凉庇佑的大地。地上岩石雕琢的形象千变万化，却也丝毫不能与这空中的奇景相媲美。云朵形成的山峰与穹顶渐渐升高，慢慢膨胀，洁白如最纯净的大理石，而且棱角分明，可谓世间最宏伟壮观的建筑。每片飘过的积雨云，即使是转瞬即逝，也都留下痕迹。花草树木的脉搏为之加速，溪流湖泊的水位为之丰盈，就连岩石表面都留有它们的印记，只是人类的眼睛不一定能看清。

自从在马蹄湾第一次见到丛状田下蓟之后，我就一直在研究这种奇特且有生命力的灌木。在科尔特维尔附近第二高原的低处斜坡上，这种灌木非常丰茂，它们生长得几乎密不透风，从远处看去就像一片黑暗的阴影。它属于蔷薇属，六到八英尺高，开白色的小花，总状花序排列的花瓣有八到十二英寸长，叶子呈圆针状，浅红色的树皮在老去后会渐渐破裂开来。它们通常生长在向阳的坡地，和野草一样经常被山火烧得一干二净，但很快又能破土重长。若有其他树种和它们生长在一起，经年累月之后大都会被肆虐的山火吞噬，而丛状田下蓟总能死后重生，这便是它们能形成那密不透风而绵延广阔的灌木带的秘诀。少量的熊果灌木，以及因为有深埋于地底的球茎可以躲过山火的以酒神菊属、麻菀属为主的菊科植物和一些百合科植物，有幸和丛状田下蓟成为邻居。许多鸟类以及"身子小巧、毛色光滑、羞涩胆怯"的动物们都将家安在了灌木丛的深处。灌木丛地带边缘的空地和小径则是冬季在暴风雪中被迫离开高原草场的鹿群栖息和觅食的去处。这是多么值得尊敬的一种植物啊！现在正值它们繁花盛开的季节，我喜欢在扣眼里别上一朵这香气袭人的花儿。

西洋杜鹃是另一种约塞米蒂海拔更高地区的迷人植物，生长在清凉的溪流旁。今天晚上，在格里利锯木场以上几英里处我们扎营的地方，我发现它们正在那里盛开。这种杜鹃跟杜鹃属非常接近，花朵夸张，香气浓郁。西洋杜鹃的生长环境里有树荫巨大的桤木、垂柳、蕨类的草地和叮咚的流水，这些环境因素加在一起，让我对这种植物是不爱也难啊！

我们今天还见到另一种针叶树——香肖楠。香肖楠树形巨大，扁平羽状的叶片是温暖的黄绿色，跟侧柏的叶片很像。它的树干则是肉桂色。老树的树干没有分枝，当阳光洒在树干上时，看上去就像闪闪发光的立柱，和树林里兰伯氏松、西黄松这样有君王风范的树木比起来也毫不逊色。这种树对我有一种奇怪的吸引力，它密实的棕色树干、小巧的鱼鳞状叶片都散发出迷人的香气，它那扁平羽状的叶片用来铺床一定很舒服，用来遮风挡雨也不错。雷雨来临时，躲在这样一棵高贵而好客的老树下，以它宽阔的枝叶当作帐篷，在树下点燃一堆枯枝，在这散发着香气的篝火旁，听着大风歌唱，这该是多么令人向往的场景啊！但今夜天气平静，我们还是只能和羊群一起扎营。目前我们已经靠近默塞德河的北汊了，夜风也已经向我们吟诵着高山的诗篇：雪国的喷泉花园、森林果园……我们甚至能从风的语调中感受高山的地形。而天上的星星，如夜空中绽放的百合一般闪耀，比起在低地的时候，它们看起来明亮了许多。远处一片塔状的松树构成的高墙，勾勒出地平线的轮廓，在阳光的照耀下，这一棵接一棵的松树构成的清晰画面就像象形文字一样。多希望我能认识这些文字啊！

营地旁的小溪轻轻地流经蕨类、百合和桤树，流水声就像是美妙的音符，不断地流进我们的耳朵。天际矗立的松树，则是献给我们眼睛的甜美歌谣。有这圣洁美景的陪伴，我仅仅需要面包和饮水就能永远生活在这里而不觉孤单；随着我对周遭一切爱得愈深，尽管我和亲爱的朋友以及邻居之间相隔千山万水，但我们之间却似乎更近了。

[选自：约翰·缪尔．夏日走过山间．邱婷婷，译．上海：上海译文出版社，2014.]

Questions for discussion

1. Could you find detailed description of a pine by John Muir?
2. Try to make a description of a tree which gives you a deep impression.
3. What is John Muir's attitude to nature?
4. What is the relationship between nature and us?

After-class reading

Read the book *Silent Spring* written by Rachel Carson.

Part B

(1)China's Fanjingshan Added to UNESCO World Heritage List

MANAMA, July 2(Xinhua)—Mount Fanjingshan, situated in the city of Tongren in China's southwestern province of Guizhou, was **inscribed** to the World Heritage List on Monday at the 42nd World Heritage Committee meeting in Bahrain's capital Manama.

UNESCO：联合国教育、科学及文化组织(United Nations Educational, Scientific and Cultural Organization)，简称联合国教科文组织，于1946年11月4日正式成立，是联合国下属的专门机构之一。

heritage['herɪtɪdʒ]：*n.* 遗产

Manama：麦纳麦，是巴林的首都，全国第一大城市，全国政治、经济、交通、贸易和文化中心，同时也是海湾地区重要的金融中心、重要港口及贸易中转站，享有"波斯湾明珠"的美誉。麦纳麦位于波斯湾中段、巴林岛的东北角。

inscribe[ɪn'skraɪb]：*v.* 在……上写(名字等)

It is the 13th site in China included on the World Natural Heritage List, making the total number of world heritage sites in China reach 53.

Fanjingshan, the highest peak in the Wuling Mountain range at an **altitude** of 2572 meters, stretches on an area of 402.75 square kilometers with a **buffer zone** of 372.39 square kilometers.

altitude['æltɪtjuːd]：*n.* 海拔高度

buffer zone：缓冲地带

The International Union for Conservation of Nature (IUCN), official **advisory** body on the natural sites of the UNESCO heritage meeting, said Fanjingshan has proved its aesthetic value as a natural heritage site and met the criteria of world natural heritage, which require the nominated sites to demonstrate outstanding **biological diversity** and **integrity**.

the International Union for Conservation of Nature(IUCN)：世界自然保护联盟，是世界上规模最大、历史最悠久的全球性非营利环保机构，也是自然环境保护与可持续发展领域唯一作为联合国大会永久观察员的国际组织。

advisory[əd'vaɪzəri]：*adj.* 顾问的；提供咨询的

biological[ˌbaɪə'lɒːdʒɪkl]：*adj.* 生物的

diversity[daɪ'vɜːsəti]：*n.* 多样化

integrity[ɪn'tegrəti]：*n.* 完整性

The ecosystem of Fanjingshan has **preserved** large numbers of ancient **relict** plants, rare and endangered creatures, as well as **unique** species. It is home to 4395 species of plants and 2767 of animals.

preserve[prɪ'zɜːv]：*v.* 保护；保存

relict['relɪkt]：*adj.* 残存的

unique[ju'niːk]：*adj.* 罕见的

As the most important **reserves** of beech forests in Asia and the world's most **gymnosperms**-rich area, the mountain is also the only **habitat** of the rare Guizhou **snub-nosed monkey** and the Fanjingshan **fir**.

reserve[rɪ'zɜːv]：*n.* (动植物)保护区

gymnosperm['dʒɪmnəspɜːm]：*n.* 裸子植物

habitat['hæbɪtæt]：*n.* (动物的)栖息地

snub-nosed monkey：金丝猴

fir[fɜː(r)]：*n.* 冷杉；枞木

In October 2013, Mount Fanjingshan was listed as the national natural heritage of China, before it was **proposed** by China as the country's only natural heritage **nomination** for the 2018 world heritage meeting.

propose[prə'pəʊz]：*v.* 提议

nomination[ˌnɒmɪ'neɪʃn]：*n.* 提名；任命

The **inclusion** of Mount Fanjingshan in the World Heritage List results from the international recognition of the natural value and the conservation work of the **wonder**, and reflects the progress that China has achieved in terms of protecting its biological diversity, said Song Xiaolu, head of the Chinese Guizhou **delegation** to the World Heritage Committee meeting.

inclusion[ɪn'kluːʒn]：*n.* 包含；被包括

wonder['wʌndə(r)]：*n.* 奇迹；奇观

delegation[ˌdelɪ'geɪʃn]：*n.* 代表团；授权；委派

"We will continue to make an effort to protect and manage the natural heritage site of Mount Fanjingshan, and improve its basic **infrastructure** on the basis of the decision of the World Heritage Committee and the Convention Concerning the Protection of the World Cultural and Natural Heritage," said Song.

infrastructure['ɪnfrəstrʌktʃə(r)]：*n.* 基础设施；基础建设

The 42nd World Heritage Committee meeting, held from June 24 to July 4, will discuss 28 nominations to the World Heritage List, including 5 natural sites, 20 cultural sites and 3 mixed ones.

参考译文

中国梵净山被列入《世界遗产名录》

（新华社麦纳麦7月2日）7月2日在巴林首都麦纳麦举行的第42届世界遗产大会上，联合国教科文组织世界遗产委员会审议通过将梵净山列入世界遗产名录。梵净山位于我国西南地区的贵州省铜仁市。

它（梵净山）成为中国第13处世界自然遗产，至此我国世界遗产总量增至53处。

梵净山是武陵山脉的主峰，海拔高度为2572米，面积为402.75平方千米，缓冲区面积为372.39平方千米。

世界遗产委员会的自然遗产评估机构——世界自然保护联盟认为，梵净山作为世界自然遗产，有其独特的魅力和美学价值。它满足了世界自然遗产生物多样性标准和完整性要求。

梵净山生态系统保留了大量古老孑遗、珍稀濒危和特有物种，拥有4395种植物和2767种动物。

梵净山是水青冈林在亚洲最重要的保护地，是全球裸子植物最丰富的地区，同时它也是黔金丝猴和梵净山冷杉唯一的栖息地和分布地。

2013 年 10 月，梵净山被列入中国国家自然遗产名录，成为中国政府 2018 年唯一向联合国教科文组织世界遗产中心申报的世界自然遗产项目。

贵州省申遗工作团团长宋晓路说，梵净山成功申遗是国际社会对梵净山自然遗产价值和保护管理工作的认可，是对世界生物多样性保护的重要贡献，是中国着力构建生态多样性保护网络取得明显成效的缩影。

宋晓路说："今后我们将严格按照世界遗产委员会的决议、《保护世界文化和自然遗产公约》的要求，完善保护管理规则，加快做好遗产地基础设施建设，加强保护管理，确保世界自然遗产资源在我们这里彰显魅力，永续传承。"

第 42 届世界遗产大会(6 月 24 日至 7 月 4 日)将主要讨论 28 项世界遗产的提名，包含 5 处自然遗产，20 处文化遗产和 3 处混合类型遗产。

(2)Smog in Europe and North America

Smog in Europe and North America could be more than 25 times more **lethal** than the average air pollution found in Chinese cities, a new study suggests.

smog[smɒg]：*n.* 雾霾

lethal[ˈliːθl]：*adj.* 致命的；致死的；有害的

In the largest ever study of its kind in the developing world, researchers tested the effects of air pollution on the health of people in 272 cities in China.

They found average **annual exposure** to **fine particles**, known as **PM2. 5**, in those cities was more than five times higher than the level **recommended** by the World Health Organization (WHO), according to a **paper** in *The American Journal of* ***Respiratory*** *and Critical Care Medicine*.

annual[ˈænjuəl]：*adj.* 每年的；一年的

exposure[ɪkˈspəʊʒə(r)]：*n.* 暴露

fine particles：细颗粒物，又称细粒、细颗粒、PM2. 5。细颗粒物指空气中空气动力学当量直径小于、等于 2. 5 微米的颗粒物。它能较长时间悬浮于空气中，其在空气中含量浓度越高，就代表空气污染越严重。

PM2. 5：细颗粒物。PM 的英文全称为 Particulate Matter。

recommend[ˌrekəˈmend]：*v.* 推荐；劝告

paper[ˈpeɪpə(r)]：*n.* 文章

respiratory[rəˈspɪrətri]：*adj.* 呼吸的

However, they also discovered that it was much less likely to increase the death rate than PM2. 5 in Europe and North America.

The researchers, led by Dr. Maigeng Zhou, of the Chinese Centre for Disease Control and Prevention, suggested this was because China is affected by large amounts of natural dust **blown** by the wind from **arid** areas, while most pollution in the West comes from industry.

blow[bləʊ]: *v.* 吹；刮风

arid['ærɪd]: *adj.* 干旱的；干燥的

They found that for every increase of 10 **micrograms** of air pollution in a cubic meter of air, the **mortality rate** increased by 0.22 percent, discounting deaths from accidents.

microgram['maɪkrəʊgræm]: *n.* 微克

mortality rate：死亡率

Professor Frank Kelly, an **expert** in environmental health at King's College London, who was not involved in the study but has studied air pollution in China, told *The Independent*: "Those **relative** risks are **considerably** less than those seen in Europe and the US."

expert['ekspɜːt]: *n.* 专家

relative['relətɪv]: *adj.* 相对的

considerably[kən'sɪdərəbli]: *adv.* 相当地；非常；颇

"For **premature** mortality (in Europe) we are working on a six percent increase per 10 micrograms." That suggests air pollution in Europe is about 27 times more **toxic** than average air pollution in China.

premature['premətʃə(r)]: *adj.* 过早的

toxic['tɒksɪk]: *adj.* 有毒的

However, Professor Kelly said cities like Beijing, Shanghai and Hong Kong were likely to suffer from Western-style air pollution.

"The natural dust component there is not of the **magnitude** that it would **dwarf** the coal, **biomass** and **fossil** fuel signals," he said.

magnitude['mægnɪtjuːd]: *n.* 量级

dwarf[dwɔːf]: *v.* 使……受阻碍；使相形见绌

biomass['baɪəʊmæs]: *n.*（单位面积或体积内的）生物数量

fossil['fɒsl]: *n.* 化石

"That (the lower mortality rate) may be true in certain cities whose pollution is not **dominated** by local power generation or major traffic **congestion.**"

dominate['dɒmɪneɪt]: *v.* 控制；支配；在……中占首要地位

congestion[kən'dʒestʃən]：*n.* 堵塞；拥挤

Natural dust particles can cause physical damage to the lungs and **trigger** an **asthma** attack. Particles of carbon produced when fossil fuels are burned can lead to similar problems but they are also coated with toxic heavy metals, chemicals and **volatile** organic compounds. These are able to pass from the lungs into the blood stream where it is thought they cause further damage to the body.

trigger['trɪgə(r)]：*v.* 引发

asthma['æsmə]：*n.* 气喘；哮喘

volatile['vɒlətaɪl]：*adj.*（液体或油）易挥发的

Areeba Hamid, an air pollution campaigner with environmental group Greenpeace, said: "Toxic air causes **havoc** to people's health wherever in the world they live."

havoc['hævək]：*n.* 大破坏；摧残

"We now know **fumes** from **diesel** vehicles are a lot more toxic than car companies **claimed** and this is a big cause of air pollution in Europe and North America."

fume[fjuːm]：*n.* 刺激性气味；刺鼻的雾

diesel['diːzl]：*n.* 柴油

claim[kleɪm]：*v.* 宣称

These companies have a lot to answer for, but so far they've managed to avoid any real **accountability**.

accountability[əˌkaʊntə'bɪləti]：*n.* 有责任

The study of cities in China found the average annual expose to PM2.5 was 56 micrograms per cubic meter, compared to the WHO guideline limit for safe air quality of 10 micrograms.

People who were older than 75, had less education or who lived in hotter places were more likely to die.

It is thought people in warmer cities were more likely to spend time outside or leave their windows open, thereby breathing more polluted air, the researchers said.

They also **speculated** that less well educated people might have poorer access to health care or experience poorer environmental health conditions.

speculate['spekjuleɪt]：*v.* 推测

参考译文

欧洲及北美的雾霾

一项最新研究发现，欧洲和北美的雾霾的致命性可能比中国城市平均空气污染的致命性高出 25 倍以上。

在有史以来针对发展中国家进行的同类研究中，该研究规模最大。研究人员测试了中国 272 个城市里空气污染对人体健康的影响。

研究人员在他们发表在《美国呼吸系统和重症护理医学杂志》上的文章中指出，在(中国的)这些城市中，人们的年均 PM2.5 接触量是世界卫生组织建议水平的 5 倍多。

但研究人员也发现，与欧洲和北美的 PM2.5 相比，中国的 PM2.5 的致命性要低得多。

中国疾病预防控制中心的周脉耕博士领导的研究团队指出，这是因为中国的空气污染源于从干旱地区吹来的大量天然尘土，而西方的污染主要来自工业。

他们发现，如果不考虑意外事故造成的死亡，中国每立方米空气里的污染物每增加 10 微克，死亡率就增加 0.22%。

英国伦敦大学国王学院环境健康专家弗兰克·凯利教授告诉《独立报》记者："这些相对的风险明显比欧洲和美国小得多。"凯利没有参与此项研究，但研究了中国的空气污染。

凯利说："就(欧洲的)过早死亡率来看，每立方米空气污染物每增加 10 微克，死亡率将增加 6%。"这表明，欧洲空气污染的毒性约为中国的 27 倍。

但是，凯利教授说，北京、上海和香港这样的城市可能也存在"西式"空气污染。

"那儿的空气中的天然尘土的数量还不足以使煤炭、生物物质和化石燃料等因素相形见绌。"

他说："在污染物主要不是来自当地电厂或严重交通拥堵的某些城市，(死亡率较低)可能是事实。"

天然粉尘可能使肺部受损，引发哮喘。燃烧化石燃料时产生的碳微粒可能导致类似问题，但它们外表还包裹着有毒的重金属、化学物质和挥发性有机物。这些物质可能从肺部进入血液，据称这会给身体造成进一步损害。

环保绿色和平组织的反空气污染活动家阿丽芭·哈米德说："有毒空气会给世界各地人们的健康造成严重损害。"

"如今我们知道，柴油车排放的废气毒性比汽车公司宣称的要大得多，而这是欧洲和北美空气污染的一大原因。"

"这些公司要承担很大责任，但到目前为止它们都避免承担任何真正的责任。"

对中国城市的这项研究发现，PM2.5 的年均接触量为每立方米 56 微克，而世界卫生组织的空气质量安全标准为每立方米 10 微克。

75 岁以上、教育水平较低或生活在较热地区的人死亡风险更高。

研究人员说，在较热城市生活的人到户外去或开窗的时间可能更长，因此会吸入更多的污染空气。

他们还推测说，教育水平较低的人享受医疗服务的机会较少，他们接触的环境卫生状况也较差。

(3) Explosion Rocks Volcano's Summit as Kilauea Continues to Erupt

There have been thousands of earthquakes in the month since Kilauea began erupting, with 505 measured by **the Hawaiian Volcano Observatory** in the past 24 hours alone.

rock[rɒk]：*v.* 摇晃；摇动；震动

volcano[vɒl'keɪnəʊ]：*n.* 火山

summit['sʌmɪt]：*n.* 顶点

Kilauea：基拉韦厄火山，位于美国夏威夷岛东南部，是世界上最大和最壮观的火山口之一，从 1983 年至今就没有停止过喷发。

the Hawaiian Volcano Observatory：夏威夷火山天文台

Today's earthquake occurred at 4：45 a. m. local time (3：45 p. m. BST) and was associated with an explosive eruption at the summit.

The Pacific Tsunami Warning Centre has said there is no risk of a **tsunami** following the earthquake, as it was too small to trigger any activity.

The Pacific Tsunami Warning Centre：太平洋海啸预警中心，位于夏威夷檀香山附近，是目前全球唯一的多国海啸预警系统，于 1949 年成立，并于 1965 年扩大参与国范围，包括中国、日本、澳大利亚等环绕太平洋的 26 个国家都参与其中，中国于 1983 年加入。

tsunami[tsuː'nɑːmi]：*n.* 海啸

The eruption was similar to explosions that have happened **previously** at the summit, said the **US Geological Survey.**

previously['priːviəsli]：*adv.* 先前

US Geological Survey：美国地质勘探局，简称 USGS。

Past explosions have sent **ash** plumes up to 10000 feet above sea level.

ash[æʃ]：*n.* 灰烬；灰

A smaller earthquake also shook the summit at 12：46 local time (11：46 a. m. BST), reported by the USGS to be within the **magnitude** 4 range.

magnitude['mægnɪtjuːd]：*n.* (地震)级数

The volcanic **alert** level for Kilauea remains red, meaning that eruption is underway with **significant** ash plumes entering the **atmosphere**.

alert[ə'lɜːt]：*n.* 警戒；戒备

significant[sɪg'nɪfɪkənt]：*adj.* 大量的；重大的

atmosphere['ætməsfɪə(r)]：*n.* 空气

Fissure 8 continues to **spew** **lava** high into the air, with the USGS reporting three closely spaced fountains of lava at the fissure.

fissure['fɪʃə(r)]：*n.* 狭长裂缝或裂隙

spew[spju]：*v.* 涌出；射出；喷出

lava['lɑːvə]：*n.* 岩浆

The fountains have reached heights of between 150 and 180 feet and continue to feed lava into a north-flowing channel towards the ocean.

This channel reaches the ocean at **Kapoho Bay**, entering the sea and causing huge plumes of deadly laze to enter the atmosphere.

Kapoho Bay：卡波霍海湾

Minor steam explosions have also been seen at the ocean entry, said the USGS, as **molten** lava meeting the cool water reacts along the edge.

minor['maɪnə(r)]：*adj.* 小型的

molten['məʊltən]：*adj.* 熔化的

This channel of lava has created a new **landmass** where Kapoho Bay once was, known as a lava **delta**.

landmass['lændmæs]：*n.* 陆地

delta['deltə]：*n.* 三角洲

Lava deltas occur when molten lava enters the ocean, as when the lava cools and **solidifies** it builds on unstable lava **fragments** where the land meets the sea creating a mass of land.

solidify[sə'lɪdɪfaɪ]：*v.* (使)凝固；变硬

fragment['frægmənt]：*n.* 碎片

The USGS report that the lava delta at Kapoho Bay has reached 200 acres in size, and is continuing to expand.

More than 600 homes have been destroyed by lava since explosive eruptions began on May 3, said Hawaii County Mayor Harry Kim.

Geologist Janet Babb of USGS told a **news conference** that these events are somewhat becoming predictable as scientists **track indicators** that could lead to the next eruption.

geologist[dʒiˈɒlədʒɪst]：*n.* 地质专家；地质学家

news conference：新闻发布会

track[træk]：*v.* 跟踪；追踪；监测

indicator[ˈɪndɪkeɪtə(r)]：*n.* 迹象

Ash eruptions and earthquakes seem to be on a 24-48 hour cycle when the activity is repeated，Babb reported to the conference.

However，scientists are unable to predict when Kilauea will stop erupting or when **seismic** activity will **cease.**

seismic[ˈsaɪzmɪk]：*adj.* 地震的；由地震引起的

cease[siːs]：*v.* 停止；终止

参考译文

夏威夷基拉韦厄火山持续爆炸性喷发

本月自基拉韦厄火山喷发以来，已发生千余次地震。在最近 24 小时内夏威夷火山天文台就已监测到 505 次。

今天的地震发生在当地时间早上 4：45(英国夏令时间下午 3：45)，这与山顶爆炸性的火山喷发密切相关。

太平洋海啸预警中心认为，这次地震规模过小，还不足以引发任何活动，因此地震过后不会有海啸的危险。

美国地质勘探局认为，此次火山喷发是由先前发生于山顶的爆炸引起的。

先前的爆炸已导致大量的灰羽流喷出，超出海平线一万英尺。

又一次小型地震发生在当地时间 12：46(英国夏令时间上午 11：46)，震级为四级，美国地质勘探局报道。

基拉韦厄火山区仍处于红色警报状态，这也就意味着火山喷发仍在继续，同时伴随着大量的灰羽流混入空气中。

美国地质勘探局报道称，8 号裂缝中的岩浆继续涌出，裂缝处有三处相邻的岩浆喷射口。

裂缝岩浆喷发高度在 150～180 英尺，喷射出的岩浆形成一条向北流动的沟渠，一直流向海洋。

这条熔岩沟渠一直抵达卡波霍海湾，流入海洋，并在空气中形成大量的烟雾。

美国地质勘探局说，当灼热的熔岩遇海水发生反应时，入海口的小型蒸汽爆炸随时可见。

这条熔岩沟渠形成一块新的陆地，称为熔岩三角洲，正如曾经的卡波霍湾一样。

熔岩三角洲是炙热熔岩流入海洋后，冷却、凝固形成的，它是不稳定的熔岩碎片遇海水堆积而成的一片陆地。

美国地质勘探局称，卡波霍湾的熔岩三角洲已达200英亩，并且面积还在继续扩大。

夏威夷市市长哈利·金说："自5月3日爆发性的火山喷发开始以来，夏威夷大岛上已有600多栋房屋被基拉韦厄火山喷出的熔岩吞噬。"

美国地质勘探局的地质专家珍妮特·巴比特在新闻发布会上说："随着科学家对那些引起新的火山喷发的迹象进行跟踪，这些事件从某种程度上来说是可以预测的。"

巴比特在新闻发布会上说，随着地震性运动的反复出现，火山灰的喷发和地震看似已形成了24～48小时间隙的循环。

然而，科学家还无法预测基拉韦厄火山何时停止喷发或这样的地震性运动何时能结束。

Part C

British Education System

Introduction

Many people think school is just about teaching children what are often called the three Rs—"reading, riting and rithmetic"(reading, writing and arithmetic). In other words, the purpose of school is to provide children with **literacy** and the other basic skills they will need to become active members of society. But the purpose of the British education system is also to **socialize** children. Children are taught practical skills; but in school they also learn the rules and values they need to become good citizens, to participate in the community, and to contribute to the economic prosperity of an advanced industrial economy.[①]

literacy[ˈlɪtərəsi]: *n.* 读写能力

socialize[ˈsəʊʃəlaɪz]: *v.* 使合群；使适应社会生活

It is no surprise, then, that the state is heavily involved in deciding when, where, how and what children are taught. It is also no surprise that these decisions are often very **controversial.** Should naughty pupils be punished physically? **Corporal punishment** is currently banned in the UK, but some people—including the government minister responsible for education—would like to see the return of the cane. ② What sort of English should children learn to speak? Should children be forced to speak in a standardized way rather than with regional accents and idioms? Or do local **variations** in the way people talk contribute to the richness of British culture?

controversial[ˌkɒntrəˈvɜːʃl]: *adj.* 有争议的

corporal punishment: 体罚

variation[ˌveəriˈeɪʃn]: *n.* 变化

Such controversies are not just about education. They reflect the deeper divisions in Britain society as a whole. Britain is a society in which social class is still very important. Class inequality can be **erased** or continued according to educational policy. ③ If you understand the importance of the relationship between education and social class, you can understand a great deal about British culture and society.

erase[ɪˈreɪz]: *v.* 消除

The enduring feature of British education is the continuing debate over how "equal" educational opportunity should be. ④ **Sociologists** have found that 51% of British people are working class and 49% are middle class. While the split is about half and half, the opportunities for working class and middle class people can be very different. In Britain, the accent you speak with, the clothes you wear, and the schools you attend are all markers that identify your social class. ⑤

sociologist[ˌsəʊsiˈɒlədʒɪst]: *n.* 社会学家

The school (or college) **tie** is a clear marker of social class. Even on informal occasions you will sometimes see men wearing their school ties as belts to hold up their trousers—proudly displaying their attendance at a certain school. To have attended the "right" schools—particularly the famous boy's public schools like Eton and Winchester⑥—and the "right" universities—Oxford and Cambrige⑦ (those two rival universities have been nicknamed "Oxbridge")—is still the single best way to **guarantee** a successful career. In 2005, 46% of Conservative Party Members of Parliament were graduates of Oxbridge. Most senior **civil servants** are also Oxbridge graduates. When people in Britain talk about "the old boys network"⑧, they mean this **elite** group of men who went to school and university together. Not only do they dominate government, but they are also very influential in banking, the media, the arts and education. In Britain, where you are educated is still very important to your future.

tie[taɪ]：*n.* 领带

guarantee[ˌgærən'tiː]：*v.* 保证；担保

civil servant：公务员

elite[eɪ'liːt]：*n.* 精英

The present education system

Education in the UK is **compulsory**. Children are legally **obliged** to attend school from the age of 5 (4 in Northern Ireland) to 16. In 1992 there were 9.5 million full-time school/college students.

compulsory[kəm'pʌlsəri]：*adj.* 义务的

obliged[ə'blaɪdʒd]：*adj.* 义不容辞的

Parents can choose between sending their children to state schools or to private schools. State schools are funded by local and central government. About 93% of pupils receive free education from the public sector. The government also sometimes **assists** schools established by religious groups.

assist[ə'sɪst]：*v.* 帮助

Since 1993, parents have the right to express a preference for a particular state school for their children.⑨ A system of "league tables"—comparative tables which rank schools according to public examination results, **truancy** rates, destinations of school leavers, and so on—are published in order to help parents make choices.⑩ While children usually attend the school they live closest to, now ambitious parents sometimes move to a different neighborhood in order to be close to a well-performing school. Needless to say, good schools tend to be in middle class neighborhoods and it is the wealthier middle classes who can most easily afford to move if they think it is necessary.

truancy['truːənsi]：*n.* 逃学；旷课

In the private sector there are independent schools which are commonly, but confusingly, called public schools⑪. (They are called public schools because they were originally seen as "public" alternatives to having private tutors in aristocratic households.) Independent schools receive their funding through the private sector and through **tuition rates**, with some government assistance. Independent schools are not part of the national education system, but the quality of instruction and standards are maintained through visits from Her Majesty's Inspectors of Schools⑫. Parents choose to pay fees in order to send their children to these schools because the quality of education is such that their children have a better chance of getting into good universities and/or getting better jobs when they leave school. ⑬

tuition rate：学费

Up to age 5, children may have some pre-primary schooling in nursery schools, **daycare**, or play groups. The government has no obligation to provide such **facilities** and so many are private enterprise arrangements. However, the state realizes such provision is important, especially now that many mothers work, and so they provide some financial support.

daycare[ˈdeɪkeə]：*n.* 日托

facility[fəˈsɪləti]：*n.* 设备；设施

Between the ages of 5 to 11, pupils mainly attend state sector primary schools. These schools are called **co-educational** or mixed schools because they admit both boys and girls.

co-educational[ˌkəʊedʒuˈkeɪʃənl]：*adj.* 对男女学生开放的(学校)

From the age of 11 up to around the age of 19, students attend secondary schools. More than 80% of pupils in secondary schools in England and Wales attend mixed schools; 60% in Northern Ireland; Scotland, nearly all.

About 90% of secondary schools are comprehensive schools which admit children without reference to their academic abilities. Such schools provide a general education. Pupils can study everything from academic subjects like literature and sciences, to more practical subjects like cooking and **carpentry**.

carpentry[ˈkɑːpəntri]：*n.* 木工手艺；木工活

Foreign languages are taught as an **integral** part of the National Curriculum, reflecting the importance of Britain's relationship with Europe. ⑭

integral[ˈɪntɪgrəl]：*adj.* 不可或缺的

Those children who do not attend comprehensive schools attend grammar schools instead. Grammar schools select children, usually at the age of 11, through an examination called "the 11-plus". Those who show academic potential are admitted to the grammar schools where the emphasis is on advanced academic work rather than the more general curriculum of the comprehensive schools. In Northern Ireland the grammar school/non-grammar school division is still common, but throughout the rest of Great Britain grammar schools are becoming increasingly rare.

After 5 years of secondary education, (at about age 16) English, Northern Irish and Welsh students sit their GCSE (General Certificate of Secondary Education⑮) exams. GCSEs are the main means of assessing pupils' progress in their final 2 years of compulsory education. Based on these results, pupils then decide what avenue of education they would like to follow.⑯ They have a number of choices. At the age of 16, they can decide to **quit** school and find a job; or they can prepare to sit exams for university entrance; or they can concentrate on vocational training. Every 16 or 17 year old is guaranteed a place in full-time education or training.

quit[kwɪt]：*v.* 放弃

Pupils who hope to attend university carry on their academic study in the sixth **form** for a further two years and then sit A-levels exams (General Certificate of Education-Advanced⑰). Most pupils try to achieve 3 or 4 A-levels in the subjects they are most **proficient** at.⑱ Since admittance to universities depends largely on A-level results, the two years spent in the sixth form are very important and often very **stressful** for British pupils. Among first year university students getting to know each other, the most common question after "What's your name?" and "Where are you from?" is "What A-levels did you take?"⑲

form[fɔːm]：*n.* 年级

proficient[prəˈfɪʃnt]：*adj.* 熟练的；精通的

stressful[ˈstresfl]：*adj.* 紧张的；压力重的

Other pupils who decide not to go to university may choose to take vocational training. The vocational equivalent of A-levels are GNVQs (General National Vocational Qualifications⑳), which provide a broadly based preparation for work or for taking further vocational training.

Higher education

British universities are public bodies which receive funds from central government. This differs from the United States which, in addition to public universities, also has privately funded universities which are often very wealthy. In the UK, the amount of funding each university receives is based on its size, the number of students it teaches, and the research it conducts.㉑ So far, the UK has only one privately funded university, the University of Buckingham.

Higher education has a long history in the UK. Oxford and Cambridge date from the 12th and 13th centuries, while the Scottish universities of St. Andrews, Glasgow, Edinburgh and Aberdeen from the 14th and 15th centuries. The rest were founded in the 19th and 20th centuries. In the 1960s there was a large expansion in the numbers of universities and many new universities were built. In 1992 the number grew again when polytechnics[22] and other higher education establishments were given the right to become universities. By 2008, Britain had 129 universities.

University campuses are full of people of different ages and nationalities studying many different things. In 2008/9 there were 1540035 full-time students, 305885 who came from overseas. While most of the students are studying for their first degrees, about 268000 were working on **postgraduate** qualifications. There are about 117465 full time university teachers paid wholly from university funds.

postgraduate[ˌpəʊstˈgrædʒuət]: *n.* 研究生

UK educational institutions are world class. The excellence of their teaching, research and scholarships is acknowledged worldwide. Such is the reputation of British education that, every year, UK institutions attract hundreds of thousands of international students. Many who come to study here pay for their courses privately and some receive financial help. UK government departments and the **devolved** administrations of Scotland, Wales and Northern Ireland offer a variety of scholarships and other awards to help international students study in the UK. These awards are a sign of the UK's strong commitment to the rest of the world. They also show the UK's awareness of the many benefits that come from sharing the excellence of its schools, colleges and universities with visiting students and scholars from abroad.

devolved[dɪˈvɒlvd]: *adj.* 移交的；下放的

Universities, reflecting the trend throughout the education system, have traditionally been rather **elitist**. Most students were from the middle classes, attended good schools, performed well in their A-levels and received a fully-funded place in a university. In recent years, great efforts have been made to increase the numbers of and kinds of people that pursue higher education. For example, whereas in 1980, 1 in 8 pupils went on to university, by 1990 it was 1 in 5, and by 2000 it was to be 1 in 3. Access for mature students and students without traditional A-level qualifications is widening.[23]

elitist[eɪˈliːtɪst]：*n.* 优秀人才；杰出者

The Open University[24] offers a non-traditional route for people to take university level courses and receive a university degree. People can register without having any formal educational qualifications. They follow university courses through textbooks, TV and radio broadcasts, **correspondence**, videos, **residential schools** and a network of study centers. Tens of thousands of Britons, from housewives to coal miners, from teachers to ballet dancers "attend" the Open University each year. It was the Open University which provided the **inspiration** for the founding of China's TV and Radio University. Degree titles vary, but usually one receives a Bachelor of Arts (BA) or a Bachelor of Science (BSc), for a second degree Master of Arts (MA) or Science (MSc) and Doctor of Philosophy (PhD).[25] In the older Scottish universities, Master is used for a first degree in Arts subjects, and in Oxford and Cambridge the BA converts to an MA several years later, upon payment of a fee.[26]

correspondence[ˌkɒrəˈspɒndəns]：*n.* 函授
residential schools：寄宿制学校
inspiration[ˌɪnspəˈreɪʃn]：*n.* 灵感

Notes

①Children are taught… of an advanced industrial economy：学生在学校不仅要学习各种技能，还要学一些作为好公民所应具备的道德规范和价值观，以便能走上社会，为一个发达的工业化国家的经济繁荣做贡献。

②Corporal punishment is… to see the return of the cane：体罚目前在英国是禁止的，但有些人，包括教育大臣，仍然希望学校能够重新使用体罚。cane，意为"手杖"，是传统的体罚工具，因此 the return of the cane 意为 the return of corporal punishment。

③Class inequality can be erased or continued according to educational policy：教育政策可以铲除地位的不平等，也可以使这种不平等继续存在。这说明在英国，是否受到良好教育直接影响一个人的社会地位。

④The enduring feature of British education is… how "equal" educational opportunity should be：英国教育中的一个长期特点就是在就学机会"平等"的问题上争论不休。

⑤In Britain, the accent you speak with… identify your social class：在英国，从你说话的口音、你穿的衣服和你所上的学校都能看出你的社会地位。

marker：标记。

⑥Eton and Winchester：伊顿公学位于伦敦以西，温彻斯特公学位于英格兰南部，这两所公学都是英国著名的私立贵族学校。

⑦Oxford and Cambridge：牛津大学和剑桥大学是英国最古老的两所大学，分别建立于12世纪和13世纪。这两所大学有着悠久的历史，在世界上享有盛誉。英国大部分政治家和政府官员都毕业于这两所大学。

⑧"the old boys network"："老男孩关系网"，指毕业于私立贵族公学，而后又毕业于牛津和剑桥大学的老同学。因英国公学只收男孩，因此他们被称为"老男孩"。他们过去是校友，现在又占据了政府部门的要职，形成一张"关系网"。他们不仅在政府部门有地位，在银行、新闻、艺术和教育界也很有影响力。

⑨Since 1993, parents have the right…school for their children：1993年以来，家长有权替他们的孩子选择某一所公立学校。

⑩A system of "League tables"…to help parents make choices：学校等级表是一种用来反映各类学校的考试成绩、逃学比例、毕业去向等情况的表格，人们以此划定各个学校的等级。公布这些情况是为了让家长替子女挑选最好的学校。

⑪public schools：公学，也叫私立学校。学费昂贵，一般有钱人家的子女才上得起这样的学校。英国有名的公学有伊顿、哈罗和拉格贝。

⑫Her Majesty's Inspectors of Schools：皇家督学。英国皇家督学制度已有160余年历史，其主要职责是：保证每所学校在规定的期限内接受监督，并保证教育大臣能及时了解学校的教学质量，学生的精神、道德、社会和文化发展情况，学校的财政管理情况等。1992年，英国成立了专门督导机构——教育标准局，独立于英国教育部，统管全国教育监督和评价工作。其首脑为首席皇家督学(Her Majesty's Chief Inspector of School)，由女王直接任命，其成员为皇家督学。

⑬Parents choose to pay fees…when they leave school：家长们之所以付钱让孩子们上这样的学校，是因为这些学校的教学质量好，能使自己的孩子有机会进好大学，或者毕业后找到好工作。

⑭Foreign languages are taught…Britain's relationship with Europe：外语教学是全国教学大纲不可或缺的组成部分，反映了英国与欧洲国家之间的重要关系。

⑮General Certificate of Secondary Education：中学毕业证书。英国的义务教育制度到16岁结束。学生16岁后分流，一部分选择几门课程进一步深造，通过高级水平考试，从而获得进大学的资格；另一部分则以多种方式走向

职业技术教育。

⑯Based on these results，pupils then decide…to follow：然后学生根据这些结果选择自己喜欢的教育途径。avenue of education：教育途径。

⑰General Certificate of Education-Advanced：高级水平测试结业证书。16岁的学生通过中学毕业考试后，如果想进高等学府继续深造，必须通过高级水平测试。在16岁至18岁的两年时间里，学生根据自己想读的大学专业选定数门有关课程进行学习，一般选三门。通过A级水平考试者均可入大学深造。

⑱Most pupils try to…most proficient at：大部分学生试图在自己学得最好的三至四门课程中取得A级水平。A-Level：advanced-level，即高级水平。

⑲Among first year university students … is "What A-Levels did you take?"：大学一年级学生初次见面时，在问过"你叫什么名字"和"你从哪儿来之后"，最常问的问题就是"你的A级水平测试选的是哪几门课程"。

⑳General National Vocational Qualifications：国家专业资格证书。这一证书是为职业技术学校毕业的学生设置的，共分为五个级别，这就便于人们按照阶梯逐级攀登，根据自身条件通过实际工作和专业培训由低级向高级发展。获四级国家专业资格证书相当于学士学位，获五级国家专业资格证书相当于研究生水平。

㉑In the UK，the amount of funding each university receives … the research it conducts：在英国，每所大学的经费是根据它的规模、学生数量和从事的研究项目而定的。

㉒polytechnics：理工学院，1992年后转为大学。

㉓Access for mature students…is widening：成人以及没有通过传统的A级测试的学生，进入高等学府的渠道正在拓宽。

㉔the Open University：开放大学。对任何人都开放，无须正式学历。学生在完成大学的必修课程后均可拿到大学文凭。开放大学的特点就在于通过电视、广播、录像、函授等方式为学生提供就地学习的条件。开放大学不限年龄，最小的学生不到20岁，最大的学生90多岁，大多数为20～40岁。

㉕Degree titles vary…and Doctor of Philosophy：学位名称不同，一般先获得文学学士或理科学士(也称第一学位)，第二学位指文科硕士或理科硕士以及哲学博士。

㉖In the older Scottish universities…upon payment of a fee：在古老的苏格兰大学，文学硕士只相当于文学学士。在牛津和剑桥大学获得学士学位的毕业生，数年后，只要交纳一定费用，就可转为硕士学位。

Questions

1. What are the purposes of the British education system? Please comment on those purposes. What are the main purposes of the Chinese education system? Are there any differences or similarities in the education of the two nations?

2. How does the British education system reflect social class?

3. What is the Open University in Britain? What do you think of this system?

Part D

Pre-reading activities

1. What is the regional feature of the border town?

2. Do you like the border town? Please give the reasons.

边城(片段1)

这小城里虽那么安静和平，但地方既为川东商业交易接头处，故城外小小河街，情形却不同了一点。也有商人落脚的客店，坐镇不动的理发馆。此外饭店、杂货铺、油行、盐栈、花衣庄，莫不各有一种地位，装点了这条河街。还有卖船上用的檀木活车、竹缆与锅罐铺子，介绍水手职业吃码头饭的人家。小饭店门前长案上，常有煎得焦黄的鲤鱼豆腐，身上装饰了红辣椒丝，卧在浅口钵头里，钵旁大竹筒中插着大把朱红筷子，不拘谁个愿意花点钱，这人就可以傍了门前长案坐下来，抽出一双筷子捏到手上，那边一个眉毛扯得极细脸上擦了白粉的妇人就走过来问："大哥，副爷，要甜酒？要烧酒？"男子火焰高一点的，谐趣的，对内掌柜有点意思的，必故意装成生气似的说："吃甜酒？又不是小孩子，还问人吃甜酒！"那么，酽冽的烧酒，从大瓮里用木滤子舀出，倒进土碗里，即刻就来到身边案桌上了。这烧酒自然是浓而且香的，能醉倒一个汉子，所以照例也不会多吃。杂货铺卖美孚油及点美孚油的洋灯，与香烛纸张。油行屯桐油。盐栈堆四川火井出的青盐。花衣庄则有白棉纱、大布、棉花以及包头的黑绉绸出卖。卖船上用物的，百物罗列，无所不备，且间或有重至百斤以外的铁锚搁在门外路旁，等候主顾问价的。专以介绍水手为事业，吃水码头饭的，在河街的家中，终日大门必敞开着，常有穿青羽缎马褂的船主与毛手毛脚的水手进出，地方像茶馆却不卖茶，不是烟馆又可以抽烟。来到这里的，虽说所谈的是船上生意经，然而船只的上下，划船拉纤人大都有一定规矩，不必作数目上的讨论。他们来到这里大多数倒是在"联欢"。以"龙头管事"作中心，谈论点本地时事、两省商务上情形，以及下游的"新事"。邀会的，集款时大多数皆在此地，扒骰子看点数多少轮作会首时，也常常在此举行。真真成为他们生意经的，有两件事：买卖船只，买卖媳妇。

参考译文

The Border Town (Excerpt 1)

For all its quiet **tranquility**, this little town is a centre of trade and communications for east Sichuan, and therefore the small **waterfronts** have a **character** all their own. There are inns where merchants put up, barbers' establishments, **not to mention** restaurants, general stores, oil and salt **depots** and **drapers**' shops. There are **ship-chandlers** too, and "**wharf rats**" who make a living by **recruiting** boatmen. The long tables in front of the **modest** eating houses often **bear crisp** brown **carp** fried with **beancurd** and **garnished** with **slivers** of **paprika** in **shallow** dishes next to **bamboo** holders filled with scarlet **chopsticks**. For a few cents anyone can sit down at the table and pull out a pair of chopsticks. Then a woman with **plucked eyebrows** and a powdered face will come to ask, "Would you care for **sweet wine** or rice wine, master?"A spirited man who likes to **tease** will **retort**, "Sweet wine? What do you take me for—a child?" Then rich yellow wine is **ladled** out of the **vat** into an earthen bowl and brought **promptly** to the table. This **potent**, fragrant **brew** can knock a strong man out if he drinks too much. The general stores sell **paraffin**, paraffin lamps, candles and paper. The oil depots purchase tung oil. The salt merchants store the dark rock salt from Sichuan's salt **wells**. The drapers stock white cotton yarn, cloth, cotton and black silk headscarves. The ship-chandlers have everything a junk can need down to **anchors** weighing a good hundred catties displayed outside to **tempt** the customers in. The doors of the "wharf rats" on the waterfront remain open all day long as in and out troop **jolly** boatmen or boat-owners in dark **satin** jackets over long **gowns**. These places are like tea-houses where no tea is sold. They are not **opium dens**, yet you can smoke opium there. Although men come here on business, from the boat—owners down to the **oarsmen** and towmen they make it a rule never to mention figures. Most of them drop in here to have a good time. They discuss local happenings, the state of trade in both provinces, and news from down-river. Meetings and **financial transactions** take place here too, not to mention **dicing** and **gambling**. But the two main **items** of business are **deals** in boats and in wives.

tranquility[træŋˈkwɪləti]：*n*. 宁静
waterfront[ˈwɔːtəfrʌnt]：*n*. 滨水路
character[ˈkærəktə(r)]：*n*. 特点
not to mention：更不用说，后可接名词或动词-ing 形式。
depot[ˈdepəʊ]：*n*. 仓库
draper[ˈdreɪpə(r)]：*n*. 布商；服装商
ship-chandler[ʃɪpˈtʃændlə(r)]：*n*. 船用杂货商
wharf rats：指的是专门介绍水手职业、吃码头饭的人，含贬义。
recruit[rɪˈkruːt]：*v*. 招聘
modest[ˈmɒdɪst]：*adj*. 不太大的
bear[beə(r)]：*v*. 承担
crisp[krɪsp]：*adj*. 脆的
carp[kɑːp]：*n*. 鲤鱼
beancurd[ˈbiːnkəːd]：*n*. 豆腐
garnish[ˈɡɑːnɪʃ]：*v*. 装饰(尤指食物)
sliver[ˈslɪvə(r)]：*n*. 细片；长条
paprika[ˈpæprɪkə]：*n*. 红辣椒
shallow[ˈʃæləʊ]：*adj*. 浅的
bamboo[bæmˈbuː]：*n*. 竹子
chopstick[ˈtʃɒpstɪk]：*n*. 筷子
pluck[plʌk]：*v*. 扯
eyebrow[ˈaɪbraʊ]：*n*. 眉毛
sweet wine：甜酒
tease[tiːz]：*v*. 挑逗；戏弄
retort[rɪˈtɔːt]：*v*. 反驳；回嘴
ladle[ˈleɪdl]：*v*. (用勺)舀或盛很多(食物)
vat[væt]：*n*. 大瓮；大桶
promptly[ˈprɒmptli]：*adv*. 迅速地；立即地
potent[ˈpəʊtnt]：*adj*. 烈性的
brew[bruː]：*n*. 酿造的饮料
paraffin[ˈpærəfɪn]：*n*. 煤油
well[wel]：*n*. 井
anchor[ˈæŋkə(r)]：*n*. 锚
tempt[tempt]：*v*. 引诱；吸引
jolly[ˈdʒɒli]：*adj*. 快活的；愉快的；兴高采烈的

satin['sætɪn]：*adj.* 绸缎做的
gown[gaʊn]：*n.* 长袍
opium dens：鸦片烟馆
oarsman['ɔːzmən]：*n.* 划手；划桨者
financial[faɪ'nænʃl]：*adj.* 金融的；财务的
transaction[træn'zækʃn]：*n.* 事务；交易
dicing['daɪsɪŋ]：*n.* 掷骰子
gambling['gæmblɪŋ]：*n.* 赌博
item['aɪtəm]：*n.* 项目
deal[diːl]：*n.*（一笔）交易

[选自：沈从文．边城(英汉双语对照)．杨宪益，戴乃迭，译．南京：译林出版社，2013.]

After-reading activities

1. How much do you know about the folk customs in western Hunan?

2. There are many well-known "border towns" with unique appeal of regional features in China. Could you introduce one of them?

作者简介

沈从文(1902—1988)，男，原名沈岳焕，乳名茂林，字崇文，笔名休芸芸、甲辰、上官碧、璇若等，湖南凤凰县人，中国著名作家、历史文物研究者。

14 岁时，他投身行伍，浪迹湘川黔交界地区。1924 年开始进行文学创作，撰写出版了《长河》《边城》等小说。1931—1933 年在青岛大学任教，抗日战争爆发后到西南联合大学任教，1946 年回到北京大学任教，中华人民共和国成立后，在中国历史博物馆和中国社会科学院历史研究所工作，主要从事中国古代历史与文物的研究，著有《中国古代服饰研究》。1988 年 5 月 10 日病逝于北京，享年 86 岁。

写作背景

《边城》是沈从文创作的中篇小说，成书于 1931 年，那正是沈从文爱情事业双丰收的季节。1931 年，社会虽然动荡不安，但总体上还是稍显和平，这个时候中国有良知的文人都在思考着人性的本质，沈从文自然是走在前沿的。他希望通过自己对湘西的印象，描写一个近似桃花源的湘西小城，给都市文明中迷茫的人指一条明路——人间尚有纯洁自然的爱，人生需要回归自然的本性。《边城》首次出版于 1934 年。

作品鉴赏

《边城》以 20 世纪 30 年代川湘交界的边城小镇——茶峒为背景，以兼具抒情诗和小品文的优美笔触，描绘了湘西地区特有的风土人情；借船家少女翠翠的纯爱故事，展现出人性的善良美好。由于《边城》的美学艺术，这部小说在中国近代文学史上具有独特的地位。

作品中女主人公翠翠的原型是一个绒线铺的姑娘。沈从文在行军途中有一个叫赵开明的好友。赵开明在泸溪县城一家绒线铺遇到了一个叫翠翠的少女，她长相俊秀，赵开明发誓要娶她为妻。17 年后，沈从文乘坐的小船又停靠在泸溪。他站在船头上，回忆起翠翠的美丽形象，便朝绒线铺走去，在门前意外地看到了一个和翠翠长得十分相似的少女，熟悉的眼睛、鼻子，薄薄的小嘴，沈从文惊讶得说不出话来。原来这是翠翠的女儿小翠。当年的翠翠嫁给了追求她的赵开明。彼时她已死去，留下父女两个。为了不打扰赵开明，沈从文没有跟他打招呼，但感情上的震撼却久久不能平复。翠翠，这个美丽、朴实的少女，他怎么也无法忘怀。1934 年，他坐在院子里，在阳光下的枣树和槐树枝叶阴影间写《边城》时，翠翠的形象便跃然纸上。沈从文在《湘行散记・老伴》中说："我写《边城》故事时，弄渡船的外孙女明慧温柔的品性，就从那绒线铺子女孩脱胎而来。"

该小说入选 20 世纪中文小说 100 强，排名第二位，仅次于鲁迅的《呐喊》。

《边城》寄托着沈从文"美"与"爱"的美学理想，是他的作品中最能表现人性美的一部小说。《边城》极力讴歌的传统文化中保留至今的美德，是相对于现代社会传统美德受到破坏，到处充溢着物欲金钱主义的浅薄、庸俗和腐化堕落的现实而言的。《边城》中描写的湘西，自然风光秀丽，民风淳朴，人们不讲等级，真诚相待。外公对孙女的爱、翠翠对傩送的爱、天保兄弟对翠翠的爱以及兄弟间诚挚的手足之情，这些都代表着未受污染的农业文明的传统美德。作者极力状写湘西自然之明净，也是为了状写湘西人的心灵之明净。《边城》中对以歌求婚、兄弟让婚、外公和翠翠的相依之情的描写隐含着对现实生活中古老美德丢失的痛心，以及对现代文明物欲泛滥的批判。

Chapter 3　The Family

Part A

《心灵的慰藉：一部非同寻常的地域与家族史》是美国自然文学作家及诗人特丽·T. 威廉斯(Terry T. Williams)的代表作，被誉为美国自然文学的"经典之作"。作者将自己及其家族的经历、美国西部大盐湖及熊河候鸟保护区的特殊环境联系在一起，用一种独特的写作方式将人与自然之间的密切关系展示在人们面前。威廉斯生长于美国犹他州的大盐湖畔。作为摩门教徒，他们家已经在那里繁衍了六代。然而，由于位于美国核试验基地的下风口，威廉斯家族的女性多半都患有乳腺癌。她的祖母、外祖母、母亲及六位姑姨都做了乳房切除手术，其中的几位最终都死于癌症。因此，作者用"女性只有一侧乳房的家族"作为此书的跋。与此同时，威廉斯发现盐湖水在不断地上涨，这使得熊河候鸟保护区的鸟类受到威胁，有些鸟类可能会从此消亡。人类的悲剧与自然界的悲剧同时上演，这种现象使作者大胆地采用了一种独特的写作方式来展示她的生态视野。她将人类内心的情感世界与特定的自然风景融为一体。这些类似日记的优美的散文记述了作者陪同乳腺癌晚期的母亲在大盐湖畔走过人生最后一程的经历。威廉斯在书中将湖、鸟、人三者视为不可分割的整体。她从一个大视野中，感悟人与自然、人与鸟、鸟与湖共生共荣的生命真相。她希望通过自己亲历的非同寻常的地域与家族史，唤醒世人的善待自然之心。

全书共36章，每一章都以熊河候鸟保护区的一种鸟类命名。章题下面是大盐湖的水位记录。大盐湖水位的上涨与作者母亲病情的加重相呼应，自然界的悲剧与人类的悲剧交替上演，从而体现出一种博大的生态视野及土地伦理，即人类、动物及植物都属于同一个地球社区，彼此不可分离，息息相关。故事的开端是大盐湖涨水了，它的湖面海拔达 4204.70 英尺，即将超过熊河候鸟保护区的湖面(海拔 4206 英尺)。这意味着熊河候鸟保护区将被淹没，那里的鸟类将沦落为“仓皇逃离的难民”。与此同时，作者身患乳腺癌的母亲黛安娜病情恶化，癌症转移到了腹部，可是她并没有及时就医，而是隐瞒病情，去了大峡谷。因为对于她而言，在大峡谷及科罗拉多河上度过的日子堪称一种沉思冥想、一种精神的复活。穿过古老的岩石群的经历赋予她希望，使她能够承受任何必须面对的事实。她从孤寂中寻找到应对病魔的力量。在坚强地挺过手术之后，经过激烈的思想斗争，黛安娜决定做化疗。通过母女二人的对话，我们可见她们应对病魔的独特之处。“母亲说：‘或许，你能帮我想象一条河——我可以把化疗想象为一条河，它能够穿过我的身体，把癌细胞冲走。特丽，你说，是哪条河?’‘科罗拉多河怎么样?’我说。几周来，我第一次看到我母亲的脸上露出了笑容。”

大自然赋予她们母女战胜病魔的定力和毅力。作者的母亲在与癌症搏斗之中感到生命得以浓缩，每天都在用心生活。母亲从自然中汲取的活力令作者敬佩。她看到母亲从自然界获取的开朗达观，她看到母亲全身的生命节奏都在加速，她看到母亲“是一只翱翔于天地之间的鸟，羽翼上承载着新获取的对于生命价值的理解”。这本书告诉了我们，在现代社会中，当人类面对诸多不稳定的因素，甚至灾难及人生悲剧时，如何从自然中寻求心灵的慰藉和精神的升华。

这部“非同寻常的地域与家族史”，在书题、结构、章名、内容及语言方面，都堪称独树一帜：每一章都以特定的鸟类命名，章题下面是大盐湖的水位记录。水位的涨落与作者母亲的病情及熊河候鸟保护区的存亡密切相关。湖、鸟、人作为不可分离的整体，成为这部书的主角。自然不再是陪衬或背景，由此体现出一种博大的生态视野及土地伦理。这本书在 1991 年首版之后，不仅于 1994 年及 2002 年先后由不同的出版社作为有声读物出版，而且被收入文选及课本之中，走进了高校的课堂。当作者动手整理她在大盐湖畔的日记准备出书时，她本人也被确诊为乳腺癌，年仅 34 岁。她翻开这些记录母亲弥留人世时的日记，鸟的羽毛、大盐湖畔的细沙、鼠尾草的叶片纷纷从日记本中落下，触动了她内心的悲痛。如她本人所述：“我讲述这个故事，是为了抚慰自己受伤的心灵，是为了面对我尚无法理解的事物，是为了给自己铺一条回家的路，因为我认为，‘记忆是唯一回归家园之路’。我一直在避难，这个故事是我的归程。”

作者特丽 • T. 威廉斯依然健在，她依然居住在美国犹他州。虽然身为犹他州自然史博物馆的驻馆博物学家及犹他大学兼职教授，威廉斯笔耕不辍，著述颇丰，曾获美国蕾切尔·卡逊荣誉奖、华莱士·斯蒂格文学奖以及美国联邦国家野生动物保护特殊成就奖，是美国自然文学、生态批评及环境保护等领域颇具影响力的人物。1996 年之后，她离职专心进行写作，并参与环保活动。威廉斯著述颇丰，其中包括《片片白贝壳：纳瓦霍印第安人居留区之行》(*White Shells*: *A Trip to Navajo Indian Reservation*)、《土狼的峡谷》(*Coyote's Canyon*)、《心灵的慰藉：一部非同寻常的地域与家族史》、《无言的渴望：原野的故事》(*Wordless Desire*: *The Story of the Wilderness*)、《沙漠四熏奏：一片令人销魂的风景》(*Four Smoke in the Desert*: *A Fascinating Landscape*)、《红色：沙漠中的激情及耐心》(*Red*: *Passion and Patience in the Desert*)以及《在破碎的世界中寻求美》(*Seeking Beauty in a Broken World*)。以上著作均由散文体写就，以作者所熟悉的美国西部大盆地为写作背景，并将土地与人的故事融为一体。所以，有学者评论，威廉斯所采用的文体是一种"叙述式的散文"，她所用的语言是一种"抒情诗的语言"，她是"一个写散文诗的作家"。

(1) Burrowing Owls

题注：穴鸮，是鸮形目、鸱鸮科的鸟类。身体纤瘦，腿颇长，成年穴鸮体长为 19～25 厘米，以啮齿类动物遗弃的洞穴为巢，或以自己打的洞为巢。活动范围是在开阔的草地和农耕平原上，喜欢捕食个头大的昆虫、麻雀或老鼠等小动物。这种穴鸮在中国很少见，多分布于美洲地区。穴鸮被称为"受威胁的物种"，与濒临灭绝的物种仅一步之遥。

In **Mormon** culture, that is one of the things you do know—history and **genealogy**. I come from a family with deep roots in the American West. When the expense of **outfitting** several thousand immigrants to Utah was becoming too great for the newly established church, leaders decided to **furnish** the pioneers with small two-wheeled carts about the size of those used by apple **peddlers**, which could be pulled by hand from Missouri to the Salt Lake Valley. ① My **ancestors** were part of these original "handcart companies" in the 1850s. With faith, they would **endure**. They came with few **provisions** over the twelve-hundred-mile trail. It was a small **sacrifice** in the name of religious freedom. Almost one hundred and fifty years later, we are still here.

Mormon：基督后期圣徒教会(The Church of Jesus Christ of Latter-Day Saints)是泛基督信仰各宗派运动的一个分支，但其在信仰内容上与基督教有别，而坊间则有摩门教这个非官方的称呼。

genealogy[ˌdʒiːniˈælədʒi]：*n.* 族谱；家族

outfit[ˈaʊtfɪt]：*v.* 供养

furnish[ˈfɜːnɪʃ]：*v.* 为……提供

peddler[ˈpedlə(r)]：*n.* 小贩

ancestor[ˈænsestə(r)]：*n.* 祖先

endure[ɪnˈdjʊə(r)]：*v.* 忍受

provision[prəˈvɪʒn]：*n.* 供给；生活物资

sacrifice[ˈsækrɪfaɪs]：*n.* 牺牲

I am the oldest child in our family, a daughter with three younger brothers: Steve, Dan, and Hank. My parents, John Henry Tempest, and Diane Dixon Tempest, were married in the Mormon Temple in Salt Lake City on September 18, 1953. My husband, Brooke Williams, and I followed the same tradition and were married on June 2, 1975. I was nineteen years old.

Our **extended family** includes both **maternal** and **paternal** grandparents: Lettie Romney Dixon and Donald "Sanky" Dixon, Kathryn Blackett Tempest and John Henry Tempest, Jr. Aunts, uncles, and cousins are many, extending familial ties all across the state of Utah. If I ever wonder who I am, I simply attend a Romney family reunion and find myself in the eyes of everyone I meet. It is comforting and disturbing, at once. ② I have known five of my great-grandparents **intimately**. They **tutored** me in stories with a belief that **lineage** mattered. Genealogy is in our blood. ③ As a people and as a family, we have a sense of history. And our history is tied to land.

extended family：大家庭

maternal[məˈtɜːnl]：*adj.* 母系的

paternal[pəˈtɜːnl]：*adj.* 父系的

intimately [ˈɪntɪmɪtli]：*adv.* 亲密地

tutor[ˈtjuːtə(r)]：*v.* 教导

lineage[ˈlɪniɪdʒ]：*n.* 血统

I was raised to believe in a spirit world, that life exists before the earth and will continue to exist afterward, that each human being, bird, and **bulrush**, along with all other life forms had a spirit life before it came to **dwell** physically on the earth. Each occupied an assigned sphere of influence, each has a place and a purpose. ④

bulrush[ˈbʊlrʌʃ]：*n.* 灯芯草

dwell[dwel]：*v.* 居住

It made sense to a child. And if the natural world was assigned spiritual values, then those days spent in wildness were **sacred**. We learned at an early age that God can be found wherever you are, especially outside. Family **worship was not just relegated** to Sunday in a **chapel.** ⑤ Our weekends were spent camped alongside a small stream in **the Great Basin**, in the Stansbury Mountains or Deep Creeks. ⑥ My father would take the boys rabbit hunting while Mother and I would sit on a log in an **aspen grove** and talk. She would tell me stories of how when she was a girl she would paint red lips on the trunks of trees to practice kissing, or how she would lie in her grandmother's **lucerne** patch and watch clouds.

sacred[ˈseɪkrɪd]: *adj.* 神圣的

worship[ˈwɜːʃɪp]: *n.* 礼拜

relegate[ˈrelɪgeɪt]: *v.* (使)降级

chapel[ˈtʃæpl]: *n.* 小教堂

the Great Basin：美国大盆地。它是美国西部科迪勒拉山系中的高原性内陆盆地。

aspen grove：杨树林

lucerne[luːˈsɜːn]: *n.* 苜蓿

"I have never known my full capacity for solitude," she would say.

"Solitude?" I asked.

"The gift of being alone. I can never get enough."⑦

The men would return anxious for dinner. Mother would cook over a green Coleman stove as Dad told stories from his childhood—like the time his father took away his BB gun for a year because he shot off the heads of every red **tulip** in his mother's garden, row after row. He laughed. We laughed. And then it was time to bless the food.

tulip[ˈtjuːlɪp]: *n.* 郁金香

After supper, we would spread out our sleeping bags in a circle, heads pointing to the center like **a covey of quail**, and watch the Great Basin sky fill with stars. Our **attachment** to the land was our attachment to each other. ⑧

a covey of quail：一群鹌鹑

attachment[əˈtætʃmənt]: *n.* 依附

[选自：Terry T. Williams. *Refuge: An Unnatural History of Family and Place*. New York: Vintage Books, 1992.]

Notes

①犹他州：位于美国西部，人口主要由摩门教信众的后代和北欧移民的后

裔组成。盐湖城：是美国犹他州的首府和最大城市，以紧靠大盐湖而得名，1847 年，由杨百翰率领一批摩门教的信徒在此拓荒所建成。此后，该教会的总会一直位于盐湖城。目前超过半数的该地人士为该教会教徒。

译文：当新建立的教堂无力承担供养涌向犹他州的几千移民的巨大费用时，宗教领袖决定给拓荒者提供卖苹果小贩用的那种两轮手推车，以便他们从密苏里迁移到盐湖流域。

②译文：假若我搞不清楚自己的身份，只需参加一个罗姆尼家庭聚会，就可以从我遇到的每个人的目光中认识自己。那是一件既令人安慰又令人不安的事情。

③译文：他们的故事引导我相信一脉相承的重要性。传宗接代的概念已经融入我们的血液中。

④译文：每一种生物都被赋予特定的影响范围，每一种生物都有其特定的位置及目标。

⑤译文：一家人做礼拜不仅仅局限于周日的教堂。

⑥译文：周末，我们常在西部大盆地、斯坦斯伯里山或迪普克里克山的小溪边露营。

⑦译文："享受孤寂的天赋，我真喜欢独处，没个够。"

⑧译文：我们对土地的依附如同我们彼此之间的依附。

Remarks

威廉斯的母亲戴安娜在病情恶化后，先去了大峡谷和科罗拉多河，在临终前 10 天，她选择去看湖畔的飞鸟、细沙和鼠尾草。威廉斯陪伴着她，一边观察母亲从大自然中汲取的活力，一边审视水位的涨落并思考候鸟的保护问题。她将湖、鸟、人三者视为不可分割的整体，她从一个大视野中，感悟人与自然、人与鸟、鸟与湖共生共荣的生命真相。

母亲带着微笑和无限的遗憾离开了人世。家中的男人不再拿着猎枪去屠杀湖区的鸟儿了，就连酷爱打猎的弟弟在进山时也只是端着望远镜看活跃奔跑的雄鹿。威廉斯记下了曾经的猎手们由悲伤之情发展而成的怜悯之心。虽然她知道大盐湖畔以及熊河候鸟保护区已经很难恢复到原来的状态，但她还是努力将母亲弥留之际的言语和行动留在她的记忆与文字里，希望由此唤醒世人的善待自然之心。这里的风景曾给她以温柔与慰藉，让她远离人们的争斗、贪婪，使她的心灵受到震撼，且萌生出新的欢欣和信心。

文中的描述，无论是对人，还是对鸟，乃至对大自然和人居环境，都带有强烈的感情色彩。威廉斯家族是典型的"单乳族"，她自己饱经病痛折磨，但她仍然对候鸟充满关注。大盐湖周边有不少鸟儿走了，死了。望着盐湖风起时大浪此起彼伏的情景，威廉斯心中涌起越来越强烈的忧患感。

威廉斯以文体独特、深情动人的文章，试图警示盲目破坏生态平衡的世人，期待人们能同她一样医治自己，给自己铺一条回家的路。她对土地满怀深情，对自然充满爱恋。残酷的现实生活带给她许多关于人与自然的启迪，也促使她在自然文学、生态批评与环境保护等领域倾注了很多的情感与精力，形成了很多深具影响力的思想。

威廉斯的《心灵的慰藉：一部非同寻常的地域与家庭史》一书，虽不无感伤和苍凉，但她努力以一种新鲜的思想元素，将在疾病中寻求健康的家族史当成一面镜子，同时她期待人们看清貌似丰富实则满目疮痍的大自然，审视现状，反思自我，寻求人与自然的真正和解。

人类的悲剧命运与自然界的悲剧命运是一枚硬币的两面。这样的视角，导致作者的思考总是叠加着自己家族成员的悲剧命运和自然生态的失衡与恶化。她将内心的悲痛情感与其周围的自然风物融会贯通。这些声情并茂、文质兼美的思考札记，详细记述了威廉斯陪同乳腺癌晚期的母亲在大盐湖畔走向生命边缘的刻骨铭心的内心体验和对生存环境日益恶化的深切忧愤。

在患病期间，特丽·T. 威廉斯的母亲把大自然当作心灵的慰藉，她说：“当我与自然独处的时候，我找到了内心的平静与安宁。”在治疗的时候，她也没有放弃对美好生活的追求。尤其令人感动的是，书中这位 79 岁的母亲 4 点钟起床，为的是去看 76 年出现一次的哈雷彗星。“那是一个多么美妙的早晨，看着光缓缓出现在东方——色彩瞬息万变；日出时是桃红色和粉红色，深紫色，蓝色和灰色——我不是去看哈雷彗星的，大地及天空的魅力使我不虚此行。”诚如中国作家丰子恺所言：“一切自然，常暗示我们爱和美。”威廉斯的写作是对美好自然感悟的一种回应，也是对自我与自然关系的一种深切关怀。她坚守自由、诗意的言说伦理，凝视个体内部的尊严，尊敬个体与自然之间的精神对决，并试图由此重建自然写作的悲剧意识和生命自身的尊严。在一个崇尚科技和发展速度的时代，她的写作是有精神重量的。她把个人际遇与自然命运相结合，深感真相的挖掘才是更内在的人文关怀，而作品中所表达的个人常被自然理想裹挟的无力感，又说出现代人在生存意义上的根本困境。正是在这种沉痛、矛盾和紧张感中，她描述出了人与自然双重罹难时灵魂粗粝的面影和良知残存的价值。

参考译文

穴鸮

在摩门文化中，有一件事情你必须知道，那就是历史和地理。我来自一个根深蒂固的美国西部家庭。当新建立的教堂无力承担供养涌向犹他州的几千移民的巨大费用时，宗教领袖决定为拓荒者提供卖苹果小贩用的那种两轮手推车，以便他们从密苏里迁移到盐湖流域。我的祖先就是19世纪50年代这些最初的“手推车大队人马”中的一部分。心存信仰，他们不畏艰难。在供给不足的情况下，他们徒步走了1200英里的小路来到此地。为了获得宗教自由，这点牺牲不足挂齿。在将近一百五十年之后，我们还居住在此地。

我是我们家中最大的孩子。身为长女，我有三个弟弟：史蒂夫、丹及汉克。我的父母约翰·亨利·坦皮斯特三世及黛安娜·狄克逊·坦皮斯特于1953年9月18日在盐湖城的摩门教堂结婚。我与我的丈夫布鲁克·威廉斯依照同样的传统于1975年6月2日举行了婚礼。当时我19岁。

我们的大家庭包括外祖父母和祖父母：莱蒂·罗姆尼·狄克逊与唐纳德·“桑基”·狄克逊，凯瑟琳·布莱克特·坦皮斯特与约翰·亨利，坦皮斯特。还有众多的姑姑姨姨、叔叔舅舅以及堂表兄弟姐妹。这个大家庭的成员遍及犹他州。假若我搞不清楚自己的身份，只需参加一个罗姆尼家庭聚会，就可以从我遇到的每个人的目光中认识自己。那是一件既令人安慰又令人不安的事情。我与五位曾祖父母都有着情感上的密切联系。他们的故事引导我相信一脉相承的重要性。传宗接代的概念已融入我们的血液中。作为一个民族和一个家族，我们有一种历史感，而我们的历史是与土地紧密相连的。

我是怀着信奉精神世界的信仰长大的，即相信生命在大地出现之前就已经存在，并且在大地出现之后继续存在；相信每一个人、每一只鸟、每一株灯芯草以及所有其他生物在其生命的实体来到世上之前都有一种精神的生命。每一种生物都被赋予特定的影响范围，每一种生物都有其特定的位置及目标。

对于一个孩子而言，这种信仰可以理解。假若自然世界被赋予了精神价值的话，那么在荒野中度过的日子便堪称神圣的。从孩提时我们就得知上帝无处不在，尤其是在野外。一家人做礼拜不仅仅局限于周日的教堂。周末，我们常在西部大盆地、斯坦斯伯里山或迪普克里克山的小溪边露营。通常是父亲带着男孩去猎兔，而母亲与我则坐在杨树林的一条圆木上聊天。她总是给我讲她青春年少时的故事，比如怎样在树干上涂抹上两片红嘴唇练习接吻，怎样在祖母的紫花苜蓿地里观云。

“我从来都不知道自己独处的能力有多强。”她总是这样说。

“独处?”我问道。

“享受孤寂的天赋，我真喜欢独处，没个够。”

男人们一返回，就急着要吃晚饭。母亲通常是用一个绿色科尔曼汽炉烧饭，而父亲则给我们讲他儿时的故事，诸如有段时间，他父亲没收了他的气枪，原因是他一排一排地把他母亲花园里的所有红色郁金香的花头全都打落了。他笑了，我们大家都笑了。接着就该祈祷吃晚饭了。

晚饭后，我们把各自的睡袋呈圆形依次铺开，头都冲着中央，像是一群鹌鹑，观望着西部大盆地那繁星点点的夜空。我们对土地的依附如同我们彼此之间的依附。

[选自：特丽·T. 威廉斯. 心灵的慰藉：一部非同寻常的地域与家族史. 程虹，译. 北京：生活·读书·新知三联书店，2010.]

Questions for discussion

1. How do you understand the relationship between environment and human beings?

2. Where is the writer's refugee?

3. How do you stay calm when you are in trouble?

(2) California Gulls

题注：加州鸥，属于鸥科。鸥科是人们最熟悉的海洋鸟类，在沿海和内陆水域活动，分布遍及全球，有些种类，如北极燕鸥，每年都往返于南北两极之间，是迁徙距离最长的动物。鸥科分为鸥和燕鸥两大类，常被进一步划分为鸥科和燕鸥科两科。鸥和燕鸥均翅长，极善于飞行，飞行姿态优雅，脚上有蹼，雌雄同色，以灰、褐为主，腹部多为白色，有些种类不易区分。鸥和燕鸥之间的区别也很明显，鸥嘴端具钩，而燕鸥不具；鸥尾常为圆形，燕鸥尾常为叉形，似燕；鸥体型通常比燕鸥要大；鸥擅长在水面游泳而不能潜水，燕鸥擅长俯冲潜水，但多不常游泳。鸥和燕鸥多以鱼虾等为食，但有些鸥类，特别是一些大型种类，有类似贼鸥的掠夺习性，比较具有攻击性。

I have seen hundreds of gulls **nesting** not on the islands of Great Salt Lake, but on the old **dike** at the Bear River **Migratory Bird Refuge.**[①] To wander through a gull **colony** is **disorienting.** In the midst of **shrieking** gulls, you begin to speak, but your voice is silenced. They pull the clouds around you as you walk on eggshells. You quickly realize that you do not belong.

nest[nest]：*v.* 筑巢

dike[daɪk]：*n.* 堤坝

Migratory Bird Refuge：候鸟保护区

colony[ˈkɒləni]：*n.* 聚居地

disorient[dɪsˈɔːrɪənt]：*v.* 使迷失方向

shriek[ʃriːk]：*v.* 尖叫

Hundreds of gulls **hovered** inches above my head, making their **shrill** repetitive cries, "Halp! Halp! Halp!" Several wing tips struck my forehead, a warning that I was too close to their nests. There were so many nests, I didn't know where to step, much less how to behave. Finally, I just stood in one place and watched.

hover[ˈhɒvə(r)]: *v.* 盘旋

shrill[ʃrɪl]: *adj.* 尖锐的

Most of the gulls I watched at the Bird Refuge were **incubating** eggs, an activity which takes from twenty-three to twenty-eight days. Both sexes share in the responsibility.

incubate[ˈɪnkjubeɪt]: *v.* 孵化

I wondered in the midst of so many gulls and so many eggs, how the birds could **differentiate** between them. They do. Parental recognition. The **subtle** distinctions in patterning and **coloration** among individual egg clutches test my eye for **discrimination.** Each **brood** bears its own **coat of arms.** ②

differentiate[ˌdɪfəˈrenʃieɪt]: *v.* 区分；辨别

subtle[ˈsʌtl]: *adj.* 不易察觉的；不明显的

coloration[ˌkʌləˈreɪʃn]: *n.*（动物或植物的）自然色彩；自然花纹

discrimination[dɪˌskrɪmɪˈneɪʃn]: *n.* 区别

brood[bruːd]: *n.* 一窝鸟（动物）

coat of arms：盾型徽章，诞生于12世纪的战场，骑士用于在混战中辨认的符号，专属于某个家族或团体。

It is **tempting** to pick up a baby gull. I must confess I have tried, but only got as far as its **fierce** little **beak** would let me. ③ They come into life as **speckled warriors**, waving **egg teeth** on the tips of their upper **mandibles.** Their battle with the eggshell is tireless as they struggle anywhere from twenty minutes to ten hours. They stand in wet **armor** ready to face the world.

tempting[ˈtemptɪŋ]: *adj.* 诱人的

fierce[fɪəs]: *adj.* 凶猛的

beak[biːk]: *n.* 鸟喙

speckled[ˈspekld]: *adj.* 有斑点的

warrior[ˈwɒriə(r)]: *n.* 斗士

egg teeth：破壳齿

mandible[ˈmændɪbl]: *n.* 上颚

armor[ˈɑːmə]: *n.* 盔甲

All around me, eggs were moving, cracking, and breaking open. I would **stoop** a few feet from a nest and find myself staring eye-to-eye with a chick.

stoop[stuːp]：*v.* 俯身

A month from now, in June, the young will be in **juvenile plumage**, looking like gulls who **ventured** too close to a campfire. **Smoked** feathers. They will **stretch** and beat their wings wildly until one day their own force will surprise them, lifting them a foot or two off the ground. ④ Gradually, with a few running steps, their wings will carry them. In a matter of weeks, **adolescent** gulls will be **agile** fliers.

juvenile[ˈdʒuːvənaɪl]：*adj.* 年少的

plumage[ˈpluːmɪdʒ]：*n.* 鸟类羽毛

venture[ˈventʃə(r)]：*v.* 冒险

smoked[sməʊkt]：*adj.* 烟灰色的

stretch[stretʃ]：*v.* 伸展

adolescent[ˌædəˈlesnt]：*adj.* 少年的

agile[ˈædʒaɪl]：*adj.* 灵巧的

By July, the California gulls will prepare to leave their breeding grounds, taking their young with them. **Banding records** from Bear River indicate that most of the Great Salt Lake population **winters** along the Pacific coast from northern Washington to southern California. ⑤

banding records：环志记录。戴在候鸟身上的金属或塑料环形标志，用作研究候鸟迁徙规律的依据。

winter[ˈwɪntə]：*v.* 过冬

I love to watch gulls **soar** over the Great Basin. It is another trick of the lake to **lure** gulls inland. On days such as this, when my soul has been **wrenched**, the simplicity of flight and form above the lake **untangles** my grief. ⑥

soar[sɔː(r)]：*v.* 翱翔

lure[lʊə(r)]：*v.* 诱惑

wrench[rentʃ]：*v.* 使痛苦

untangle[ʌnˈtæŋgl]：*v.* 解除

"Glide!" the gulls write in the sky—and, for a few brief moments, I do.

glide[glaɪd]：*v.* 滑行

I go to the lake for a **compass** reading, to **orient** myself once again in the midst of change. ⑦ Each trip is unique. The lake is different. I am different. But the gulls are always here, ordinary—black, white, and gray.

compass[ˈkʌmpəs]：*n.* 指南针

orient[ˈɔːrient]：*v.* 定位

I have refused to believe that Mother will die. And by denying her cancer, even her death, I deny her life. Denial stops us from listening. I cannot hear what Mother is saying. I can only hear what I want.

But denial lies. It protects us from the **potency** of a truth we cannot yet bear to accept. ⑧ It takes our hands and leads us to places of comfort. Denial **flourishes** in the familiar. It **seduces** us with our own desires and cleverly constructs walls around us to keep us safe.

potency[ˈpəʊtnsi]：*n.* 效力

flourish[ˈflʌrɪʃ]：*v.* 繁荣

seduce[sɪˈdjuːs]：*v.* 引诱

I want the walls down. Mother's **rage** over our **inability** to face her illness has burned away my defenses. I am left with **guilt**, guilt I cannot tolerate because it has no courage. I hurt Mother through my own desire to be cured.

rage[reɪdʒ]：*n.* 愤怒

inability[ˌɪnəˈbɪləti]：*n.* 无能

guilt[ɡɪlt]：*n.* 内疚

I continue to watch the gulls. Their **pilgrimage** from salt water to fresh becomes my own. ⑨

pilgrimage[ˈpɪlɡrɪmɪdʒ]：*n.* 朝圣之旅；人生的旅途

（选自：Terry T. Williams. *Refuge：An Unnatural History of Family and Place*. New York：Vintage Books，1992.）

Notes

①译文：我曾在熊河候鸟保护区的老堤坝上见过几百只海鸥集群营巢，但却从未在大盐湖的岛屿上见过。

②译文：每一窝又都拥有其家族的独特标志。

③译文：谁都忍不住要去捧起一只小鸥。我得承认我尝试过，不过它那厉害的小鸟喙却不容我接近。

④译文：它们会拼命地伸展身体，拍打翅膀，直到有一天，体内一种惊奇的力量令它们跃跃欲试，离开地面。

⑤译文：据熊河候鸟保护区的环志记录记载，多数大盐湖的加州鸥都会在太平洋沿岸过冬，北自华盛顿，南至加利福尼亚。

⑥译文：在我悲伤的日子里，大盐湖上空那简单的飞行和简朴的身影总能化解我的哀愁。

⑦译文：我到大盐湖去寻求方向，在变化之中给自己重新定位。

⑧译文：但拒绝也会撒谎，它使我们对于自己无法承受的事实真相听而不闻、视而不见。

⑨译文：它们那由盐水浸泡过的羽毛变得清新，那羽毛的变化仿佛发生在我自己身上。

Remarks

大盐湖在美国犹他州，是一片不能饮用的碧水。那里有一个曾生活着208种鸟类的熊河候鸟保护区。在这个水禽保护区，威廉斯通过实地亲历、切身感悟，写下了自然文学的经典之作——《心灵的慰藉：一部非同寻常的地域与家族史》。书中涉及鸟类与人类共同面对的生态困境，同时也书写了癌症晚期患者及家属直面病魔和家庭悲剧的心路历程。书中的一些生活细节，如母亲病情恶化时，威廉斯赴大盐湖向加州鸥寻求心理援助；她在冰冻的湖畔，听母亲谈托尔斯泰的短篇小说；她精心装饰一只被洪水淹死的小天鹅，甚至在母亲去世后，跑到大自然中寻觅熟悉的声影……这一切都能见证威廉斯母女迎战病魔的顽强。威廉斯通过类似日记体的优美散文，将对鹗、鹬、鹭、燕、鸥、鸦、鹃、鹊、雁、雀等数十种鸟类的真切印象，生动地记录了下来。

关注人与自然的关系，是最现实的人文关怀，因为人类生存的环境一旦被破坏和干扰，想要再恢复到原来的模样，需要的时间不是十年二十年，而是数个世纪甚至万年。保护生态，保持人与自然的和谐关系，是造福千秋万代的伟业。诚如中国作家张炜所说的："人与自然的关系是世界上无数法则、无数关系之中最重要的一个，如果这方面出现问题，其他所有方面的条理都显得微不足道了。如果人类文明与地球灾难一块发展和扩大，这种文明最终就会将世界引向死亡。"因为，一旦把人与自然恶化的关系推向极致，就会出现毁灭性的重大灾难，这是一个最可怕的结局，我们必须采取一切手段避免走到这一步。文明的火种要世代延续，我们必须把文明赖以生生不息、繁衍兴盛的人文环境和自然环境保护好。

参考译文

加州鸥

我曾在熊河候鸟保护区的老堤坝上见过几百只海鸥集群营巢，但却从未在大盐湖的岛屿上见过。漫步于加州鸥群落的地盘，令人迷失。在海鸥的尖叫声中，你欲开口说话，可是你的声音却被淹没。当你走在鸟蛋壳上时，它们会铺天盖地，一拥而上。你立即会意识到自己是个外来人。

几百只海鸥在我头顶上方的几英寸处盘旋，不停地发出“哈噗！哈噗！哈噗！”的尖叫声。有几只海鸥的翅尖触到了我的前额，警告我离它们的鸟巢太近了。地上有那么多的鸟巢，我不知道在何处下脚，更不知道该怎么做才好。最后，我只好原地不动，静而观之。

我在候鸟保护区看到的多数加州鸥正值孵化期，此过程需要23～28天。雌雄鸟共同承担这项责任。

我疑惑在如此众多的加州鸥和鸟蛋中，这些鸟如何辨识自己的鸟巢和鸟蛋。可它们没问题。那就像父母认自己的子女一样。每一窝鸟蛋的色彩和形态仅有着细微的差别，考验着我的眼力，而每一窝又都拥有其家族的独特标志。

谁都忍不住要去捧起一只小鸥。我得承认我尝试过，不过它那厉害的小鸟喙却不容我接近。它们一出壳就是浑身斑点的小斗士，摇晃着上颚的破壳齿。它们与蛋壳的搏斗不屈不挠，从20分钟到10小时不等。它们脱壳后，身披湿乎乎的“盔甲”，直面世界。

我的周围到处是正在晃动、破碎、裂开的鸟蛋。我在离鸟巢几步远的地方，俯身观望，发现自己正与一只雏鸟相互凝视。

从现在起一个月之后，也就是6月，雏鸟就会披上幼鸟的羽毛，看上去就像离篝火太近的鸥，浑身烟灰色。它们会拼命地伸展身体，拍打翅膀，直到有一天，体内一种惊奇的力量令它们跃跃欲试，离开地面。渐渐地，随着几步助跑，它们的翅膀便将它们送上天空。几周之后，少年的加州鸥就可以轻快自如地飞行了。

到了7月，加州鸥便会携带幼鸟离开繁殖地。据熊河候鸟保护区的环志记录记载，多数大盐湖的加州鸥都会在太平洋沿岸过冬，北自华盛顿，南至加利福尼亚。

我喜欢观看加州鸥在西部大盆地翱翔。将加州鸥引诱到内陆是大盐湖的又一个骗局。在我悲伤的日子里，大盐湖上空那简单的飞行和简朴的身影总能化解我的哀愁。

“滑行!”海鸥用身体在天空中书写道。而我，在片刻之中，做到了这一点。

我到大盐湖去寻求方向，在变化之中给自己重新定位。每去一次都不同凡响。湖在变，我也在变。不变的总是这里的海鸥，平凡依旧——黑色、白色和灰色。

我拒绝相信母亲会死。由于拒绝承认她的癌症，拒绝相信她的死亡，我拒绝了她的生命。拒绝使得我们听而不信。我无法听到母亲的话。我只听到了我想听的话。

但拒绝也会撒谎，它使我们对于自己无法承受的事实真相听而不闻、视而不见。它牵着我们的手，将我们引向安乐之乡。拒绝在熟悉的土壤中开花结果。它迎合我们的欲望把我们拉下水，并聪明地在我们周围建上一垛墙，以确保我们的安全。

我想拆毁围墙。由于我们无法正视母亲的病情而使她产生的怒火烧毁了我心中的防线。我深感内疚。这是一种无法饶恕的内疚，因为它是由缺乏勇气所致的。出于自己急于治愈的欲望，我伤害了母亲。

我继续观望着海鸥。它们那由盐水浸泡过的羽毛变得清新，那羽毛的变化仿佛发生在我自己身上。

［选自：特丽·威廉斯．心灵的慰藉：一部非同寻常的地域与家族史．程虹，译．北京：生活·读书·新知三联书店，2010.］

Questions for discussion

1. In the last paragraph how do you understand the word "pilgrimage"?
2. What are your suggestions to protect wildlife and natural environment?
3. Can you talk about the natural environment of your hometown?

After-class reading

Read *Refuge: An Unnatural History of Family and Place.*

Part B　News

(1)China's Vaccination Efforts Deserve Kudos

Mobile vaccination vehicles, songs encouraging **inoculation** and coupons for vaccinated shoppers… with various types of support and **incentives**, China is conducting a massive vaccine **rollout** for its 1.4 billion people.

inoculation[ɪˌnɒkjuˈleɪʃn]：*n.* 接种

incentive[ɪnˈsentɪv]：*n.* 激励

rollout[ˈrəʊlaʊt]：*n.* 新产品的推出

Such stepped-up inoculation drive, coupled with China's vaccine support to other countries, is bringing the world a step closer to the final victory against COVID-19. The challenge of realizing herd immunity for the world's most populous country is obvious, as it can only occur when the vaccination rate reaches around 70 to 80 percent among the whole population.

By the end of August, more than 2 billion doses of COVID-19 vaccines had been administered. The pace of vaccination is accelerating. China has clearly stated that people's life and health should be the top priority in the fight against the virus. The country encourages voluntary vaccination and has been making efforts to ensure that everyone eligible for vaccination has full access to it. In addition, China has been making contributions to the accessibility and affordability of vaccines in other developing countries, despite its own huge population and supply shortage at home. It has provided vaccine assistance to over 80 countries and three international organizations, and has exported vaccines to over 50 nations. Recently, the **Sinopharm** vaccine has been listed for emergency use by the World Health Organization (WHO). China has also announced offer of vaccines to UN peacekeeping missions and the International Olympic Committee. All the moves are in line with the idea that COVID-19 vaccines should be a global public good, a solemn commitment made by the Chinese leadership from the very beginning. As a developing country and a responsible member of the international community, China has promised to do all things that are conducive to developing nations' fight against the virus and support all actions that can help them acquire vaccines in an equitable way.

Sinopharm：国药集团

According to WHO statistics, variations in the novel coronavirus are increasingly frequent, adding more uncertainty to the battle against the virus. Human society must ensure that the speed of COVID-19 vaccination is faster than the pace of **mutation.** China's contributions are crucial to the race and its efforts deserve **kudos.**

mutation[mjuːˈteɪʃn]：*n.*（生物物种的）变异，突变

kudos[ˈkjuːdɒs]：*n.* 荣誉

参考译文

中国在接种疫苗方面的努力值得称赞

流动疫苗接种车、鼓励接种的歌曲和接种疫苗购物者的优惠券……在各种形式的支持和激励下，中国正在为14亿人口大规模推广疫苗。

如此加紧的疫苗接种工作，加上中国对其他国家的疫苗支持，使世界距离战胜新冠病毒的最后胜利又近了一步。对于这个世界上人口最多的国家来说，实现群体免疫的挑战是显而易见的，因为只有当疫苗接种率达到总人口的70%到80%时，才能实现群体免疫。

截至8月底，中国新冠疫苗累计接种已经突破20亿剂次。疫苗接种的步伐正在加快。中国明确提出，在抗击病毒的战役中，要把人民的生命健康

放在最重要的位置。国家鼓励自愿接种疫苗，并一直努力确保每个适合接种疫苗的人都能充分获得疫苗。此外，尽管中国人口众多，国内供应短缺，但中国一直在为其他发展中国家疫苗的可获得性和可负担性做出贡献。它向80多个国家和三个国际组织提供疫苗援助，并向50多个国家出口疫苗。最近，国药集团疫苗已被世界卫生组织列入紧急使用名单。中国还宣布向联合国维和特派团和国际奥委会提供疫苗。所有这些举措都符合新冠疫苗应该成为“全球公益”的理念，这是中国领导层从一开始就做出的庄严承诺。作为一个发展中国家和国际社会负责任的一员，中国承诺做一切有利于发展中国家抗击病毒的事情，支持一切有利于发展中国家公平获得疫苗的行动。

根据世界卫生组织的统计数据，新冠病毒的变异越来越频繁，这给对抗该病毒的战斗增加了更多的不确定性。人类社会必须确保新冠疫苗接种的速度快于病毒突变的速度。中国的贡献对这场比赛至关重要，中国的努力值得称赞。

(2) Varkey Foundation Global Teacher Prize

A teacher who learned to greet her pupils in the 35 languages spoken at her **deprived** inner city school has been named the best teacher in the world.

deprived[dɪ'praɪvd]：*adj*. 贫穷的；贫困的

Andria Zafirakou, 39, was selected from thousands of **applicants** around the world for her work with **migrant** children at Alperton Community School in Brent. And now the teacher has won the fourth annual Varkey Foundation Global Teacher Prize worth one million dollars (£715000). The award honors one **exceptional** teacher every year who has made a significant contribution to the profession. Andria beat some 30000 applicants from around the world to **scoop** the prize, becoming the first UK teacher to do so.

applicant['æplɪkənt]：*n*. 申请人

migrant['maɪgrənt]：*n*. 移民

exceptional[ɪk'sepʃənl]：*adj*. 杰出的；优秀的

scoop[sku:p]：*v*. 抢先获得

Andria received her award during a **star-studded** Oscars-style ceremony on Sunday **hosted** by Trevor Noah of *The Daily Show*. Other **celebrities** present included Hollywood star Charlize Theron and Indian actress Priyanka Chopra. And the **trophy** was delivered by **Formula One**'s Lewis Hamilton. In a **congratulatory** video message, **Prime Minister** Theresa May said the prize was a "**fitting** tribute" for everything Ms Zafirakou had done for her students.

star-studded[ˈstɑːstʌdɪd]：*adj.* 明星荟萃的

host[həʊst]：*v.* 主持

celebrity[səˈlebrəti]：*n.* 名人

trophy[ˈtrəʊfi]：*n.* 奖杯；奖品

Formula One：一级方程式赛车

congratulatory[kənˌɡrætʃuˈleɪtəri]：*adj.* 庆祝的；祝贺的

Prime Minister：首相

fitting[ˈfɪtɪŋ]：*adj.* 合适的；恰当的

A high **proportion** of the pupils Andria teaches come from migrant families. In an effort to build bridges within the school community, she learned the greetings for the 35 languages spoken by her pupils, so she could talk to them and their parents at the gates. These include **Gujarati**, **Hindi**, **Tamil**, **Portuguese**, **Somali**, **Arabic**, **Romanian**, **Polish**, **Urdu** and Italian. Judges **shortlisted** her for the annual Varkey Foundation Global Teacher Prize after hearing about how she reached out to families in her **diverse** community. She said that greeting someone in their language "helps to break down **barriers** and enables families to **engage** more in the school community".

proportion[prəˈpɔːʃn]：*n.* 比例

Gujarati[ˌɡuːdʒəˈrɑːti]：*n.* 古吉拉特语

Hindi[ˈhɪndi]：*n.* 印地语(印度官方语言之一)

Tamil[ˈtæmɪl]：*n.* 坦米尔语

Portuguese[ˌpɔːtʃuˈɡiːz]：*n.* 葡萄牙语

Somali[səʊˈmɑːli]：*n.* 索马里语

Arabic[ˈærəbɪk]：*n.* 阿拉伯语

Romanian[rəʊˈmeɪnɪən]：*n.* 罗马尼亚语

Polish[ˈpɒlɪʃ]：*n.* 波兰语

Urdu[ˈʊəduː]：*n.* 乌尔都语

shortlist[ˈʃɔːtlɪst]：*v.* 把……列入入围名单

diverse[daɪˈvɜːs]：*adj.* 不同的；多种多样的

barrier[ˈbæriə(r)]：*n.* 障碍

engage[ɪnˈɡeɪdʒ]：*v.* 从事；参与

Brent has the largest proportion of black, Asian and **minority** ethnic (BAME) people in England and Wales, and more than 140 languages are spoken. As a member of the school's senior leadership team, Miss Zafirakou redesigned the curriculum to make it "**relevant**" to her pupil's lives. She helped a music teacher **launch** a Somali school **choir** and also **pioneered** girls-only sports so that those from **conservative** religious communities would be more willing to take part in. Her **colleagues** also **credit** her with helping the school to win a number of awards and **boost** pupil performance.

minority[maɪˈnɒrəti]：*adj.* 少数的；属于少数派的
relevant[ˈreləvənt]：*adj.* 相关的；切题的
launch[lɔːntʃ]：*v.* 开展(活动、计划等)
choir[ˈkwaɪə(r)]：*n.* 公开表演的合唱团
pioneer[ˌpaɪəˈnɪə(r)]：*v.* 开辟；首倡
conservative[kənˈsɜːvətɪv]：*adj.* 保守的
colleague[ˈkɒliːg]：*n.* 同事
credit[ˈkredɪt]：*v.* 赞扬
boost[buːst]：*v.* 提高

参考译文

瓦尔基基金会全球教师奖

在一所贫困的市区中学里，一位老师学会用35种语言欢迎学生，而她已被评为“世界上最好的老师”。

39岁的安德莉亚·扎菲拉科在布伦特地区的艾伯顿社区学校任教。在全世界成千上万名申请者中，她因对移民子女的良好教育而被评选为“世界上最好的老师”。如今这位老师赢得了第四届瓦尔基基金会年度全球教师奖，奖金为100万美元(715000英镑)。该奖项每年都会授予一位在教育领域做出重大贡献的优秀教师。安德莉亚击败了全球近30000名申请者，赢得了该奖项，成为英国第一位获此殊荣的老师。

星期日，在一场如奥斯卡一般明星荟萃的颁奖典礼上，安德莉亚拿到了她的奖项，而该颁奖礼的主持人是《每日秀》的特雷弗·诺亚。到场的其他名人有好莱坞明星查理兹·塞隆以及印度女演员朴雅卡·乔普拉。奖杯则是由一级方程式赛车锦标赛(F1)冠军刘易斯·汉密尔顿颁发的。在一段祝贺视频中，英国首相特丽莎·梅表示，对于扎菲拉科女士为学生所做的一切，该奖项是一份“十分合适的礼物”。

安德莉亚教授的学生有很多人都来自移民家庭。为了在学校社区内建立纽带，她学会了用35种语言来欢迎学生，这样她就可以在校门口与学生和他们的父母交谈。这其中包括古吉拉特语、印地语、坦米尔语、葡萄牙语、索马里语、阿拉伯语、罗马尼亚语、波兰语、乌尔都语和意大利语。在了解到她是如何在这样多元化的社区中深入学生们的家庭之后，评审员把她列为“瓦尔基基金会年度全球最佳教师奖”的候选人。她表示，用学生们的语言来问候他们“有助于打破障碍，使学生的家人们更多地参与到学校社区的活动中”。

在英格兰与威尔士，布伦特地区拥有最多的黑人、亚洲人和少数族裔群体，而且当地居民的语言有140多种。作为学校高层管理团队的一员，扎菲拉科重新设计了课程，以使之“切合”学生们的生活。她还帮助一位音乐老师成立了一个索马里语校园合唱团，并倡导了只有女孩子参加的体育运动，这样那些来自保守宗教团体的学生会更愿意参与其中。她的同事也称赞她帮助学校赢得了众多奖项，并提高了学生们的成绩。

(3)An African-American Woman Mayor in New Orleans

New Orleans **made history** last night. For the first time ever, the city has elected a woman as mayor—LaToya Cantrell. But Cantrell says that there are other big numbers that matter more.

make history：创造历史

Nearly 300 years—that's how long the city's been around. And not once has it had a woman for a **chief executive**. That long **streak** ended **unofficially** last month when both LaToya Cantrell and Desiree Charbonnet, a fellow **Democrat**, **qualified** for a **runoff** election. It was only a matter of whose name earned an **entry** in the history books. Well, Cantrell won that honor Saturday night with a **commanding** 60 percent of the vote. But in her victory speech at the New Orleans Jazz Market, she said, “The city has more important things to think about than just my place in history. ”“ This **campaign** did not start about self. It only started with and has been **routed** in the people of the city of New Orleans. ”

chief[tʃiːf]：*adj*. 主要的；首要的

executive[ɪɡˈzekjətɪv]：*n*. 执行者；主管人员

streak[striːk]：*n*.（不断经历成功或失败的）一段时期

unofficially[ˌʌnəˈfɪʃəli]：*adv*. 非官方地；非正式地

democrat[ˈdeməkræt]：*n*. 美国民主党派的成员

qualify[ˈkwɒlɪfaɪ]：*v*. 使具备资格

runoff[ˈrʌnɒf]：*n*. 决胜投票

entry[ˈentri]：*n*. 进入；进入权

commanding[kəˈmɑːndɪŋ]：*adj*. 领先的

campaign[kæmˈpeɪn]：*n*. 竞选

route[ruːt]：*v*. 为……安排路线

Before this election, Cantrell earned attention as a community **activist** with another kind of campaign—the **quest** to save the neighborhood of Broadmoor after **Hurricane** Katrina.

activist[ˈæktɪvɪst]：*n.* 活动分子；积极分子

quest[kwest]：*n.* 探索；寻求

hurricane[ˈhʌrɪkən]：*n.* 飓风

Katrina **battered** Broadmoor. An **unidentified** man once said, "There is no Broadmoor. We're destroyed. It looked like a **napalm bomb** had been dropped on the area, and everything was dead."

batter[ˈbætə(r)]：*v.* 猛击；打坏

unidentified[ˌʌnaɪˈdentɪfaɪd]：*adj.* 身份不明的

napalm[ˈneɪpɑːm]：*n.* 凝固汽油

bomb[bɒm]：*n.* 炸弹

Cantrell led efforts to bring it back from the **brink**. In her victory speech Saturday night, the mayor-elect **pledged** to have every neighborhood in mind when she steps into office.

brink[brɪŋk]：*n.* 边缘

pledge[pledʒ]：*v.* 发誓；保证

"What I'm here to say to you tonight—we have spoken. The people of our city have spoken. And no one will be left out."

Cantrell officially takes office in about six months when she **takes over** for **current** Mayor Mitch Landrieu.

take over：接任

current[ˈkʌrənt]：*adj.* 现在的

参考译文

新奥尔良的非裔美籍女市长

昨晚新奥尔良市创造了历史。该市破天荒选举出一位女性作为市长——拉托亚·坎特雷尔。坎特雷尔称，除了上述情况外，还有其他更多紧要的事需要处理。

近三百年的历史，这座城市历经如此之久，但从未有过女性成为这个城市的市长。那样的历史轨迹在上个月以非正式的情况结束了，拉托亚·坎特雷尔和民主党人德西蕾·查伯内特都进入了候选人名单之列。目前只存在一个问题，即谁的名字将名垂青史。然而，坎特雷尔在星期六晚上以60%的绝对领先票数获此殊荣。但是她在新奥尔良爵士市场胜选演讲上这样讲道：

"这座城市还有比名垂青史更重要的事去考虑。""这场活动不只是从自我开始，而要从并且已经从新奥尔良这座城市的人民开始。"

在这场选举之前，坎特雷尔作为社区的活动参与者在另一种活动中获得民众的关注，即拯救卡特里娜飓风过后布罗德莫尔社区的邻里居民。

卡特里娜飓风强袭了布罗德莫尔社区。一位身份不明的男性曾经说过："布罗德莫尔社区不存在了。我们被摧毁了。就像一枚凝固汽油弹坠落至此，一切都被毁掉了。"

坎特雷尔努力把这个社区从消亡的边缘拯救回来。在星期六晚上的胜选演讲上，当这位市长踏进大厅时，她的誓言已经留在了每一个社区居民的脑海中。

"我今天晚上在此所说的，其实都已经讲过了。整个城市的人民都讲过了。没有一个人被落下！"

坎特雷尔在六个月后将接任现任市长米奇·兰德里欧正式就职。

Part C

British Sports

Having a drink at the local **pub**, going for a walk in the country, working in the garden or watching sports on the telly (television)—these are all ways in which many British people like to relax on weekends or when their daily **shifts** at work have ended. Such activities tell us about how modern **Brits** like to spend their free time; but if we look more closely, we can see these activities are not just recent inventions, but are deeply rooted in the British experience over centuries. Going to a **public house** for a glass of **ale**, working the land or going to watch a ball game were familiar activities in Shakespeare's time. ① If today's British person were to be transported 500 years into the past, he or she would find many familiar **pursuits** and games played in rough but recognizable forms. ② And because many of the sports we see played throughout the world today were born in Britain, the history of such activities is of interest to people everywhere. ③

pub[pʌb]: *n.* 酒吧

shift[ʃɪft]: *n.* 轮班

Brit[brɪt]: *n.* (口语)英国人

public house: 酒吧

ale[eɪl]：*n.* 麦芽酒

pursuit[pəˈsjuːt]：*n.* 娱乐活动

In the past, Britain was a mainly agricultural society with most people involved in farming. Britain was also a very religious society and the influence of Christian Church on peoples' lives was very great. Such influences are still evident in today's sports and **leisure** activities. One very obvious example is how Sunday—the day of the week when everyone traditionally went to Church—is still the day that most people have off in the UK. ④ In recent years the government has changed the laws and now some shops and pubs are allowed to open on Sundays, but such changes are very recent and very controversial.

leisure[ˈleʒə(r)]：*n.* 休闲

Football

The idea of sports having seasons—like the football season—also comes from the natural rhythms of an agricultural society, where the timing of harvests and the general weather affected how people spent their times. ⑤ Football is a **boisterous** sport still played in winter and early spring when the weather is cool and often wet. In the winter, bad weather kept people in doors and there was not so much work to do on the farm. Men used to doing hard, physical labor found they needed to release their energies and so got together regularly to play rough, fast games like football. ⑥ There are legends that suggest that games like football and **rugby** actually derived from the "sport" of ancient warriors celebrating victory by kicking around the **decapitated** head of an enemy. ⑦ There is a similar grisly tale told about origins of **bowling**: it is said that in ancient times, Scottish warriors rolled the **skulls** of their enemies along the grass for sport.

boisterous[ˈbɔɪstərəs]：*adj.* 粗鲁的；喧闹的

rugby[ˈrʌgbi]：*n.* 英式橄榄球

decapitate[dɪˈkæpɪteɪt]：*v.* 斩首

bowling[bəʊlɪŋ]：*n.* 保龄球

skull[skʌl]：*n.* 头骨；颅骨

While all social classes used to join in the local football match, during the Renaissance the idea began to emerge that some sports were too rough for **aristocratic** young men. One influential writer of the era described football as "nothing but **beastly fury** and extreme violence" and not at all suitable for gentlemen. In Shakespeare's time, football was played in the cities as well as the countryside. Visitors from abroad sometimes complained about **stumbling** into the midst of a rough and dangerous game when walking the streets of London, while local householders and merchants were troubled by having their windows broken by **stray** footballs. Drinking hard went along with playing hard and at half-time, players and spectators often got very drunk which led to even more unrefined behavior. ⑧

aristocratic[ˌærɪstəˈkrætɪk]: *adj.* 贵族的

beastly[biːstli]: *adj.* 野兽般的；野蛮的

fury[ˈfjʊəri]: *n.* 愤怒

stumble[ˈstʌmbl]: *v.* 跌跌撞撞地走

stray[streɪ]: *adj.* 跑偏的

Today, violence is still associated with football. "Football **hooligans**", supporters of rival teams, sometimes clash before, during and after matches and occasionally run riot through the town, breaking windows and beating each other up. ⑨ Some football fans paint their faces and sing or chant football songs and it is not too difficult to imagine their warrior-ancestors. While football violence gets a lot of attention, before big matches when trouble is expected, police patrol the streets, pubs near the football grounds are closed, and shops lock their doors and shutter their windows. The selling of tickets, the seating in stadiums and security in general is more strictly controlled and every effort is made to ensure that spectators can just sit down and enjoy the game, which they do in their millions. ⑩ Over 20 million tickets are sold to Football Association (FA) games each season. The FA is the league or association that the major teams compete in, for a trophy title known as the FA Cup. ⑪

hooligan[ˈhuːlɪgən]: *n.* 流氓；无赖

Tennis

A more gentle sport that is a sure sign that summer has arrived is the popular game of tennis. Wimbledon, actually a London suburb, is where the world's best players gather to compete on grass courts. ⑫ It is one of the major events of the British sporting calendar and probably the most famous tennis event in the world. Besides actually watching the tennis matches, other activities closely associated with the "Wimbledon **fortnight**" are eating strawberries and cream, drinking champagne and hoping that it doesn't rain⑬.

fortnight[ˈfɔːtnaɪt]: *n.* 十四天；两星期

Tennis was invented in Britain and it owes its origins, literally, to the church. [14] Church records indicate that by the mid-15th century, people were making a game of **bouncing** a ball off the side of their local churches or **cathedrals**, first using the hand, and later a **racquet**.

bounce[baʊns]：*v.* 弹起

cathedral[kəˈθiːdrəl]：*n.* 大教堂

racquet[ˈrækɪt]：*n.* 球拍

Cricket

Cricket was one of the very first team sports in Britain to have organized rules and to be played according to the same rules nationally. [15] By 1787 the rules were fixed, a full century before national rules were fixed for other sports like tennis, rugby and football. (In other sports, each local village or county played by different rules, and even today Americans and Canadians play football according to different rules.) The reason that fixed rules were applied to cricket so early on was a financial one: aristocrats loved betting on cricket matches and if people were going to risk money on a game, they wanted to ensure that the game would be played fairly.

Before the Victorian era, and in modern Britain, people from all walks of life play cricket, but in the 19th century, cricket became a sport associated with the upper classes. It was a kind of a "snob" game played by boys who attended public school. [16] Cricket also became popular in places where the public school system was adapted, like in the colonies of Australia, New Zealand, India and Pakistan.

As generations of public school boys grew up to become the civil servants and rulers of the UK and its colonies, cricket became associated with a set of moral values, in particular the idea of "fair play" which characterized British government. [17] Sir lan Bancroft, a high level civil servant in the 1980s, remembered that when he began his career in Whitehall, one day his government minister was so angry that he threw the telephone at him. Sir Ian said he knew exactly how to respond—"Having played cricket I was able to catch it and hand it back to him politely." [18]

British English is still full of references and phrases to cricket which those not familiar with the game will be **baffled** by. [19] To be "on a sticky **wicket**" is to face difficulties [20]; to "throw a **googly**" is to act unpredictably [21]. And if someone tells you that what you are doing is "not cricket" it means that you are not

behaving ethically or honorably in a situation, whereas if you are "playing with a straight bat", you are an honest person.

baffle['bæfl]: *v.* 使困惑

wicket['wɪkɪt]: *n.*（板球）三柱门

googly['guːgli]: *n.*（曲棍球、板球的）曲线球

ethically['eθɪkli]: *adv.* 合乎道德地

The rules of cricket are as **obscure** as the language. With most sports, you can understand what is going on by simply watching for a while, but with cricket this is not the case. However, whether you understand the game or not, it is enjoyable to watch. It is a very distinctive sport: the players wear white trousers and appear quite formally dressed. Spectators gather around the "green", a large field, in chairs, enjoying the sun, sipping drinks and watching the teams play. Another unusual thing about cricket is that matches do not last just a few hours. They can go on for days.

obscure[əb'skjʊə(r)]: *adj.* 晦涩的；费解的

Golf

The game of golf was invented by the Scottish and today **avid** golfers around the world dream of playing on the famous and ancient golf course at St. Andrews, not far from Edinburgh.[22] The Scots took their recreation seriously: by the 16th century, golf was already so popular that the **Archbishop** of St. Andrews was only allowed to keep his rabbit **warrens** on the links (golf course) as long as his rabbit-raising activities didn't interfere with people who wanted to play golf.[23] And while many students of British history have heard of Mary Queen of Scots[24], the tragic and beautiful queen who was **beheaded** in the 16th century during a controversy over the succession to the throne, few know that she liked to play golf. Indeed, she became the object of gossip and criticism because she was seen out on the links shortly after the death of her second husband.

avid['ævɪd]: *adj.* 劲头十足的

archbishop[ˌɑːtʃ'bɪʃəp]: *n.* 大主教

warren['wɒrən]: *n.* 养兔场

behead[bɪ'hed]: *v.* 斩首

Horse racing, hunting and equestrianism

The true sport of British Kings (and Queens) is not skiing or golfing, but horse racing. Organized national horse races have been held throughout Britain for hundreds of years. At the heart of medieval life was the horse，a symbol of authority and wealth and necessary to travelling，hunting and warfare.[25] The age of English **chivalry** is full of stories，songs，poems and depictions of the brave **Knight** on his **steed.** History records that knights raced for 3 miles in the year 1190，for a prize purse of £40. In fact，racing was not a good sport for knights who were clad in heavy iron **armor.** Medieval **tournaments** more commonly had activities to show off the bravery and military **prowess** of the knights，such as **jousting.** Sports which involve the riding of horses are still considered rather **snobbish** or aristocratic sports because of course the average British family cannot afford to own a horse. However，there are **stables** which rent horses and offer riding lessons at affordable prices. And of course just about everyone can afford to place a bet on a horse race now and then.

equestrianism[ɪˈkwestriənɪzəm]：*n.* 马术
chivalry[ˈʃɪvəlri]：*n.* 骑士精神；骑士制度
Knight[naɪt]：*n.*（中世纪）骑士
steed[stiːd]：*n.* 坐骑；骏马
armor[ˈɑːmə]：*n.* 盔甲
tournament[ˈtʊənəmənt]：*n.*（中世纪骑士）马上比武
prowess[ˈpraʊəs]：*n.* 英勇；勇猛
jousting[ˈdʒaʊstɪŋ]：*n.* 马上长枪比武
snobbish[ˈsnɒbɪʃ]：*adj.* 势利的
stable[ˈsteɪbl]：*n.* 马厩

There are two kinds of horse racing：flat racing，where horses and riders compete on a flat，oval track；and **steeplechasing**，which is racing either across the countryside，or around a course designed to represent the obstacles you might encounter in the countryside（**hedges**，ponds，hills，and so on）. The Grand National[26] is the world's most famous steeplechase. Established in 1837，in recent years the Grand National has become increasingly controversial because of the dangers involved. Every year some horses（and riders too）can be injured in trying to **negotiate** a jump for example. Badly-hurt horses are usually shot，and animal lovers find it unacceptable that animals should be hurt and killed just for our enjoyment.[27] Now the Grand National course is designed to be difficult enough to be exciting，but not so difficult as to cause serious injuries.

steeplechasing[stiːplˈtʃeɪsɪŋ]：*n.* 障碍赛马；越野赛马

hedge[hedʒ]：*n.* 围栏；障碍物

negotiate[nɪˈɡəʊʃieɪt]：*v.*（口）顺利通过

While it is the sport of kings, kings and **commoners** alike enjoy betting on the horses. In any town center you can go into a betting shop and place a bet on the horses. The biggest social event associated with horse racing is the Royal Ascot[28], where people dress up and go to show off how fashionable they are as well to watch the races and place their bets. Women especially wear very elaborate and exotic hats and after the races, the television and newspapers will often have stories featuring the sorts of hats and outfits that were worn.

commoner[ˈkɒmənə(r)]：*n.* 平民

Another horsy sport associated with the aristocracy is equestrianism, sports which can involve riding skills such as show jumping and carriage driving, as well as speed.

Hunting for wild **game** was born of necessity, but it developed into a recreational pursuit in medieval England.[29] It became so popular that great lords surrounded their houses with deer parks where they could go hunting conveniently. They sometimes arranged for the servants to **herd** the deer into a corner of the park so that even the delicate aristocratic ladies could take their bows and arrows and **bag** a deer for dinner. Many of the ancient **manor** houses you can still visit in Britain have their herds of deer, although now these are more for decoration than for sport.

game[ɡeɪm]：*n.* 猎物；打猎的目标

herd[hɜːd]：*v.* 把……赶在一起

bag[bæɡ]：*v.* 猎获；捕杀

manor[ˈmænə(r)]：*n.*（封建领主的）领地；庄园

More common than hunting within an enclosed park was chasing an animal across the countryside on horseback, with a spear, arrows, and dogs and servants to assist.[30] In the Middle Ages, the **boar** was the favorite **quarry**, and later the wolf. Both were hunted into near **extinction**. Modern hunters usually chase foxes nowadays: their medieval **forebears** would sneer at such an insignificant quarry. Hunting foxes and rabbits is also disapproved of by many British animal lovers who think such "blood sports" are unnecessarily cruel.

boar[bɔː(r)]：*n.* 野猪；公猪

quarry[ˈkwɒri]：*n.* 猎物

extinction[ɪkˈstɪŋkʃn]：*n.* 消亡；灭绝

forebear[ˈfɔːbeə(r)]：*n.* 祖先

A hunting meet is a very exciting thing to watch：huntsmen and women mounted，traditionally clad in red jackets，white **jodhpurs** and high boots，on their beautiful horses surrounded by barking，excited hunting dogs and anxious servants，charge across the green fields and **hedgerows** of the countryside. But as the reason for all this activity is to chase and kill a tiny rabbit or fox，Animal Rights groups find this an unacceptable recreation for a society that is supposed to be civilized. ㉛ There have been recent attempts to pass laws in Parliament to ban blood sports. These attempts have been defeated by narrow margins. Since many MPs and Lords are from wealthy families which enjoy hunting，they tend to vote against these efforts to ban one of their **pastimes.**

jodhpurs[ˈdʒɒdpəz]：*n.* 马裤

hedgerow[ˈhedʒrəʊ]：*n.* 栅篱

pastime[ˈpɑːstaɪm]：*n.* 消遣

Notes

①Going to a public house for a glass of ale，working the land … in Shakespeare's time：去酒吧喝一杯麦芽酒，在地里干活，或去观看球赛，这些活动在莎士比亚时代就习以为常了。

②If today's British person were to be transported 500 years … rough but recognizable forms：假设今天的英国人回到500年前的过去，他或她会看到许多熟悉的娱乐活动和比赛，虽然这些活动的形式比较粗糙，但完全可以辨认。

③And because many of the sports we see played throughout the world … people everywhere：而且由于我们现在看到的世界上的许多体育项目都发源于英国，因此了解这些运动的历史对其他地方的人们是有一定意义的。

④Such influences are still evident in today's sports … that most people have off in the UK：这些影响在当今体育和休闲活动中依然存在。一个非常显而易见的例子是，英国人大多还是礼拜天休息，因为传统上礼拜天是去教堂做礼拜的日子。作者这里所说的休息是指商店、娱乐场所大多关门，不营业。

⑤The idea of sports having seasons—like the football season … how people spent their times：体育运动也有季节，如足球赛季，这一点来自农业社会的自然节奏。在农业社会里，收获的时间以及天气影响着人们如何度过他们的时光。

⑥Men used to doing hard，physical labor found … play rough，fast games like football：习惯于干粗重体力活的男人们发现他们需要释放一下剩余的精力，于是他们经常聚在一起开展足球一类的粗野快速的运动比赛。

⑦There are legends that suggest that games like football and… head of an enemy：根据有些传说，像足球和英式橄榄球实际上来源于古代勇士的“体育”：他们将斩首的敌人的头颅踢来踢去，以此庆祝胜利。

⑧Drinking hard went along with playing hard and at half-time… unrefined behavior：豪饮伴随着疯狂的比赛，赛到一半时，运动员和观众都烂醉如泥，这往往导致更加粗鲁的行为。

⑨“Football hooligans”，supporters of rival teams … and beating each other up：那些“足球流氓”，也就是支持比赛队的球迷们，常常在赛前、赛中和赛后发生冲突，有时骚乱扩展到整个城镇，他们砸碎窗户，互相殴打。

⑩The selling of tickets，the seating in stadiums and security… they do in their millions：从售票、体育场座位的安排到安保措施都受到更加严格的控制，所有的措施都是为了保障成千上万的观众能坐下来欣赏比赛。

⑪The FA is the league or association that the major teams compete in… the FA Cup：主要球队都在英国足球协会里比赛，争夺足总杯的冠军称号。英国足球协会成立于 1863 年，是主管英国职业和业余足球队的组织。

⑫ Wimbledon，actually a London suburb，is where the world's best players… grass courts：温布尔登，实际上是伦敦的一个郊区，它是世界上最优秀的网球手聚会进行草地比赛的场所。室外网球比赛场地分为草地、红土以及硬地三种。

⑬hoping that it doesn't rain：希望不要下雨。因为温布尔登是室外场地，而英国的天气又多阵雨，比赛进行时经常下雨，这时比赛不得不中断，等待天晴才能继续。

⑭Tennis was invented in Britain and it owes its origins，literally，to the Church：网球是英国发明的，它的真正起源要追溯到教会。

⑮Cricket was one of the very first team sports in Britain to … the same rules nationally：板球比赛是英国最早有统一规则，并且全国遵守同一规则进行比赛的团体运动项目之一。

⑯It was a kind of a “snob” game played by boys who attended public schools：板球是种“势利”的比赛项目，玩板球的都是就读于公学的男孩。

⑰ As generations of public school boys grew up to become the civil servants… British government：当一代又一代的公学男孩长大成人，当了公务员或者英国及其殖民地的统治者时，板球便与一整套道德价值观产生了联系。具体地说，“公平竞争”的思想成为英国政府的特点。

⑱Having played cricket I was able to catch it and hand it back to him politely：由于打过板球，我能接住他扔过来的电话机，然后礼貌地递还给他。

⑲British English is still full of references and phrases to cricket… will be baffled by：英式英语里有许多关于板球的典故和短语，那些不熟悉这项运动的人会感到困惑。

⑳ To be "on a sticky wicket" is to face difficulties："在泥泞的三柱门"的意思是面对困境。sticky wicket 原指雨后场地泥泞的三柱门，因这种情况使球跳不高而难以击打，因而用于比喻困难的处境。

㉑to "throw a googly" is to act unpredictably：googly，原指"变向曲线球"，喻指"行动无法预测，捉摸不透"。

㉒The game of golf was invented by the Scottish and today… not far from Edinburgh：高尔夫球由苏格兰人发明，今天全世界的高尔夫球迷们都梦想在圣安德鲁和爱丁堡著名的古老的球场上打球。

㉓The Scots took their recreation seriously：by the 16 century… wanted to play golf：苏格兰人对待娱乐的态度十分严肃。比如说，到 16 世纪，高尔夫球已很风行，以至于当时的圣安德鲁大主教必须保证他养兔子不会干扰人们打高尔夫球才得到允许将养兔场留在高尔夫球场上。

㉔Mary Queen of Scots：苏格兰的玛丽女王(1542—1587)，出生六天即继承王位，成为苏格兰女王后嫁给法王法兰西斯二世，1561 年返苏格兰后两次再嫁，被迫逊位，逃亡英格兰，后因图谋暗杀英格兰女王伊丽莎白一世而被斩首。

㉕At the heart of medieval life was the horse，a symbol … travelling，hunting and warfare：中世纪生活的中心是马，马是权威与财富的象征，并且是旅行、打猎和战争的必需之物。

㉖The Grand National：一年一度在利物浦举行的全国越野障碍赛马。

㉗ Badly-hurt horses are usually shot，and animal lovers find it unacceptable… just for our enjoyment：重伤的马通常被射杀(以免遭受痛苦)。动物爱好者认为，动物为了人们的娱乐而不得不受伤害，甚至遭到杀戮，这是不能接受的。

㉘the Royal Ascot：皇家阿斯科特赛马会。每年 6 月在伯克郡的阿斯科特举行的为期 4 天的赛马会，是英国最重要的赛马会之一，王室成员常参加。

㉙ Hunting for wild game was born of necessity，but it developed … in medieval England：捕猎野兽最早是出于生存的需要，但是到了中世纪，打猎发展成为英国的娱乐消遣活动。

㉚More common than hunting within an enclosed park… dogs and servants to assist：比在一个圈围起来的公园里打猎更寻常的是骑在马背上在田野里追逐动物，这些猎手手持长矛和弓箭，有猎狗和仆人相助。

㉛Animal Rights groups find this an unacceptable recreation for a society that is supposed to be civilized：维护动物权利组织认为这项娱乐活动对于一个文明社会来说是不可接受的。

Questions

1. Find some examples from the text to demonstrate how Christian Church has influenced the sports and leisure activities of the British.

2. Why is cricket very English? Why does the author believe that cricket was associated with a set of English values?

Part D

Pre-reading activities

1. Which season do you like best? Why?

2. What's the winter like in your hometown?

济南的冬天

对于一个在北平住惯的人，像我，冬天要是不刮风，便觉得是奇迹；济南的冬天是没有风声的。对于一个刚由伦敦回来的人，像我，冬天要能看得见日光，便觉得是怪事；济南的冬天是响晴的。自然，在热带的地方，日光是永远那么毒，响亮的天气，反有点叫人害怕。可是，在北中国的冬天，而能有温晴的天气，济南真得算个宝地。

设若单单是有阳光，那也算不了出奇。请闭上眼睛想：一个老城，有山有水，全在天底下晒着阳光，暖和安适地睡着，只等春风来把它们唤醒，这是不是个理想的境界？小山整把济南围了个圈儿，只有北边缺着点口儿。这一圈小山在冬天特别可爱，好像是把济南放在一个小摇篮里，它们安静不动地低声地说："你们放心吧，这儿准保暖和。"真的，济南的人们在冬天是面上含笑的。他们一看那些小山，心中便觉得有了着落，有了依靠。他们由天上看到山上，便不知不觉地想起："明天也许就是春天了吧？这样的温暖，今天夜里山草也许就绿起来了吧？"就是这点幻想不能一时实现，他们也并不着急，因为有这样慈善的冬天，干啥还希望别的呢！

最妙的是下点小雪呀。看吧，山上的矮松越发的青黑，树尖上顶着一髻儿白花，好像日本看护妇。山尖全白了，给蓝天镶上一道银边。山坡上，有的地方雪厚点，有的地方草色还露着；这样，一道儿白，一道儿暗黄，给山们穿上一件带水纹的花衣；看着看着，这件花衣好像被风儿吹动，叫你希望看见一点更美的山的肌肤。等到快日落的时候，微黄的阳光斜射在山腰上，那点薄雪好像忽然害了羞，微微露出点粉色。就是下小雪吧，济南是受不住大雪的，那些小山太秀气！

古老的济南，城里那么狭窄，城外又那么宽敞，山坡上卧着些小村庄，小村庄的房顶上卧着点雪，对，这是张小水墨画，也许是唐代的名手画的吧。

那水呢，不但不结冰，倒反在绿萍上冒着点热气，水藻真绿，把终年贮蓄的绿色全拿出来了。天儿越晴，水藻越绿，就凭这些绿的精神，水也不忍得冻上，况且那些长枝的垂柳还要在水里照个影儿呢！看吧，由澄清的河水慢慢往上看吧，空中，半空中，天上，自上而下全是那么清亮，那么蓝汪汪的，整个的是块空灵的蓝水晶。这块水晶里，包着红屋顶，黄草山，像地毯上的小团花的小灰色树影。这就是冬天的济南。

［选自：老舍．老舍经典作品集．北京：北京工艺美术出版社，2018.］

参考译文

Winter in JiNan

For someone like me who is used to living in Beiping, a winter without any wind is a bit of a miracle. Well, one never hears any whistling winter winds in JiNan. For someone like me who has just returned from London, sunshine in the winter seems quite unusual. Well, JiNan has bright sunny winter weather. I know that in tropical regions, the **blazing** sun and the **perpetual** harsh glare can be intimidating, but here in north China, a mild sunny winter season is a **boon** that makes JiNan a very special place indeed.

blazing[ˈbleɪzɪŋ]：*adj*. 酷热的

perpetual[pəˈpetʃuəl]：*adj*. 不间断的；持续的

boon[buːn]：*n*. 非常有用的东西；恩惠

But there is more than just sunshine. Close your eyes and picture to yourself: an ancient town, with mountains and lakes, dozing in the sunlight, warm and comfortable, waiting for the spring breezes to blow it awake. Doesn't that sound **idyllic**? Low hills practically encircle JiNan, leaving just one small dip on the north side. In the winter, they are especially endearing, as if cradling the town and murmuring to it. "Don't worry, it's warm and safe here." And it's a fact that the people of JiNan seem to smile throughout the cold season. All they have to do is to see those hills to feel secure and protected. Looking up and around, they say to themselves, "Maybe spring will come tomorrow. It's so mild, maybe tonight the grass on the hills will sprout." And even if this is just daydreaming, they don't really mind, because with this kindly winter why wish for more?

idyllic[aɪˈdɪlɪk]：*adj*. 田园诗般的

A light snow makes the scene even prettier. Look at the short dark pine trees crowned with white nurse caps. Or the line of white **etching** the hilltops like a silver **hemline** on the **azure** sky. Or the hillsides, **patchily** dusted so that in some places the grass shows through, clothing the slopes in a wavy pattern of tan and pale stripes. As one gazes, these seem to shift in the breeze as if baring the hill for a better look at its lovely shape. As the sun sets, the golden rays **slant** on to the light snow that suddenly blushes a shy pink. Just a light snowfall, nothing heavier, turns those low hills into real beauties.

etching[ˈetʃɪŋ]：*n*. 蚀刻画；蚀刻术；蚀刻法

hemline[ˈhemlaɪn]：*n*.（衣裙的）底边，下摆

azure[ˈæʒə]：*adj*. 天蓝色的；蔚蓝色的

patchily[ˈpætʃɪli]：*adv*. 散落地；零散地

slant[slænt]：*v*. 倾斜

JiNan is an ancient town with **cramped** and narrow streets, but surrounded by wide open space. Villages dot the slopes, their cottage roofs dusted with snow. Oh yes, this is a traditional ink and wash painting and probably one by a Tang Dynasty master too.

cramped[kræmpt]：*adj*. 狭窄的；拥挤的

As for the lakes and ponds, they don't freeze over, but even give off wisps of warm vapor. The water weeds remain bright green as if showing off color stored up over the year, and the clearer the weather the greener they glow. Anyway, how can the water freeze over when all those weeping willows want to see their reflections? As you raise your eyes slowly from the transparent depths and look up gradually to the sky, everything is so clear and bright and blue, like a giant hollow block of crystal, in which are encased red roofs, tan hills and little **copses**, like the design on a carpet. This is JiNan in the winter.

copse[ˈkɒps]：*n*. 矮林；灌木林

After-reading activities

1. Is JiNan pretty in winter? If yes, please find out the sentences in details.

2. Please describe your hometown in winter using figures of speech according to the essay above.

作者简介

老舍(1899—1966)，现代小说家、戏剧家、作家，原名舒庆春，字舍予，满族，北京人。出身寒苦，自幼丧父，北京师范学校毕业，早年任小学校长、劝学员。1924 年赴英国伦敦大学东方学院教中文，开始写作，连续在《小说月报》上发表长篇小说《老张的哲学》《赵子曰》《二马》，成为我国现代长篇小说奠基人之一。归国后先后在齐鲁大学、山东大学任教，同时从事写作，其间代表作有长篇小说《猫城记》《离婚》《骆驼祥子》，中篇小说《月牙儿》《我这一辈子》，短篇小说《微神》《断魂枪》等。抗日战争爆发后到武汉和重庆组织中华全国文艺界抗敌协会，对内总理会务，对外代表"文协"，创作长篇小说《四世同堂》，并对现代曲艺进行改良。1946 年赴美讲学，四年后回国，主要从事话剧剧本创作，代表作有《龙须沟》《茶馆》，荣获"人民艺术家"称号，被誉为语言大师。曾任全国文学艺术界联合会副主席、全国作家协会副主席及北京文联主席。

写作背景

老舍 1930 年前后来到山东，先后在济南齐鲁大学和青岛山东大学任教 7 年之久，对山东产生了深厚的感情，山东被称为他的"第二故乡"。据老舍夫人胡絜青回忆，老舍生前"常常怀念的是从婚后到抗战爆发，在山东度过的那几年"。该文是老舍 1931 年春天在济南齐鲁大学任教时写成的，原为一系列直接描写济南风景名胜的长篇散文《一些印象》中的第五节，发表在《齐大月刊》欧一卷第六期(1931 年 4 月出版)。

作品鉴赏

老舍一反以往厚重、富有沧桑感的现实主义风格，以轻快、自然的笔调描绘了一块冬天里的宝地。该文的主题思想即对济南特有的冬景的喜爱和赞美。作者通过对济南冬天场景的描述，充分体现了对济南的冬天的喜爱之情，对济南这座城市的热爱之情，以及热爱大自然、热爱生活、热爱生命的生活情操。

作者多用温情的意象来描绘济南冬天之景，营造出一种温婉的整体性语感。语言层面写的是济南的"温晴"，所要表达的是济南冬天的温情："温晴"是所见的外象，是借以表现心象的客体和媒介；"温情"是心象（心灵感受），它蕴含的是作家的主观情感、生命和人生感悟以及审美感受。文章不惜笔墨写景，实际是抒发对济南冬天的喜爱、赞美之情，这才是文章的真正意蕴、文章的核心。

Chapter 4 The Life

Part A

查尔斯·弗雷泽(Charles Frazier)在北卡罗来纳的山区长大。目前，他与妻子、女儿居住在罗利。他们在那里养马度日，过着隐士般的生活。《冷山》(*Cold Mountain*)是他的第一部小说。该作品因“描写了人与土地的复杂情感与关系”而获美国国家图书奖、美国书商协会年度图书大奖，成为美国十大畅销书之一，与《飘》(*Gone with the Wind*)并称为“20 世纪美国文学双璧”。他的第二部小说《十三月》(*Thirteen Moons*)继承了第一部小说的风格，将美国的风土人情、人文历史展现得淋漓尽致，获得了广泛好评。

《冷山》是一部不同凡响的小说，讲述了美国南北战争结束之际，一位士兵为了自己的所爱而返回家园的多灾多难的旅途。伟大的爱情故事与孤单凄惨的迢遥长路融为一体。伴随着《冷山》的诞生，美国文学界出现了一位耀目的新天才。

《冷山》以当地历史为背景，以从作者的高祖父起代代相传的家族故事为基础，叙述了受伤的士兵英曼，离开残酷的战场，穿过那片残破的、即将遭受败衄的南方土地，回到自己心上人艾达身边的故事。与此同时，艾达正在勇敢顽强的年轻姑娘鲁比的帮助下，努力重振父亲留下的农场。英曼的“奥德赛”与艾达的奋斗互相交织，他们长期隔绝的生活随着战争的临近终局而即将交汇，两人分别面对着一个面目全非的世界所带来的巨大挑战。查尔斯·弗雷泽深刻地洞察到人与土地的关系以及孤独状态的危险。他对于社会的变迁，具有与那些 19 世纪的伟大小说家同样敏锐的观察力。《冷山》重新创造了一个已经消失的世界，在我们的时代依然具有振聋发聩的意义。

Cold Mountain(Excerpt)

题注：美国南北战争即将结束，一位名叫英曼的士兵身受重伤，备受折磨，时日不多。他拖着疲惫的身体逃离部队，想赶回偏僻遥远的故乡冷山，只为见上心上人艾达一面。而此时，艾达在家乡冷山正遭受着煎熬，在生存底线上痛苦地挣扎。艾达原本是当地山区传教士的女儿，南北战争爆发后，父亲离开人世，留她孤苦一人。因为她是大家闺秀出身，根本没有生存的经验，所以连基本的生活都无法自理。她不会喂养牲畜，不会料理庄稼，不会烹饪，甚至不会清洗衣物。她所习得的技能是刺绣、阅读、外语，等等，可这些能力对于她自主谋生一点帮助也没有。面对一只四处逃窜的母鸡，她竟也束手无策。

Ada sat on the **porch** of the house that was now hers, a **portable** writing desk balanced across her lap①. She wet the **nib** of a pen in ink and wrote:

porch[pɔːtʃ]: *n.* 门廊

portable[ˈpɔːtəbl]: *adj.* 轻便的

nib[nɪb]: *n.* 钢笔尖

This you must know②: that despite your long absence, such is the light in which I view the happy relation existing between us, that I will never ***conceal*** *a single thought from you. Let such fears not trouble you. Know that③ I consider it a* ***mutual*** *duty, that we* ***owe to*** *each other, to communicate in a spirit of the* ***utmost*** *frankness and* ***candor****. Let it ever be done with unlocked hearts.*

conceal[kənˈsiːl]: *v.* 隐藏

mutual[ˈmjuːtʃuəl]: *adj.* 共同的

owe to: 欠……(某物)

utmost[ˈʌtməʊst]: *adj.* 极度的

candor[ˈkændə]: *n.* 坦率

She blew the paper to dry it and then scanned over what she had written with a **critical** eye. She mistrusted her handwriting, for no matter how she tried, she had never mastered the flowing **whorls** and arcs of fine **penmanship.** The characters her hand insisted on forming were instead blocky and dense as runes.④ Even more than the penmanship, she disliked the **tenor** of the letter. She **balled up** the paper and **tossed** it into a **boxwood bush.**

critical[ˈkrɪtɪkl]: *adj.* 批评的；爱挑剔的

whorl[wɜːl]: *n.* 螺纹

penmanship['penmənʃɪp]：*n.* 书法；书写技巧

tenor['tenə(r)]：*n.* 要旨；大意

ball up：滚成球

toss[tɔːs]：*v.*（轻轻或漫不经心地）扔

boxwood bush：黄杨木灌木（丛）

Aloud she said, that is just the way people talk and has nothing to do with the real matter at hand. ⑤

She **looked off** across the yard to the kitchen garden where the beans and **squash** and tomatoes **bore** vegetables hardly bigger than her thumb despite the fullness of the growing season. Many of the leaves were eaten away to their **veins** by bugs and worms. Standing thick in the rows and towering over the vegetables were weeds⑥ that Ada could not name and had neither the energy nor the heart to fight. Beyond the failed garden stretched the old cornfield, now grown up shoulder high in **poke** and **sumac**. Above the fields and pastures, the mountains were just becoming visible as the morning fog **burned away**. Their pale outliness stood at the horizon, more like the ghosts of mountains than the actual things.

look off：掉转视线

squash[skwɒʃ]：*n.* 南瓜

bear[beə(r)]：*v.* 结（果实）

vein[veɪn]：*n.* 叶脉

poke[pəʊk]：*n.* 商陆

sumac['suːmæk]：*n.* 漆树

burn away：消散

Ada sat waiting for them to **reveal** themselves clearly. Her thinking was that it would be a comfort to see something that was as it should be⑦, for otherwise her mind troubled itself with the thought that everything else in her sight was marked by **neglect**. Since her father's **funeral**, Ada had hardly turned her hand around the farm. She had at least milked the cow, which Monroe had named Waldo with disregard for gender, and fed the horse, Ralph, but she had not done much more, for she did not know how to do much more. ⑧ She had left the chickens to fend for themselves and they had gotten **skinny** and **skittish**. The hens had **abandoned** the little chicken house and roosted in trees and dropped their eggs wherever the mood **struck** them. They **vexed** Ada with their inability to settle on nesting places. She had to investigate every **cranny** of the yard to find the eggs, and lately she believed they had taken on a strange taste since the hens' diet had changed from table **scraps** to bugs.

reveal[rɪ'viːl]：*v.* 显露

neglect[nɪ'glekt]：*n.* 忽略

funeral['fjuːnərəl]：*n.* 葬礼

skinny['skɪni]：*adj.* 极瘦的；皮包骨的

skittish['skɪtɪʃ]：*adj.* 易惊的

abandon[ə'bændən]：*v.* 抛弃；离弃

strike[straɪk]：*v.* 撞击

vex[veks]：*v.* 使烦恼；使苦恼；使生气

cranny['kræni]：*n.* 裂缝；裂隙

scrap[skræp]：*n.* 残羹剩饭

Cookery had become a pressing issue for Ada. She was **perpetually** hungry, having eaten little through the summer but milk, fried eggs, salads, and plates of **miniature** tomatoes from the **untended** plants that had grown wild and bushy with **suckers**. Even **butter** had proved beyond her means, for the milk she had tried to **churn** never **firmed up** beyond the **consistency** of **runny clabber**. She wanted a bowl of chicken and dumplings and a peach pie but had not a clue how one might arrive at them. ⑨

perpetually[pə'petʃʊəli]：*adv.* 永恒的；永久的

miniature['mɪnətʃə]：*adj.* 微型的

untended[ʌn'tendɪd]：*adj.* 未受到照料的

sucker['sʌkə(r)]：*n.* 东西；玩意儿

butter['bʌtə(r)]：*n.* 黄油

churn[tʃɜːn]：*v.* 搅拌

firm up：凝固

consistency[kən'sɪstənsi]：*n.* 浓度

runny['rʌni]：*adj.* 水分过多的

clabber['klæbə(r)]：*n.* 凝奶

Ada cast one more look to the far mountains, still faint and pale, and then she rose and went in search of eggs. She checked the weeds along the fence by the lane, parted the long grass at the base of the pear tree in the side yard, **rattled** among the **clutter** of the back porch, ran her hands along the dusty shelves in the **toolshed**. ⑩ She found nothing.

rattle['rætl]：*v.* 发出咯咯的声音

clutter['klʌtə(r)]：*n.* 杂乱

toolshed[ˈtuːlʃed]：*n.* 工具房

She recalled that a red hen had sometimes lately taken to hanging about the big boxwoods at either side of the front steps. She went to the bush that she had thrown the letter into and tried to part the **dense** leafage and **peer** inside, but she could see nothing in the **dim** center. She folded her skirts tightly about her legs, and on hands and knees she worked her way inside the boxwood. ⑪ Its branches scratched at her forearms and face and neck as she pushed forward. The ground beneath her hands was dry and littered with chicken feathers and old chicken shit and the hard dead leaves of the bush. Inside, there was a **hollow** place. The thick outer growth of leaves was just a **husk** enclosing a space like a tiny room.

dense[dens]：*adj.* 浓密的

peer[pɪə(r)]：*v.* 仔细看；端详

dim[dɪm]：*adj.* 昏暗的

hollow[ˈhɒləʊ]：*adj.* 空的

husk[hʌsk]：*n.* 外皮；外壳

Ada sat up in it and looked about on the ground and in the branches for eggs but found only a broken shell, dried **yolk** the color of rust in one jag-edged cup. She fitted herself between two limbs⑫ and rested with her back against the **trunk**. The boxwood bower smelled of dust and of the sharpness and bitterness of chickens. Its light was dim, and it reminded her of childhood play in caves made by **draping** sheets over tables or by tenting carpets over clothes lines. Best of all were the **tunnels** she and her cousin Lucy dug deep into **haystacks** on her uncle's farm. They had spent entire rainy afternoons **snug** and dry as denned foxes, whispering secrets to each other.

yolk[jəʊk]：*n.* 蛋黄

trunk[trʌŋk]：*n.* 树干

drape[dreɪp]：*v.* 覆盖

tunnel[ˈtʌnl]：*n.*（动物栖息的）穴

haystack[ˈheɪstæk]：*n.* 干草堆

snug[snʌg]：*adj.* 温暖舒适的

It was with a familiar delicious **tingle** of pleasure, a tightening in her breathing, that she realized she was now similarly hidden away, that anyone walking from the gate to the porch would never know she was there. If one of the ladies from the church made an **obligatory** visit to see about her **welfare**, she could sit motionless as they called her name and knocked at the door. ⑬ She would not come out until long after she had heard the gate latch clack shut. ⑭ But she expected no one to call. The visits had **tapered off** in the face of her indifference to them.

tingle[ˈtɪŋgl]：*n.* 激动

obligatory[əˈblɪgətri]：*adj.* 义务的

welfare[ˈwelfeə(r)]：*n.* 幸福；安宁

taper off：逐渐停止

Ada looked up with some disappointment to the faint lacework of pale blue sky visible through the leaves. She wished rain were falling so she would feel even more protected as it **rustled** the leaves overhead. The occasional drop that might find its way through, **plopping** a tiny **crater** into the dust, would only **emphasize** that though inside she remained dry, outside rain fell **wholesale.** ⑮ Ada wished never to leave this fine **shelter**, for when she considered the pass she had lately reached, she wondered how a human being could be raised more impractically for the demands of an exposed life.

rustle[ˈrʌsl]：*v.* 发出沙沙的声音

plop[plɒp]：*v.* 扑通地坠落

crater[ˈkreɪtə(r)]：*n.* 弹坑

emphasize[ˈemfəsaɪz]：*v.* 强调；使突出

wholesale[ˈhəʊlseɪl]：*adv.* 大量地

shelter[ˈʃeltə(r)]：*n.* 避难所

She had grown up in Charleston and at Monroe's **insistence** had been educated beyond the point considered wise for females. She had become a knowledgeable companion for him, a lively and attentive daughter. She was filled with opinions on art and politics and literature, and ready to argue the **merits** of her positions. But what actual talents could she claim? What gifts? A fair command of French and Latin. A hint of Greek. A **passable** hand at fine needlework. A **competency** at the piano, though no **brilliance.** The ability to **render** landscape and still life with accuracy in either pencil or watercolor. And she was well read⑯.

insistence[ɪnˈsɪstəns]：*n.* 极力主张

merit[ˈmerɪt]：*n.* 价值；优点

passable[ˈpɑːsəbl]：*adj.* 过得去的；尚可的

competency[ˈkɒmpɪtənsi]：*n.* 能力

brilliance['brɪljəns]: *n.* (卓越的)才华

render['rendə(r)]: *v.* 绘制

Those were the abilities to be marked down in her favor.[17] None of them seemed exactly to the point when faced with the hard fact that she now found herself in possession of close to three hundred acres of steep and bottom, a house, a barn, outbuildings, but no idea what to do with them.[18] It gave her pleasure to play on the piano, but not enough to **compensate for** her recent realization that she could not weed a row of young bean plants without pulling half of them out along with the **ragweed.**

compensate for: 弥补

ragweed['rægwiːd]: *n.* 豚草

A certain amount of **resentment** came upon her when she thought that a measure of applied knowledge in the area of food production and preparation would stand her in better **stead** at that particular time than any fine understanding of the principles of **perspective** in painting.[19] All her life, though, her father had kept her back from the hardness of work. As long as she could remember he had hired **adequate** help, sometimes freed blacks, sometimes unlanded whites of good character, sometimes slaves, in which case the wages were paid directly to the owner. For most of the six years of their mission to the mountains, Monroe had employed a white man and his part-Cherokee wife to manage the place, leaving Ada with little to do other than **devise** a weekly menu. She had therefore been free, as always, to **occupy** her time with reading and needle work, drawing and music.

resentment[rɪ'zentmənt]: *n.* 愤恨；不满

stead[sted]: *n.* 用处

perspective[pə'spektɪv]: *n.* 透视法

adequate['ædɪkwət]: *adj.* 足够的

devise[dɪ'vaɪz]: *v.* 设计

occupy['ɒkjupaɪ]: *v.* 占用

But now the hired people were gone. The man had been **lukewarm** toward **secession** and counted himself lucky to be too old to volunteer in the first years of the war. But that spring, with the armies in Virginia desperately shorthanded, he had begun to worry that he might soon be **conscripted.** So, shortly after Monroe died, he and his wife had taken off unannounced and headed over the mountains to cross the lines into **territory** held by the Federals, leaving Ada to make a living on her own. [20]

lukewarm[ˈluːkwɔːm]：*adj.* 冷淡的；不热心的

secession[sɪˈseʃn]：*n.*（1861 年美国南方十一州的）脱离联邦

conscript[kənˈskrɪpt]：*v.* 征兵

territory[ˈterətri]：*n.* 领地

Since then, she had discovered herself to be frighteningly ill-prepared in the craft of **subsistence**, living alone on a farm that her father had run rather as an idea than a **livelihood**. Monroe never developed much interest in the many **tiresome** areas of agriculture. [21] He had held the opinion that if he could afford to buy feed corn and meal, why bother growing more than they could eat as **roasting** ears? [22] If he could buy bacon and **chops**, why be drawn into the more inconvenient details of pork?

subsistence[səbˈsɪstəns]：*n.* 存活；谋生

livelihood[ˈlaɪvlihʊd]：*n.* 生计；谋生之道

tiresome[ˈtaɪəsəm]：*adj.* 无聊的

roast[rəʊst]：*v.* 烤；烘；焙

chop[tʃɒp]：*n.* 排骨

Ada once heard him instruct the hired man to buy a dozen or so sheep and put them into the pasture below the front yard to mix in with the milk cow. The man had **objected**, pointing out to Monroe that cows and sheep do not do well pastured together. The man asked, Why do you want sheep? The wool? Meat?

object[əbˈdʒekt]：*v.* 不赞成；反对

Monroe's answer had been, for the atmosphere. But it was hard to live on atmosphere, and so the boxwood appeared to offer about all the feeling of protection Ada could soon expect. She decided she would not quit the shrub until she could **count off**, at minimum, three convincing reasons to do so. But after several minutes' thought she could only come up with one: she did not particularly wish to die within the boxwood.

count off：数出

At that moment, though, the red hen came bursting through the leaves, her wings partially opened and trailing in the dust. She **hopped** onto a limb near Ada's head and **sounded off** with an **agitated gabble**. Immediately behind her came the big black-and-gold rooster that always frightened Ada a little with his **ferocity**. [23] He **was intent on** treading the hen but pulled up short, **startled** when he saw Ada in so unexpected a place. The rooster cocked his head at an angle and fixed a shining black eye on her. He took a step back and scratched at the ground. He was close enough for Ada to note the dirt lodged between the scales on his yellow legs. The **amber** spurs looked long as a finger. The golden helmet of feathers at his head and neck **fluffed** and **swelled** and in their **glossiness** seemed almost macassared. He shook himself to settle them back into place. The black of his body had a blue-green **sheen** like oil on water. His yellow beak opened and closed.

hop[hɒp]：*v.* 跳上(下)；齐足(或双足)跳行

sound off：明确而大胆地说出

agitated[ˈædʒɪteɪtɪd]：*adj.* 焦虑不安的；激动的

gabble[ˈɡæbl]：*n.* 急促而含混不清的话

ferocity[fəˈrɒsəti]：*n.* 凶猛

be intent on：坚持要

startle[ˈstɑːtl]：*v.* 使大吃一惊；使惊跳

amber[ˈæmbə(r)]：*n.* 琥珀色

fluff[flʌf]：*v.* 变得松软

swell[swel]：*v.* 膨胀

glossiness[ˈɡlɒsɪnɪs]：*n.* 有光泽

sheen[ʃiːn]：*n.* 光泽

If he weighed a hundred and fifty pounds he'd kill me where I sit without a doubt, Ada thought.

She shifted about onto her knees and waved her hands and said, Shoo! When she did, the rooster launched himself at her face, twisting in the air so that he arrived spurs first, wings **flogging** away. ㉔ Ada threw up a hand to fend him off and was cut across the wrist by a spur. Her blow knocked the bird to the ground, but he rose and came at her again, wings fanning. As she **scrambled crablike** to get out from under the bush, the rooster **dug** at her with a spur and hung it up in the folds of her skirt. ㉕ She **burst** from the bush with a great **thrash** and rose to run, the rooster still attached to her skirt at knee level. The bird **pecked** at her **calves** and struck again and again with the spur of his free leg and beat at her with his wings. Ada hit at it with open-handed blows until it fell away, and then she ran to the porch and into the house.

flog[flɒg]：*v.* 剧烈抖动

scramble[ˈskræmbl]：*v.* 爬

crablike[ˈkræblaɪk]：*adv.* 似蟹行般地

dig[dɪg]：*v.* 戳；刺

burst[bɜːst]：*v.* 闯

thrash[θræʃ]：*n.* 拍打

peck[pek]：*v.* 啄

calf[kɑːf]：*n.* 腿肚子

She sank into an armchair and examined her wounds. There was a smear of blood at her wrist. She wiped it away and with relief saw that she was little more than scraped. She looked at her skirt and found it dusty and smeared with chicken droppings and rent in three places, and then she drew it up and looked to her legs. [26] They were marked variously by scratches and nips, none of them deep enough to draw blood. Her face and neck stung from scratches taken when she scrabbled out of the bush. She **patted** at her hair and found it **moiled** all about her head. This is the place I have reached, she thought. I am living in a new world where these are the fruits of even looking for eggs.

pat[pæt]：*v.* 轻拍

moil[mɒɪl]：*v.* 弄乱；弄脏

She rose from the chair and climbed the steps to her room and removed her clothes. At her marble-topped **washstand**, she poured water from the pitcher into the **basin** and washed off with a piece of **lavender** soap and a cloth. She ran her fingers through her hair to rake out the boxwood leaves and then just let it fall loose below her shoulders. She had abandoned both of the current hair styles—either gathered all around and swept into two big rolls that hung from the sides of a woman's head like the ears of a hound, or pulled tight to the scalp and **bunned** at the back like a mud-tailed horse. She no longer had need or patience for such updos. She could go about looking like a mad woman in a bookplate and it didn't matter, for she sometimes went up to a week or ten days without seeing another soul.

washstand[ˈwɒʃstænd]：*n.* 脸盆架

basin[ˈbeɪsn]：*n.* 脸盆

lavender[ˈlævəndə(r)]：*n.* 薰衣草

bun[bʌn]：*v.* 梳成圆发髻

She went to her chest of drawers for clean underdress and found none, laundry having been neglected for some time[27]. She put on **linens** she drew from near the bottom of the dirty clothes pile, **theorizing** that perhaps time had made them fresher than the ones she had just taken off. She topped them with a somewhat clean dress and wondered how she might get through the hours until bedtime.[28] When had things altered so that she no longer thought of how to pass the day pleasantly or profitably and began to think merely of how to pass the day?

linen[ˈlɪnɪn]：*n.* 亚麻衣物

theorize[ˈθɪəraɪz]：*v.* 提出关于……的理论

［选自：Charles Frazier. *Cold Mountain*. New York：Grove Press，2006.］

Notes

①a portable writing desk balanced across her lap：此句是前面主句部分的伴随状语，过去分词 balanced 表被动，可以理解为 a portable writing desk was balanced across her lap。

②This you must know：这是倒装句，正常语序为 you must know this，that 后面是 know 的宾语，such is the light in which I view the happy relation existing between us，that I will never conceal a single thought from you，该句为 such… that 句型，light 在上下文中可理解为"高兴、开心"的意思，"in which…"是"介词＋关系代词"引导的定语从句，修饰前面的先行词 the light。

③Know that：是接前面的 this you must know，that 后是 know 的并列宾语，第二个 that 也是并列，to 引导的是方式状语。

④her hand insisted on forming：是一个省略了关系代词 that/which 的定语从句，insist on doing sth. 意为"坚持做某事"。

⑤Aloud she said：是将副词提前的倒装句，原句为 she said aloud，that 引导的是 said 的宾语从句，has nothing to do with 意为"与……没有关系"。

⑥Standing thick in the rows and towering over the vegetables were weeds：此句为倒装句，可理解为"weeds were standing thick and towering over…"，介词短语 in the rows 作方式状语。

⑦something that was as it should be 这部分中的 that 引导的是定语从句，修饰 someting；"as it should be"意为"理当如此"。

⑧for she did not know how to do much more 句中 for 是并列连词，对前一分句进行补充，说明理由。

⑨had not a clue 意为"一点头绪也没有；一点也不懂"。arrive at 此处不是到达的意思，是"做成"的意思。

⑩本句中有四个并列的动作：checked、parted、rattled 和 ran。

⑪folded her skirts tightly about her legs：用裙子把腿紧紧包裹。on

hands and knees：四肢着地。work one's way：努力前进。

⑫limbs 在此处不是指四肢，而是指树木的枝干，相当于 branches。"She fitted herself between two limbs"意思是"她在两根树枝间找了个空当"。

⑬made an obligatory visit：出于义务来访/来询问。sit motionless：毫无表情地坐着。"as they called her name…"，as 引导的是时间状语从句。

⑭"not…until…"："直到……才……"。long after：很久之后。

⑮本句的主干部分为"The occasional drop… would only emphasize that…"。drop 后面的 that 从句是定语从句，修饰先行词 drop；plopping 是现在分词作后置定语，也修饰 drop；emphasize 后面的 that 引导宾语从句。

⑯well read：博览群书的；知识渊博的。

⑰mark down：记下。in one's favor：对……有利。

⑱to the point：切题的。face with：面对。fact 后面的 that 引导同位语从句，解释说明 fact 的内容。find oneself：发现自己处于某种状态。in possession of：拥有。

⑲"A certain amount of resentment came upon her"是主句，"when she thought that…"是 when 引导的时间状语从句，that 引导宾语从句。

⑳shortly after：不久之后。take off：出发。unannounced 是过去分词作状语，修饰 taken off，意为"没有通知地；不告知地"。head over："前往……"。

㉑develop interest：培养兴趣。in the area of：在……领域(方面)。

㉒hold the opinion：持有……观点；认为。opinion 后面的 that 引导宾语从句，从句中又有 if 引导的条件状语从句。afford to do sth.：有条件做某事；能支付得起某物。why bother doing sth.：为什么要劳烦去做某事。

㉓Immediately behind her came the big black-and-gold rooster，此部分为倒装句，可还原为"the big black-and-gold rooster came behind her immediately"。后面的 that 引导定语从句，修饰先行词 the rooster.

㉔twisting 和 flogging 是现在分词作伴随状语，修饰谓语动词 launched。在"When she did"中，did 起动词性替代作用，代替前面提及的动作 shifted、waved 和 said。

㉕As 引导的是时间状语从句，主句主语是 the rooster。with a spur 是方式状语，hung it up 与动词 dug 并列。

㉖本句中有多个并列谓语动词：looked、found、smeared、rent、drew、looked。

㉗laundry having been neglected for some time：此句是独立主格结构，表原因。

㉘topped them with：“在外面套上……”。get through：度过；挨过；撑过(一段时间、日子)。

Remarks

《冷山》重新创造了一个已经消失的世界，在我们的时代依然具有振聋发聩的意义。

“这是很长时间以来我读到的最好的一部书，读至结尾，泪水涌上了我的眼睛。它是一个奇迹。”——拉里·布朗

“《冷山》是一个让人心碎的美丽故事，叙述优雅，最细枝末节之处也同样让人信服，久久难忘。”——约翰·伯伦特

“《冷山》是继麦克尔·厦拉的《杀手天使》之后最优秀的以内战为题材的小说，风格堪与谢尔比·福特媲美。这部小说有资格获得当今所有的、任何的奖项。”——卡伊·吉朋斯

“这部小说实在是太伟大了——在任何可以想见的，以及那些读此书之前根本梦想不到的方面都是如此——以致我想到，它所达到的高度，还有我阅读时获得的快乐，会使我今后读的每一本书相形见绌。它是如此完美，甚至我可能再也不会想读别的书了。《冷山》是美国文学中最辉煌的成就之一。”——里克·巴斯

“查尔斯·弗雷泽的小说笔触简约，却意味深长，是一幅徐徐展开的壮丽画卷，点染出一位呼之欲出的人物——一个奋力从已经毁灭的世界中逃离的士兵——英曼。那些被太多的哀伤所包围的温情时刻，既真实，又感人肺腑。当艾达说‘想告诉他自己是怎样变成今天的样子’时，那种压抑的表达——在《冷山》中类似的表达方式绝不少见——几乎让人心碎，然后是更让人心痛的结局。”——安·毕替

“查尔斯·弗雷泽的《冷山》，是我很长时间以来读到的最为精彩、出众的处女作。它叙事宏大，塑造出一个个栩栩如生的人物形象，写景状物笔力超凡，读来让人欲罢不能。虽然背景选在内战时期，从最深刻的意义上来说，却是指向当代，与《永别了，武器》遥相呼应。”——威廉·莫里斯

参考译文

冷山(片段)

艾达坐在现在已经属于她的房子的门廊上，膝头搭着一张轻便写字台，她把钢笔在墨水里蘸了一下，写道：

> 你必须知道：尽管你走了很久，我们之间的一切仍然是美好的，我永远不会对你隐瞒任何想法。不要为类似的担心而烦恼。要知道，我认为以

最坦率和真诚的态度进行沟通，是我们双方共同的责任。让我们的心永远对彼此敞开。

她把纸吹干，用挑剔的目光重新浏览一遍刚才写下的内容。她对自己的书法很不满，不论如何努力，她从来都写不出行云流水般的漂亮字体。相反，她老是把字写得粗壮密实，仿佛如尼文。比书法更让她不满的，是行文的腔调。她把信纸揉成一团，丢到黄杨树篱里。

她自言自语地说：不过是些套话罢了，完全言不及义。

她向院子那边的菜园望去，尽管生长期已经很足，豆子、南瓜、西红柿的果实几乎还赶不上她的拇指大。蔬菜的许多叶子都被虫子吃到只剩筋脉。田垄里杂草繁生，高出蔬菜一头，艾达既说不出它们的名字，也没有精力和心思去铲除。荒芜的菜园旁边从前是一片玉米地，现在却被肩膀高的有毒的商陆和漆树所侵占。晨雾方散，在农田和草场尽头耸立的山脉刚刚露出苍白的轮廓，与其说它们是山，还不如说是大山的鬼魂。

艾达坐着不动，等待它们现出清晰的面目。对于她来说，能看到什么东西一如既往，是一种安慰。不然，她就会因眼前其他一切都冷落萧条而心生沮丧。自父亲的葬礼以来，艾达对农场几乎不闻不问。不过，她毕竟挤了牛奶，还喂了马。马叫拉尔夫，奶牛则被门罗命名为瓦尔多，也不管她是不是公牛（美国哲学家爱默生全名为拉尔夫·瓦尔多·爱默生——译注）。但是她没有再做更多，也不知如何去做。至于鸡，她就任它们自生自灭了。它们一个个变得精瘦，见人就躲。艾达对母鸡非常恼火，因为它们放弃了原来的小鸡窝，飞到树上藏身，蛋想下就下，不管在哪儿。为了找鸡蛋她得搜遍院子的每一个犄角旮旯。最近，她觉得鸡蛋的味道有些异样，因为母鸡的食谱已经从残羹剩饭变成了虫子。

解决烹调问题成了艾达的当务之急。一整个夏天，她没有不饿的时候。除了一点牛奶、煎蛋、色拉，外加几盘从没人侍弄而枝蔓繁生的秧上摘的微型西红柿，她基本上没吃到别的东西，甚至黄油都成了可望而不可即的宝贝。经她手搅拌的牛奶从来不会凝到足够的浓度，最多形成些稀溜溜的凝乳。她真想喝一碗热腾腾的鸡肉面团汤，吃一只黄桃派，但始终无计可施。

艾达再看一眼远方的山峦，依旧是朦胧而迷茫的。她站起来去找鸡蛋，先沿着小路查看篱笆边生长的一溜杂草，再到侧院，分开桃树根那儿的一大蓬野草细看，接着在后院堆放的杂物中一阵翻弄，又在工具室落满灰尘的架子上摸索了一番。她什么也没找到。

她想起有一只红母鸡，最近经常在门前台阶两侧的黄杨树丛中出没。艾达走到刚才扔信进去的那片树丛前，尽力拨开浓密的枝叶向内窥视，但里面一片昏暗，什么也看不见。她把裙子紧紧裹在腿上，四肢着地向里硬挤进去，枝条在小臂、脸和脖子上划来刮去。手掌下面的土地非常干燥，散落着鸡毛、干鸡屎还有枯败的树叶。爬到里面，中间是一片空地。外面密密匝匝的树叶恰似一重帷幕，围出了一个封闭的空间，像一间小屋。

艾达坐起来，环顾地面和周围的树枝，只看到一只边缘呈锯齿形的破蛋壳，里面装着红褐色的干蛋黄。她在两根树枝间找了个空当，背靠一棵树干坐着休息。黄杨树的阴凉里充斥着尘土味和鸡身上刺鼻的味道。光线暗淡，让她想起小时候把桌布铺在桌子上或把地毯搭在晒衣绳上，假装下面是洞穴，在里头玩。最好玩的是在舅舅的农场上，她和表姐露西在干草堆里掏出深深的洞穴。下雨天，整个下午她们都猫在里面，说着悄悄话，又干爽又舒服，像躲在窝里的小狐狸。

随着熟悉的快感流遍全身，艾达的呼吸一阵紧促，她意识到自己又和从前一样藏了起来。任何人从大门走到门廊，都绝不会发现她躲在这儿。如果某位虔诚的女士出于义务前来探问，她就可以一动不动地坐在此处，不管她们怎么敲门、呼唤她的名字，一直等到院门的门闩啪的一声划上很久以后再出来。不过估计没有谁会来了，由于她的冷淡，客人已经逐日稀少，渐趋于无。

艾达仰起头，透过树叶的缝隙看着略显苍白的蓝天。她有些失望，要是下雨就好了，雨水打着头上的树叶发出沙沙声，会让她更有安全感。偶尔一两滴穿过空隙洒落下来，在灰尘中打出一个小坑，只会使对比更加强烈——外面虽然下着瓢泼大雨，她这里却干爽怡人。艾达希望永远都不用离开这个可爱的避风港，回想最近的遭遇，她想不出还有谁受的教养，比她更不切合抛头露面的艰苦生活。

艾达在查尔斯敦长大，由于父亲门罗的主张，她所受的教育已经超出公认的对于女性来说明智的程度。她既是他博学的伙伴，又是一个活泼而乖巧的女儿。满脑子里都是对艺术、政治和文学的见解，并且她从不吝于表明自己的观点。但是，她能说得上有什么真正的才能和天赋吗？熟知法文和拉丁文；掌握一点希腊语；差强人意的刺绣；弹得一手纯熟的钢琴，但并不突出；能用铅笔或水彩精确地描绘风景和静物；她还博览群书。

这都是些对她没有好处的能力，有还不如没有。似乎没一样有助于应对她当前面临的严峻现实：拥有将近三百英亩的坡地和谷地、一栋房子和外屋、一个牲口棚，却两眼一抹黑，不知拿它们怎么办好。弹钢琴可以带来快乐，但无补于她最近陷入的窘境——给一垄豆苗除草，却连带着拔出一半的秧苗。

在这个时刻，一点粮食生产和加工方面的实用知识于她而言，比对绘画透视法原则的任何精妙理解都更为有用。每当想到这一点，她心头就愤恨不已。父亲向来对她娇生惯养，不让她干一点累活。从她能记事起，父亲一直雇佣足够的帮工，有时是解放的黑人，有时是人品端正但没有土地的白人，也有奴隶，如果是这样，工资就直接付给奴隶主。在山区传教的六年，门罗雇了一个白人和他的有切诺基血统的老婆来料理家务。艾达除了设计一下每周的食谱，不用做任何事情，所以她一直都是把时间花在阅读、刺绣、绘画和音乐上。

但是现在雇工们已经走掉了。那个男人对脱离联邦一直就不热心，战争开头几年，他庆幸自己上了岁数，不必自愿参军。但是今年春天，随着弗吉尼亚军队严重缺员，他开始担心征兵很快也要落到自己头上，所以在门罗死后不久，他和老婆就不辞而别，越过山区边界，逃到北方控制区，丢下艾达自谋生路。

自从农场上只剩她孤家寡人一个，艾达才发觉自己谋生的技能少得可怕。从她父亲经营农场的方式来看，与其说是为了生计，还不如说是为了实现心中的某些想法来得贴切。门罗对农业枯燥无聊的一面从来没培养出什么兴趣。他的观点是，如果买得起饲料和粮食，何必种太多的玉米，只要够烤着吃的就行了；如果可以买咸肉和猪排，何必还要和肮脏的生猪打交道！

有一次艾达听到他指派帮工去买十几只绵羊，放到院子前面的坡地上与奶牛混养。帮工不同意，说奶牛和绵羊不适合在一起放牧。他问门罗："你要绵羊做什么？是为了羊毛，还是羊肉？"

门罗回答说，他要的是一种氛围。但人不能靠氛围活着，而这黄杨林在可以预见的时间内似乎是唯一能给她安全感的所在。她决定就在这里待着不动，除非能想出至少三条有说服力的理由让她离开。但琢磨了几分钟，她只想出一条理由来：死在黄杨林里可不是一件特别称心的事。

正想之间，红母鸡穿过枝叶冲了进来，她的翅膀没有完全展开，耷拉着拖在尘土中。她蹿到靠近艾达头部的一根树枝上，兴奋地咯咯直叫。紧随其后的是那只生着黑金两色羽毛的大公鸡，它凶悍的样子经常把艾达吓一跳。公鸡正一门心思追着母鸡交配，在这个地方猛然瞧见艾达，吃了一惊，骤然停住。它竖起头，一只乌黑发亮的眼睛盯住艾达，向后退了一步，爪子在地面上来回扒着。公鸡离艾达非常近，她可以看清黄色鸡足上角质鳞片之间积累的污垢，长长的鸡足刺像手指头一样伸出来，头上和脖子上覆盖的金色羽毛蓬松涨起，光泽闪闪，似擦了头油。它抖动脖子让羽毛恢复原位，黄色的尖嘴巴张开又合上。

如果这家伙有150磅的体重，它肯定会就地把我干掉，艾达想。

她挪动身子，膝盖跪地，挥着双手，口中嘘嘘作声，想把它轰开。不想公鸡迎面蹿过来，凌空一拧身，鸡足刺伸在前面，同时翅膀还不停地扑腾着。艾达抬起一只手想把它挡开，手腕却给它的足刺划了一下子。她一巴掌把公鸡打到地上，但它旋即又拍打着翅膀再次扑来。艾达像只螃蟹一样趴在地上往外爬，公鸡赶上来用足刺戳她，结果给裙褶钩住缩不回来了。艾达连滚带爬地从树丛里闯出来，起身便逃，公鸡的一只脚仍然在她裙子靠近腿弯的地方吊着。

它用嘴叼她的小腿，并用另外一只脚上的足刺反复蹬她，翅膀也不闲着，狠命地拍打。艾达挥掌一通乱拍，终于把公鸡打脱，然后一溜烟跑上门廊冲进屋去。

她靠进扶手椅里检查自己受的伤。手腕上有一道血迹，她把血擦干，松了口气，只不过是擦破了点皮。裙子破了三个洞，脏兮兮的，还沾着鸡粪。她掀起裙子瞧瞧自己的两条腿，到处是各式各样的擦伤和啄痕，但没有一处深到要流血。脸和脖子也在往外爬的时候被树枝划伤，阵阵刺痛。她抬手摸了摸自己的头发，满脑袋乱糟糟的一团。看看我落到了什么地步，她想，这可真是一个全新的世界，连找鸡蛋都有这样的下场。

她从椅子里起身爬上楼梯，来到自己的房间，脱去衣服，把水罐中的水倒进大理石台上的脸盆，用薰衣草香皂和毛巾清洁自己。她叉开手指，穿过头发，篦出里面的黄杨树叶，然后就让头发披散在肩膀上。当时流行的两种发式她都放弃了——不管是全部拢起，梳成两个发卷，像狗耳朵一样垂在脑袋两边，还是紧贴着头皮梳到脑后，打成一个发髻，像尾巴给扎起来的马。她既没有必要也没有耐心打理这样的发髻了，即便像藏书票里画的披头散发的疯女人一样到处走，也没关系，因为有时候她十天半月都看不见一个人影。

她去衣柜里找干净内衣，但是一件也没有，衣服已经有一段时间没人洗了。她从脏衣服堆底下抽出几件亚麻内衣穿在身上，设想着或许时间能使它们变得比刚刚脱下来的衣服干净些。她在外面套上一条稍微干净点的裙子，琢磨着怎样挨到上床睡觉。世道从什么时候起发生了改变，使她不再考虑如何让时间过得愉快而充实，却只想着怎样把时间打发掉。

[选自：查尔斯·弗雷泽．冷山．丁宇岚，译．北京：中信出版社，2018.]

Questions for discussion

1. How do you make a living with little money and no help in a strange circumstance?

2. Do you think it is necessary to develop as many hobbies as possible during your school years?

3. How do you make friends with those you don't like?

After-class reading

1. Read the novel *Cold Mountain* by Charles Frazier.

2. Watch the movie *Cold Mountain*.

3. Compare the novel with the movie, and then discuss with your classmates.

Part B

(1) World's First Machine to Clean up the Planet's Largest Mass of Ocean Plastic Is Launching

Scientists are preparing to launch the world's first machine to clean up the planet's largest mass of ocean plastic. The system, originally dreamed up by a teenager, will be shipped out this summer to the Great Pacific Garbage **Patch**, between Hawaii and California, and which contains an **estimated** 1.8 **trillion** pieces of plastic. It will be the first ever attempt to **tackle** the patch since it was discovered in 1997. The experts believe the machine should be able to collect half of the **detritus** in the patch—about 40000 metric tons—within five years.

patch[pætʃ]：*n.* 碎片

estimated[ˈestɪmeɪtɪd]：*adj.* 预计的；估计的

trillion[ˈtrɪljən]：*n.* 万亿

tackle[ˈtækl]：*v.* 着手处理

detritus[dɪˈtraɪtəs]：*n.* 碎片；瓦砾

In the past few weeks they have been busy **welding** together giant **tubes** that will sit on the surface of the sea and form the **skeleton** of the machine, creating the largest floating barrier ever made. The Great Pacific Garbage Patch **spans** 617763 square miles—more than twice the size of France, and contains at least 79000 tons of plastic, research found last month. Most of it is made up of "ghost **gear**"—parts of abandoned and lost fishing gear, such as nets and ropes—often from illegal fishing **vessels.** Ghost gear kills more than 100000 whales, dolphins and seals each year, according to scientific surveys. Seabirds and other **marine** life are increasingly being found dead with stomachs full of small pieces of plastic. Creatures eat plastic discarded in the sea thinking it's food but then starve to death because they are not feeding properly. Others are trapped and die of starvation or are **strangled** or **suffocated** by ghost gear.

weld[weld]：*v.* 焊接

tube[tjuːb]：*n.* 管子

skeleton[ˈskelɪtən]：*n.* 框架

span[spæn]：*v.* 跨越

gear[ɡɪə(r)]：*n.* 装置；工具

vessel['vesl]：*n.* 船
marine[mə'riːn]：*adj.* 海生的；海产的
strangle['stræŋgl]：*v.* 把……勒死
suffocate['sʌfəkeɪt]：*v.* 使……窒息而死

参考译文

世界首台海洋塑料清理机将启用

科学家们正准备启用世界上第一台清理地球上最大海洋塑料垃圾堆的机器。这种由一名青少年原创的系统将在今年夏天被运往"大太平洋垃圾带"。大太平洋垃圾带位于美国夏威夷和加利福尼亚之间，总共含有大约1.8万亿片塑料。这将是自1997年发现该垃圾带以来首次尝试对它进行处理。专家相信，这种机器应该能在5年内收集垃圾带中一半的碎片，总重量约4万吨。

在过去几周里，他们一直在忙着将巨大的管子焊接在一起。这些管子将被放置在海面上，构成机器的主体框架，也成为有史以来人类制造的最大的漂浮屏障。上月的一项调查发现，大太平洋垃圾带的面积达到了617763平方英里，是法国面积的两倍多，其中含有至少7.9万吨塑料。塑料主要由"幽灵渔具"构成，包括废弃或丢失的渔网、绳索等渔具的组件，而这些渔具大都来自非法捕鱼船只。科学调查显示，幽灵渔具每年导致超过10万头鲸、海豚和海豹死亡。越来越多的海鸟和其他海洋生物被发现死亡时胃里装满了小块塑料。很多生物误食海里的废弃塑料，但因饮食不当而饿死。还有很多生物为"幽灵渔具"所困，死于饥饿或窒息。

(2) Zealandia, a New Continent Was Discovered

Geologists claim to have discovered a new continent to the east of Australia: Zealandia. At 4.9 million square kilometers of land mass, 94 percent of which is under water, Zealandia would be the world's smallest continent.

The 11 scientists behind the claim presented their findings in the study "Zealandia: Earth's Hidden Continent" in Geological Society of America, making a case for Zealandia to be recognized as the world's eighth continent in its own right.

According to their study, the land mass **comprises** all the four attributes needed to be considered a continent, including the presence of different rock types and **crucially** "the high elevation relative to regions floored by oceanic crust."

comprise[kəm'praɪz]：*v.* 包含；包括

crucially['kruːʃəli]：*adv.* 至关重要地；关键地

"It was not a sudden discovery but a gradual realization," the scientists wrote.

The term Zealandia was **coined** by **geophysicist** Bruce Luyendyk in 1995, at which time it was believed to possess three of the four necessary qualities required for continent status. A recent discovery using **satellite** technology and **gravity** maps of the sea floor have revealed that Zealandia is a large unified area, fulfilling all four requirements.

coin[kɔɪn]：*v.* 杜撰；创造

geophysicist[ˌdʒiːəʊ'fɪzɪsɪst]：*n.* 地球物理学家

satellite['sætəlaɪt]：*n.* 卫星；人造卫星

gravity['ɡrævəti]：*n.* 重力；地心引力

The political and economic implications of a new continent would be **manifold**, with the question of clearly defining what belongs to New Zealand and Australia particularly **salient** in light of offshore mining in the area.

manifold['mænɪfəʊld]：*adj.* 多重的；多方面的

salient['seɪliənt]：*adj.* 显著的；突出的；重要的

A six-year study by the GNS Science Research Institute in New Zealand has revealed that there could be tens of billions of dollars worth of fossil fuels located offshore in the region.

According to the study, the 94 percent of Zealandia currently **submerged** broke away from Australia and **sank** 60 million～85 million years ago.

submerge[səb'mɜːdʒ]：*v.* 淹没；潜入水中；沉浸

sink[sɪŋk]：*v.* 下沉

参考译文

西兰洲，一块被发现的新大陆

地质学家声称，在澳洲以东发现了一块新大陆：西兰洲。西兰洲的陆地面积为490万平方千米，其中94%都浸没在水中，是世界上面积最小的大陆。

提出新大陆说法的11位科学家在美国地质学会上发表了这一研究报告：《西兰洲：地球上隐藏的大陆》，他们请求将西兰洲认定为世界第八大洲。

根据他们的研究，这块陆地具备了成为大洲所需的四个要素，包括岩石类型多样化，关键在于它“相比那些基于海洋地壳的地区海拔要高”。

科学家在研究报告中写道：“这不是突然发现的，而是逐渐意识到的。”

1995年，地球物理学家布鲁斯·鲁岩迪克造出了“西兰洲”这个词，当时科学家认为这块陆地具备了成为大洲所需的四个要素中的三个要素。近日运用卫星技术和海底重力地图后发现，西兰洲是一整块大陆，具备了所有四个要素。

一个新大洲的出现将蕴含着多重的政治和经济意义，主要问题在于该地区的海底开采权将如何在新西兰和澳大利亚之间进行划分。

新西兰的地质与核科学研究所的一项长达六年的研究发现，该地区海底潜藏着价值成百上千亿美元的化石燃料能源。

根据该研究，西兰洲目前被海水浸没的94%的地区已经和澳洲大陆块分离，并于6000万至8500万年前沉没海中。

(3) More and More Overseas Students Return to Work after Graduation

Recently, I had lunch with a young Chinese student who studies at a college in New York. He is very bright and **aspiring** and I enjoyed our conversation. Still I felt **frustrated** and useless afterwards because I was not able to provide him with any good news on a question that had been **bugging** him lately. Graduating at the end of this year, he asked me how he could find a job in this country and fulfill his career dreams.

aspiring[əˈspaɪərɪŋ]: *adj.* 有抱负的；有志气的

frustrated[frʌˈstreɪtɪd]: *adj.* 失落的；沮丧的

bug[bʌg]: *v.* 困扰；烦扰

In recent years, international students who found a job here after graduation have had to go through a cruel lottery system to obtain their H1B working visa. And the success rates have been **declining** year after year because of the ever growing number of applicants. Last year, there were 233000 applicants, and only 30 percent of them were lucky, less than half of the rate in 2013.

decline[dɪˈklaɪn]: *v.* 下降

And it can only become worse. US President Donald Trump's **executive** order banning people from seven Muslim-majority countries from entering the US may have been halted by the courts temporarily, but the **squaring off** between the administration and the **judiciary** won't change the overall policy direction—immigration policies in this country are **tightening up** and this **trend** will continue for at least the next few years.

executive[ɪɡˈzekjətɪv]: *adj.* 行政的

square off：摆好架势

judiciary[dʒuˈdɪʃəri]：*n.* 司法部

tighten up：收紧

trend[trend]：*n.* 趋势

The US Congress is already **reviewing** a bill that requires a $100000 minimum annual salary **threshold** for H1B applicants. And Trump has indicated he will probably support the **legislation**. It is a figure that is very difficult for a young graduate to attain in their first job and a struggle for many with master's degrees. In this case, foreign students studying social sciences, a field in which starting salaries are rarely above the required amount, can kiss their visa hopes goodbye.

review[rɪˈvjuː]：*v.* 审查；重新考虑

threshold[ˈθreʃhəʊld]：*n.* 门槛

legislation[ˌledʒɪsˈleɪʃn]：*n.* 法律；法规

But, while I am sorry for my young friend, whose major in **journalism** is not likely to be considered as meeting a critical need in Trump's America, I know that for Chinese students in the US, the tighter visa policy will be much less **devastating** than 10 years ago.

journalism[ˈdʒɜːnəlɪzəm]：*n.* 新闻学

devastating[ˈdevəsteɪtɪŋ]：*adj.* 毁灭性的

Compared to the older generation of Chinese students who would kill to stay in the US after graduation, today's young people no longer consider the US as the only **option**. Many start to think China offers better opportunities in the longer term. According to China's Ministry of Education, there were 523700 Chinese students who went to study in foreign countries in 2015, and 409100 overseas Chinese students returned after graduation. The out/in ratio was 1.28∶1 compared to 2.15∶1 a decade ago.

option[ˈɒpʃn]：*n.* 选项；选择

Prospective Chinese employers have been quick to **detect** the change. In the past two years, an increasing number of Chinese companies have launched campus **recruitment** tours at US universities.

prospective[prəˈspektɪv]：*adj.* 未来的

detect[dɪˈtekt]：*v.* 发现；洞察

recruitment[rɪˈkruːtmənt]：*n.* 招募；招聘

The students I met at the job fair all told me that the **potential** for growth a job offers is the most important **criteria** on which they will make a decision. Whether the job is based in Beijing or New York is not as important.

potential[pəˈtenʃl]：*n.* 潜力；潜能

criteria[kraɪˈtɪəriə]：*n.*（批评、判断等的）标准；准则

This is not to say that Chinese students in the US are not interested in job opportunities here anymore. A few years of work experience in the US can give them better **leverage** when they finally land back in their home country. So far there are 328547 Chinese students studying in the US, making China the number one source for international students here. But if the job opportunities are largely reduced by the tightening of immigration policy, I expect there will be a decline. And if that happens, it is the American economy that will decrease from the loss of those educated, hard-working and talented immigrants.

leverage[ˈliːvərɪdʒ]：*n.* 影响力；优势

参考译文

越来越多的留学生毕业后选择回国工作

最近，我和一位在纽约上大学的年轻的中国学生吃午饭。他很聪明，很有抱负，我们一起相谈甚欢。但聊天之后我依然感到些许失落，感觉自己没用，因为当他和我诉说最近困扰他的问题时，我无法向他提供任何好消息。他问我，在年底毕业后怎么能在这个国家找一份工作，圆他事业上的梦想。

最近几年，毕业后在这里找工作的留学生要想拿到 H1B 工作签证是件很困难而且碰运气的事。因为申请数量的增长，出签成功率也在逐年下降。去年共有 23.3 万份签证申请，但其中只有 30％成了幸运儿，这一比例不及 2013 年的一半。

而且情况只会越来越糟。美国总统特朗普针对七个信奉伊斯兰教的国家的禁令暂时被法院暂停，但是行政部和司法部不会改变基本政策的走向——美国本土的移民政策正在不断收紧，而且这样的趋势将持续数年。

美国国会已经在修订申请 H1B 签证的要求，欲将年薪十万美金作为最低门槛。同时，特朗普表示他会支持此政策。那个数字对于年轻的毕业生们来说很难在第一份工作中达到，即使对于许多研究生来说也很困难。在这种情况下，一些学人文社科的留学生就基本无缘签证了，因为这一领域的起薪几乎不可能达到要求。

虽然我对那位年轻朋友很抱憾，新闻专业的他不大可能达到特朗普时期美国对留学生们的尖锐要求。但是我明白，相比十年前，更为收紧的签证政策对

于在美中国留学生来说不会是个毁灭性的打击。

老一代的中国学生在毕业后会绞尽脑汁、不惜一切代价留在美国，相比之下现如今的年轻人仅仅会把留美作为众多选项之一。许多学生开始觉得在中国会有更好的长期工作的机会。中国教育部数据显示，2015 年，海外的中国留学生有 52.37 万人，其中 40.19 万人在毕业后选择回国，留学人数与回国人数比为 1.28∶1，十年前这一比例为 2.15∶1。

未来的中国老板们将会很快觉察到这一变化。在过去两年里，在美国高校进行巡回招募的国企数量不断上升。

我在招聘会上遇见的学生们告诉我，工作机会不断增加的潜在趋势将是他们未来做决定的一个重要因素，至于工作是在北京还是在纽约并不那么重要。

这并不是说赴美的中国学生对那边的工作机会不再感兴趣。最终回国后，在美国短暂几年的工作经验会为他们个人增色不少。现在美国大约有 328547 名中国留学生，这使得中国成为输送留学生最多的国家。但是如果工作机会因为不断收紧的移民政策而被削减，我觉得这一数字将会下降。如果真是这样的话，美国经济将会因为数量下降的知识分子、勤勉工作并且优秀的移民流失而受到打击。

Part C

What an American Student Learns

American students pass through several levels of schooling—and thus, several curricula—on their way to a high school diploma. They attend:

Elementary School

In **statistical** reports published by the federal government, "elementary school" usually means grades kindergarten(K) through 8. But in some places, the elementary school includes only grades K to 6. And sometimes grades 4, 5 and 6 make up what is called a "middle grade" school. (Many Americans refer to the elementary grades as "grammar school".)

statistical[stəˈtɪstɪk(ə)l]: *adj.* 数据的

Secondary School

Again, in statistical reports, "secondary school" generally means grades 9-12. These grades are popularly called "high school". However, in many districts, "junior high school" includes grades 7-9. And when grades 7-9 are included with the 10th, 11th and 12th grades, all six are said to form a "senior high school".

Although there is no national curriculum in the United States, certain subjects are taught in all K to 12 systems across the country.

Almost every elementary school provides instruction in these subjects: mathematics; language arts (subject that includes reading, grammar, composition and literature); penmanship; science; social studies (a subject that includes history, geography, citizenship and economics); music; art; and physical education. In many elementary schools, courses in the use of computers have been introduced. And in some cases, a second language (other than English) is offered in the upper elementary grades.

Most secondary schools offer the same "**core**" of required subjects: English, mathematics, science, social studies and physical education. But school boards differ greatly from one district to another in the amount of class time they want high school students to spend on these basic subjects. In some high schools, for example, students must complete three years of mathematics before graduation. The national average is lower.

core[kɔː]: *n.* 核心

Students are guided by school **counselors** in choosing **electives**, which can range from specialized academic to **vocational** subjects.

counselor[ˈkaʊnsələ(r)]: *n.* 辅导员；顾问

elective[ɪˈlektɪv]: *n.* 选修课

vocational[vəʊˈkeɪʃənl]: *adj.* 职业的

For example, high schools offer more than one year—in most cases, several years—of math, science and the other core subjects. After they complete the required units in these core areas (for example, one year of American history), students can take additional units as electives (perhaps a year of European history and a year of world political issues).

Other elective courses vary from school to school. Some high schools specialize in particular types of subjects—business education, or industrial trades, or foreign languages, for example. A student planning to be a physician would want to attend a school offering many electives in science.

Higher Education

Out of more than three million students who graduate from high school each year, about one million go on for higher education. Simply by being admitted into one of the most respected universities in the United States, a high school graduate achieves a degree of success. A college at a leading university might receive applications from 2% of these high school graduates, and then accept only one out of every ten who apply. ① Successful applicants at such colleges are usually chosen on the basis of: (a) their high school records; (b) recommendations from their high school teachers; (c) the impression they make during interviews at the university; and (d) their scores on the **Scholastic Aptitude Tests** (**SATs**).

Scholastic Aptitude Tests (**SATs**)：学习能力测试

The system of higher education in the United States is complex. It comprises four categories of institutions: (1) the university, which may contain: (a) several colleges for undergraduate students seeking a **bachelor's** (four-year) **degree** and (b) one or more graduate schools for those continuing in specialized studies beyond the bachelor's degree to obtain a **master's** or a **doctoral degree**; (2) the four-year undergraduate institution—the college—most of which are not part of a university; (3) the technical training institution, at which high school graduates may take courses ranging from six months to four years in duration and learn a vide variety of technical skills, from **hair styling** through **business accounting** to **computer programming**; and (4) the two-year, or **community college**, from which students may enter many professions or may **transfer** to four-year colleges or universities.

bachelor's degree：学士学位

master's degree：硕士学位

doctoral degree：博士学位

hair styling：美发

business accounting：商业会计

computer programming：电脑编程

community college：社区大学

transfer[træns'fəː]：*v.* 转学

Any of these institutions, in any category, might be either public or private, depending on the source of its funding. There is no clear or inevitable distinction in terms of quality of education offered between the institutions which are publicly or privately funded. However, this is not to say that all institutions enjoy equal **prestige** nor that there are no material differences among them. ②

prestige[pre'stiːdʒ] *n.* 名声；威望

Many universities and colleges, both public and private, have gained reputations for offering particularly challenging courses and for providing their students with a higher quality of education. The great majority are generally regarded as quite satisfactory. A few other institutions, **conversely**, provide only adequate education, and students attend classes, pass examinations and graduate as merely competent, but not outstanding, scholars and professionals. The factors determine whether an institution is one of the best or one of lower prestige are quality of teaching **faculty**, quality of research facilities; amount of funding available for libraries, special programs, etc.; and the competence and the number of applicants for admission, i. e., how selective the institution can be in choosing its students. All of these factors **reinforce** one another. ③

conversely['kɒnvəːsli]: *adv.* 相反地

faculty['fækəlti]: *n.* (大学的)全体教职员工

reinforce[riːɪn'fɔːs]: *v.* 增强

In the United States it is generally recognized that there are more and less desirable institutions in which to study and from which to graduate. ④ The more desirable institutions are generally—but not always—more costly to attend, and having graduated from one of them may bring distinct advantages as the individual seeks employment opportunities and **social mobility** within the society. ⑤ Competition to get into such a college prompts a million secondary school students to take the SATs every year. But recently emphasis on admissions examinations has been widely criticized in the United States because the examinations tend to measure only competence in mathematics and English. In defense of using the examinations as criteria for admissions, administrators at many universities say that the SATs provide a fair way for deciding whom to admit when they have 10 or 12 applicants for every first-year student seat.

social mobility：社会流动性，指取得较高的社会地位。

Education for All

In 1944 Congress passed the Servicemen's Readjustment Act, soon popularly called the "GI Bill of Rights". ⑥ ("GI" at the time, was a nickname for the American soldier. The nickname came from an **abbreviation** for

"Government Issue"—the uniforms and other articles "issued" to a soldier.)[⑦] The Act promised financial aid, including aid for higher education, to members of the armed forces after the end of World War Ⅱ.

abbreviation [əbriːvɪˈeɪʃn]：*n.* 缩写；简写

The war ended in the following year. The prediction had been that 600000 war veterans would apply for aid for education. By 1955, more than two million veterans of World War Ⅱ and of the Korean War had used the GI Bill of Rights to go to college. Many of these veterans were from poor families. 30% were married when they applied for college aid; 10% had children. More than a few had to work part time while they took courses. It was difficult, but these veterans believed that a college degree (which they could not afford on their own) would improve their chances for a good job in the postwar economy. Some went to liberal arts colleges; others to technical and professional institutions. Their outstanding success in all these schools forced everyone connected with higher education to rethink its purpose and goals. Within just a few years, American **veterans** had changed the image of who should go to college.

veteran[ˈvetərən]：*n.* 老兵；退伍兵

In postwar America, other groups sought their place on America's campuses, too. The enrollment of women in higher education began to increase. Racial segregation in elementary and secondary education ended, and thus blacks achieved an equal opportunity to get into any college of their choice.

By the end of 1960s, some colleges introduced special plans and programs to equalize educational opportunities—at every level, for all groups. Some of these plans were called "Affirmative Action Programs"[⑧]. Their goal was to make up for past inequality by giving special reference to members of minorities seeking jobs or admission to college. [In the United States, the term "minority" has two meanings, often related: (a) A minority is any ethnic or racial group that makes up small percentage of the total population; (b) The term also suggests a group that is not the dominant political power.] Some colleges, for example, sponsored programs to help minority students prepare for college while still in high school.

By the 1970s, the United States government stood firmly behind such goals. It required colleges and universities receiving public funds to practice some form of affirmative action. But when colleges began to set **quotas** (fixed numbers) of minority students to be admitted, many Americans (including minority citizens) protested. They felt that this was another form of discrimination.

quota ['kwəʊtə]: *n.* 定额；配额

As with most (but not all) problems in American public life, the conflict was resolved by change and compromise. ⑨ Colleges continued to serve the goal of affirmative action—but in less controversial ways. One large university, for example, announced a new policy: It would seek to admit students who would add diverse talents to the student body. It thus dealt with all applicants—minorities included—on a basis that was not restricted to high school performance and entrance tests, but which took into account the talents, voluntary activities and "life experience" of the student. ⑩

What success did these efforts have? American college students are an increasingly diverse group. The number of women enrolled in college has been greater than male college student enrollment since 1980. In 1987, 54% were women. Women received 51% of the bachelor's and master's degrees awarded that year, and 35% of the doctorates and professional degrees. Between 1997 and 2007, men enrolled at a 32% increase rate while women were a 63% increase in enrollment. In 2009, nearly 74% of high school graduate women were enrolled in college and the number of men was about 66%. But not all groups are doing so well.

Although 59% of the students who graduated from high school in 1988 enrolled in college that same year, only 45% of the African-American high school graduates went on to college. Educators and others have been working to increase that percentage. Recent statistics show that 55% of African American high school graduates continued directly on to college. But African-Americans still lag behind in obtaining college degrees. Only 43% of African-Americans who enter college graduate—20% lower than the rate for whites.

US colleges and universities are also enrolling a higher percentage of non-traditional students—students who have worked for several years before starting college or students who go to school part-time while holding down a job. According to a recent survey, about half of college students are 25 years of age or older and nearly 60% were part-time students.

Notes

①A college at a leading university… and then accept only one out of every ten who apply：一流大学的学院也许会收到应届高中毕业生中 2%学生的申请，却只能从中录取 10%的学生。

②However, this is not to say… there are no material differences among them：但这并不意味着所有学院都享有同样的声誉，也不是说它们之间就没有实质区别。

③The factors determine whether an institution is… reinforce one another：决定一所学院是好是坏取决于教员质量，研究设施、图书馆及特殊项目等所需资金是否充足，以及申请该校的学生人数和质量，即学院筛选学生时能有多大空间。所有这些因素相辅相成。

④In the United States it is generally recognized… to study and from which to graduate：在美国，人们普遍认为既有较好的也有较差的大学供学生在其中学习并毕业获取学位。

⑤The more desirable institutions are … and social mobility within the society：好大学一般要贵一些，但也不是绝对如此，从这类学校毕业的学生在求职和社会地位提高方面会有显著优势。

⑥In 1944 Congress passed the Servicemen's Readjustment Act… the "GI Bill of Rights"：1944 年，美国国会通过了《军人重新安置法案》，很快被通俗地称为《退役军人权利法案》。GI Bill of Rights：《退役军人权利法案》由罗斯福总统在 1944 年 6 月 22 日签署，主要为"二战"老兵提供资助，资助他们购房、创业，尤其是帮助他们获得受教育的机会。该法案规定，政府为老兵们重回学校或大学提供学费、生活补助、书本以及学业咨询服务。在法案实施后的 7 年中，大约八百万老兵享受到了这些教育资助。

⑦"GI" at the time, … the uniforms and other articles "issued" to a soldier：在当时，GI 是美国士兵的绰号，是 Government Issue(免费发给士兵的军装和其他物品)的简称。

⑧Affirmative Action Programs："肯定性行动计划"(又译《平权法案》)，美国政府为弥补以往对某些特殊群体(如少数民族和妇女)的歧视而给这些群体在就业和受教育机会方面提供较为优惠的照顾性政策。该项政策始于 20 世纪 60 年代，但到 70 年代后期，因所设立的种族配额制度偏向少数族裔和妇女而被谴责为"逆向歧视"。

⑨As with most (but not all) problems… was resolved by change and compromise：一如美国公众生活中大多数(但不是所有)问题一样，这一矛盾通过改革和妥协得以解决。

⑩It thus dealt with all applicants… and "life experience" of the student：由此，对所有申请者(包括少数民族)的录取标准不再局限于高中时的学习成绩或是入学考试成绩，还包括学生的特长、志愿活动的参与程度以及"人生经历"。

Questions

1. What is the goal of education in the United States? Discuss the similarities and differences between China and the United States concerning the goals of education.

2. How is the system of American higher education?

3. What do you think are the characteristics in education that are particularly American?

Part D

Pre-reading activities

Find five ancient Chinese poems describing natural scenery, and compare them with their English editions in language and structure.

杳杳寒山道

杳杳寒山道，落落冷涧滨。
啾啾常有鸟，寂寂更无人。
淅淅风吹面，纷纷雪积身。
朝朝不见日，岁岁不知春。

参考译文

Long，Long，the Path to the Cold Hill

Long，long，the path to the Cold Hill；
Bleak，bleak the canyon **ford**，so **chill**.
Cheep，cheep，several birds in flight；
Lone，lone，no people within sight.
Sighs，sighs，the face **assaulting** blow；
Soughs，soughs，the body wrapping snow.
Day in day out，you see no sun；
Year in year out，no spring comes on.

bleak[bliːk]：*adj*. 昏暗的；荒凉的
ford[fɔːd]：*n*. 浅滩
chill[tʃɪl]：*adj*. 冷的
sigh[saɪ]：*v*. 叹气；悲叹；悲鸣
assault[əˈsɔːlt]：*v*. 袭击
sough[saʊ]：*v*. 飒飒而鸣；哗啦哗啦地响
[选自：英韵唐诗百首．赵彦春，译．北京：高等教育出版社，2019.]

After-reading activities

查尔斯·弗雷泽在《冷山》的扉页上引用了一句诗："Men ask the way to Cold Mountain，Cold Mountain：there's no through trail."而这正是寒山诗"人问寒山道，寒山路不通"的英译。请试着翻译其余的诗句。

人问寒山道，寒山路不通。
夏天冰未释，日出雾朦胧。
似我何由届，与君心不同。
君心若似我，还得到其中。

作者简介

寒山，又称寒山子，乃唐代首都长安人，出身于官宦人家，多次投考不第，被迫出家，30岁后隐居于浙东天台山，享年一百多岁。严振非在《寒山子身世考》中更以《北史》《隋书》等大量史料与寒山诗相印证，指出寒山乃隋皇室后裔杨瓒之子杨温，因遭皇室内的妒忌与排挤及佛教思想影响而遁入空门，隐于天台山寒岩。这位富有神话色彩的唐代诗人，曾经一度被世人冷落，然而随着20世纪的到来，其诗却越来越多地被世人接受并广泛流传。正如其诗所写："有人笑我诗，我诗合典雅。不烦郑氏笺，岂用毛公解。不恨会人稀，只为知音寡。若遣趁宫商，余病莫能罢。忽遇明眼人，即自流天下。"20世纪的寒山诗果然遇到了众多的"明眼人"。

寒山作为中国唐代少有的几位白话诗人之一，20世纪以来一直受到日本学者的推崇。自1905年起，寒山诗就在日本一版再版，并且有十多位学者对其诗做了大量研究、注释及翻译工作。日本著名小说家森鸥外(1862—1922)曾根据寒山诗集前闾丘胤的序言，写了名为《寒山拾得》的一篇小说。不少评论家认为，该小说是其最好的作品之一。

胡适在其《白话文学史》中将寒山、王梵志、王绩三人并列为唐代的三位白话大诗人。由此，寒山诗受到国人的青睐，学术界纷纷撰文评议寒山。中华人民共和国成立后，寒山研究更呈现出雨后春笋之态势。

从20世纪50年代起，寒山诗远涉重洋传入美国。美国“垮掉的一代”(The Beat Generation)将寒山奉为偶像。其诗一时之间风靡欧洲，被翻译成英语和法语，为众多读者所接受。在那里，他赢得了比李白、杜甫还要高的声誉。

写作背景

寒山长期住在天台山寒岩，诗就写刻在山石竹木之上，盈六百首，现存三百余首。此诗为其中一首。

作品鉴赏

此诗主要写天台山寒岩及其周围的景致，最后见出心情，通篇浸透了寒意。首联写山水。“杳杳”言山路深暗幽远，“落落”言涧边寂寥冷落。诗一开始就把读者带进一种冷森森的境界，使人顿觉寒气逼人。次联写山中幽静的环境，用轻细的鸟鸣声反衬四周的冷寂。三联写山中气候，用风雪的凛冽写出环境的冷峻。尾联写山幽林茂，不易见到阳光；心如古井，不关心春来秋去。前七句渲染环境的幽冷，后一句见出诗人超然物外的冷淡心情。

除了用景物渲染气氛、以气氛烘托心情这种传统的表现手法之外，使用叠词也是此诗的特点之一。通篇句首都用叠词，这种情况是不多见的。“杳杳”具有幽暗的色彩感；“落落”具有空旷的空间感；“啾啾”言有声；“寂寂”言无声；“淅淅”写风的动态感；“纷纷”写雪的飞舞状；“朝朝”“岁岁”虽同指时间，又有长短的区别。八组叠词，各具情状。就词性看，这些叠词有形容词、副词、象声词、名词，各不相同。就描摹对象看，或山或水，或鸟或人，或风或雪，或境或情，也不一样。这样既使文字显得变幻多姿，又增强了音乐美。借助音节的复沓、和谐贯串、一气盘旋以及形式上的划一，把原本分散的山、水、风、雪、境、情组成一个整体，使人感到回环往复，连绵不断。

Chapter 5　The Park

Part A

简·奥斯汀(Jane Austen，1775—1817)，英国女小说家，主要作品有《理智与情感》(*Sense and Sensibility*)、《傲慢与偏见》(*Pride and Prejudice*)等。奥斯汀是英国18世纪优秀的女性作家，曾被誉为唯一能与莎士比亚比肩的现实主义和浪漫主义文学家。奥斯汀生活的18—19世纪，正值英国工业革命进一步深化和法国拿破仑战争时期，近代资本主义经济模式的发展逐渐促使封建制的土地经济解体，同时近现代的民族国家观念也逐渐发展起来。这些都促使人们的价值观、世界观产生了急剧变化。在扩大生产、加紧全球殖民、争夺世界的过程中，农村经济解体，城市逐渐兴起，工业机械化程度进一步提高，旧贵族和大土地所有者逐渐被正在形成的中产阶级取代。为了加速资本的形成和积累，传统的道德观正在逐步瓦解，人们正在挣脱传统宗教道德的束缚，滑向资本主义和极端利己主义的深渊。奥斯汀冷眼观世，虽无力改变，却借小说塑造了与现实相反的美好田园与和谐村庄，极力歌颂心中完美的农村自然经济秩序。

(1) Sense and Sensibility (Excerpt)

题注：《理智与情感》是奥斯汀的处女作，也被认为是《傲慢与偏见》的姐妹篇。此章节选部分为原作第六章内容。

前情提要：苏赛克斯郡的达希伍德先生过世之前，千叮咛万嘱咐地交代长子约翰一定要对后母和妹妹们多加照顾。可是约翰待父亲一闭眼，便和夫人合计霸占了祖产诺兰庄园，驱逐后母与同父异母的三个妹妹离开家园。母亲和长女四处托亲朋好友帮忙，终于在友人的家乡巴顿寻得一处能负担得起的田园小舍。此时母女一行四人踏上旅途，带着沉重的心情离开生活了十多年的诺兰庄园，辗转于通往新居的路途之中。

The first part of their journey was **performed** in too **melancholy** a **disposition** to be **otherwise than tedious** and unpleasant. ① But as they **drew towards** the end of it, their interest in the appearance of a country which they were to② inhabit overcame their dejection, and a view of Barton Valley③, as they entered it④, gave them **cheerfulness.** ⑤ It was a pleasant, fertile spot, well wooded, and rich in pasture. After **winding along** it for more than a mile, they reached their own house. A small green **court** was the whole of its **demesne** in front; and a **neat** wicket-gate admitted them into it. ⑥

perform[pəˈfɔːm]: *v.* 完成；执行

melancholy[ˈmelənkəli]: *adj.* 忧郁的；使人悲伤的

disposition[ˌdɪspəˈzɪʃn]: *n.* 心情

otherwise than: 除了……以外。此句是想表达旅途中除了沉闷、不愉悦以外，就是忧郁了。

tedious[ˈtiːdiəs]: *adj.* 沉闷的

draw towards: 接近；朝……方向移动

cheerfulness[ˈtʃɪəflnəs]: *n.* 高兴；快活

wind along: 蜿蜒向前

court[kɔːt]: *n.* 院子

demesne[dɪˈmeɪn]: *n.* 私有地；领地

neat[niːt]: *adj.* 整齐的

As a house, Barton Cottage, though small, was comfortable and **compact**⑦; but as a cottage it was **defective**, for the building was regular, the roof was **tiled**, the window **shutters** were not painted green, nor were the walls covered with **honeysuckles**⑧. A narrow passage led directly through the house into the garden behind. On each side of the entrance was a sitting room, about sixteen feet square⑨; and beyond them were the offices and the stairs. Four bed-rooms and two **garrets** formed the rest of the house. It had not been built many years, and was **in good repair**. In comparison of **Norland**, it was poor and small indeed! —but the tears which **recollection called forth** as they entered the house were soon **dried away**⑩. They **were cheered by** the joy of the servants on their arrival, and each **for the sake of** the others **resolved** to appear happy. It was very early in September; the season was fine; and from first seeing the place **under the advantage of** good weather, they received an impression in its favor which was of material service in **recommending** it to their lasting **approbation**⑪.

compact[kəm'pækt]：*adj*. 紧凑的；简洁的

defective[dɪ'fektɪv]：*adj*. 有缺陷的；不完美的

tiled[taɪld]：*adj*. 平铺的；用瓦管排水的

shutter['ʃʌtə(r)]：*n*. 遮板；百叶窗

honeysuckle['hʌnisʌkl]：*n*. 忍冬花

garret['gærət]：*n*. 阁楼；顶楼

in good repair：修缮良好

Norland：诺兰庄园，是女主角一家人之前生活的地方。

recollection[ˌrekə'lekʃn]：*n*. 回忆

call forth：唤起

dry away：(使)干透

be cheered by：由于……而欢呼雀跃

for the sake of：为了……；为了……的利益

resolve[rɪ'zɒlv]：*v*. 决心；决定

under the advantage of：在……的优势下

recommend[ˌrekə'mend]：*v*. 推荐

approbation[ˌæprə'beɪʃn]：*n*. 赞许

The situation of the house was good. High hills rose immediately behind, and at no great distance on each side⑫; some of which⑬ were open downs, the others cultivated and woody. The village of Barton was chiefly on one of these hills, and formed a pleasant view from the cottage windows. The prospect in front was more **extensive**; it **commanded** the whole of the valley, and reached into the country beyond. The hills which surrounded the cottage **terminated** the valley in that direction; **under another name**, and **in another course**, it **branched out** again between two of the steepest of them⑭.

extensive[ɪk'stensɪv]：*adj*. 开阔的

command：原意为"命令"，在这里指"景色全收"。

terminate['tɜːmɪneɪt]：*v*. 终止

under another name：以另一个名目；冠以另一个名字

in another course：在另一条道上；另一个方向

branch out：分岔；分出

[选自：Jane Austen. *Sense and Sensibility*. London：Oxford University Press，2008.]

Notes

①此句用了被动语态，着意描写主人公一家被迫离开故乡的无奈与不舍。too melancholy a disposition 在这里表示强调，too 相当于 so。此句可译为：旅途开头一段，大家心情抑郁，只觉得道路漫长，索然无味。

②were to 是 be to 的过去时态，表示“即将”。which 在这里引导一个定语从句，修饰 country，表示“她们即将要居住的乡村”。

③Barton Valley，专有名词，巴顿山谷。

④as they entered it，在句中作插入语，表示“当她们一进入”。

⑤译文：但是，临近终点的时候，一看到马上就要居住的乡间，兴致就冒了出来，沮丧的情绪顿时被压了下去。而一走进巴顿山谷，大家便都情不自禁地兴奋起来。

⑥a neat wicket-gate admitted them into it：边门似乎在欢迎她们进入。整句可译为：沿着蜿蜒的山谷走上一英里多路，便来到她们的家。屋前只有一个绿茵小院，她们母女几个穿过一道整齐的小门，走进院里。

⑦though small 在句中作插入语。整句可译为：巴顿乡舍作为一所住宅，尽管太小，倒也舒适紧凑。

⑧nor were the walls covered with honeysuckles，nor 表示“也不”，位于句首时后面使用部分倒装。整句可译为：墙上也没有爬满忍冬花。

⑨On each side of the entrance was a sitting room，about sixteen feet square：介词短语作地点状语放在句首，句中主语和谓语完全倒装。正常语序为：“A sitting room… was on each side of the entrance.”整句可译为：过道两旁各有一间客厅，约略十六英尺见方。一英尺大约是 0.3048 米，16 英尺大约是 4.88 米。

⑩… but the tears which recollection called forth as they entered the house were soon dried away：which 引导定语从句，修饰 the tears。此句可译为：但是，她们马上擦干了刚进屋时勾起的辛酸眼泪。

⑪… they received an impression in its favor which was of material service in recommending it to their lasting approbation：which 引导定语从句，修饰 an impression。material 在句中作形容词，意为“重要的”。“be of material service”意为“起重要作用”。“lasting approbation”意为“持续的赞许”。此句可译为：这良好的印象，对于促使她们长久喜爱这个地方，起到了巨大的作用。

⑫High hills rose immediately behind，and at no great distance on each side：

此处描写屋舍所在的位置，可译为：紧靠屋后，山峦耸立；左右不远，也有峰峦依傍。

⑬some of which 中的 which 指 high hills，有的是开阔的高地，有的是耕地和林带。

⑭… under another name，and in another course，it branched out again between two of the steepest of them：在本句中，地点状语在前。整句可译为：但是在两座最陡峭的山峦之间，沿另一方向，岔出一条另有名目的支谷。

Remarks

《理智与情感》虽是奥斯汀的第一部小说，但写作技巧已经相当娴熟。故事讲述的是：埃诺莉和玛丽安娜两姐妹生在一个英国乡绅家庭，姐姐善于用理智来控制情感，妹妹的情感却毫无节制，因此在面对爱情时，她们做出了不同的反应。小说以这两位女主角曲折复杂的婚事风波为主线，通过"理智与情感"的幽默对比，提出了道德与行为的规范问题。

参考译文

理智与情感(片段)

旅途开头一段，大家心情抑郁，只觉得道路漫长，索然无味。但是，临近终点的时候，一看到马上就要居住的乡间，兴致就冒了出来，沮丧的情绪顿时被压了下去。而一走进巴顿山谷，大家便都情不自禁地兴奋起来。这地方景色宜人，土质肥沃，林木茂密，牧草丰盛。沿着蜿蜒的山谷走上一英里多路，便来到她们的家。屋前只有一个绿茵小院，她们母女几个穿过一道整齐的小门，走进院里。

巴顿乡舍作为一所住宅，尽管太小，倒也舒适紧凑。不过作为一座乡舍，却有不少缺陷，因为房子造得太正规，房顶铺瓦，窗板没有漆成绿色，墙上也没有爬满忍冬花。一条狭窄的穿堂过道，直通屋后的花园。过道两旁各有一间客厅，约略十六英尺见方，客厅向里是下房和楼梯。构成小楼其余部分的，是四间卧室和两间阁楼。房子盖好没几年，修缮得很好。同诺兰的住宅相比，的确显得寒碜、矮小！但是，她们马上擦干了刚进屋时勾起的辛酸眼泪。仆人见主人来了，一个个喜气洋洋，主人也跟着乐了。各人都看在别人的分上，硬是装出高高兴兴的样子。现在是九月初，正赶上好时节。多亏老天作美——天气晴朗，她们初次见到这个地方，就留下了良好的印象，这对于促使她们长久喜爱这个地方，起到了巨大的作用。

房子的位置选得恰到好处。紧靠屋后，山峦耸立；左右不远，也有峰峦依傍；群山之中，有的是开阔的高地，有的是耕地和林带。巴顿村大致建在一座山上，立在村口举目远眺，景色十分宜人。房舍正面，视野尤为开阔，整个山谷一览无遗，目力所及，直达远处乡间。山谷绵延到乡舍跟前，终于被三面环抱的山峦截断；但是在两座最陡峭的山峦之间，沿另一方向，岔出一条另有名目的支谷。

[选自：简·奥斯汀．理智与情感．成维安，译．哈尔滨：哈尔滨出版社，2009.]

(2) Pride and Prejudice (Excerpt)

题注：小说描写了小乡绅班纳特五个待字闺中的千金，主角是二女儿伊丽莎白。她在舞会上认识了达西，但是耳闻他为人傲慢，一直对他心生排斥。经历一番周折后，伊丽莎白解除了对达西的偏见，达西也放下傲慢，有情人终成眷属。这部作品以日常生活为素材，一反当时社会上流行的感伤小说内容和矫揉造作的写作手法，生动地反映了18世纪末19世纪初处于保守和闭塞状态下的英国乡镇生活和世态人情，并被改编成电影和电视剧。

《傲慢与偏见》的人物关系图如下。

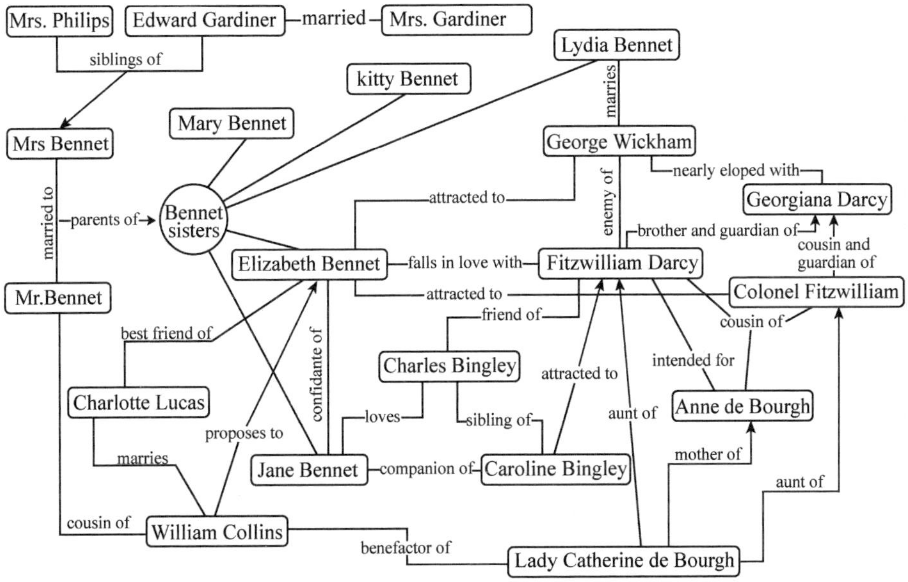

前情提要：女主人公伊丽莎白听信了威克汉的谗言，相信达西是个傲慢无礼而且自私的伪君子，而男主人公达西一方面倾心于伊丽莎白，另一方面却深深嫌弃其家庭背景和粗俗的姐妹亲戚。在达西姨母的罗新斯庄园两人再次相遇，达西终于按捺不住向伊丽莎白求婚，但同时也淋漓尽致地表达了对伊丽莎白出身和家世的鄙夷。伊丽莎白深觉所受侮辱大过被求婚的惊喜，断然拒绝了达西。达西愤然离开，然而第二天却写了一封长长的信给伊丽莎白，全力澄清之前的误会。伊丽莎白读完书信，深知自己误信了流言，正后悔不已。此时随舅父母一起出游，恰逢路过达西的庄园——彭伯里。她一面欣赏着庄园美景，一面忐忑不安，唯恐遇上庄园的男主人，两相尴尬。可是命运却总是爱和有心的人开玩笑，两个仍然思念着对方的人还是遇上了，正是这次的相聚让双方刷新了彼此的印象，才有了后来的喜结连理。

Elizabeth, as they drove along, watched for the first appearance of Pemberley Woods① with some **perturbation**; and when **at length** they **turned in** at the **lodge**, her spirits were in a high **flutter**.

perturbation[ˌpɜːtəˈbeɪʃn]：*n.* 忧虑；不安

at length：终于；最后

turn in：拐入

lodge：原意为"小屋"，在这里指"庄园"。

flutter[ˈflʌtə(r)]：*n.* 紧张；激动不安

The park was very large, and **contained** great variety of ground. They entered it in one of its lowest points, and drove for some time through a beautiful wood, **stretching over** a wide extent.

contain[kənˈteɪn]：*v.* 包含

stretch over：横跨；延续

Elizabeth's mind was too full for conversation, but she saw and **admired** every remarkable spot and **point of view**.② They gradually **ascended** for half a mile, and then found themselves at the top of a **considerable eminence**③, where the wood ceased, and the eye was instantly caught by Pemberley House④, situated on the opposite side of a valley, into which the road, with some **abruptness**, **wound**⑤. It was a large, handsome, stone building, standing well on **rising ground**, and backed by a ridge of high woody hills; —and in front, a stream of some natural importance was swelled into greater, but without any **artificial** appearance⑥. Its banks were neither formal, nor **falsely adorned**. Elizabeth was delighted. She had never seen a place for which nature had done more, or where natural beauty had been so little **counteracted** by an **awkward** taste⑦. They were all of them warm in their admiration⑧; and at that moment she felt that to be **mistress** of Pemberley might be **something**!

admire[ədˈmaɪə(r)]：*v.* 欣赏；赞赏；称赞

point of view：原意为"观点"，在这里指"景色的优美之处"。

ascend[əˈsend]：*v.* 爬坡

considerable[kən'sɪdərəbl]：*adj.* 相当大的

eminence['emɪnəns]：*n.* 高地

abruptness[ə'brʌptnəs]：*n.* 陡斜

wind[waɪnd]：*v.* 蜿蜒

rising ground：高地

artificial[ˌɑːtɪ'fɪʃl]：*adj.* 人工的；人造的

falsely['fɔːlsli]：*adv.* 虚假地

adorn[ə'dɔːn]：*v.* 装饰；修饰

counteract[ˌkaʊntər'ækt]：*v.* 抵消；阻碍

awkward['ɔːkwəd]：*adj.* 笨拙的；令人尴尬的

mistress['mɪstrəs]：*n.* 主妇；女主人

something['sʌmθɪŋ]：*pron.* 有一定意义的事

The housekeeper came; a **respectable**-looking, **elderly** woman, much less **fine**, and more **civil**, than she had any **notion** of finding her[9]. They followed her into the dining-**parlour**. It was a large, **well-proportioned** room, handsomely **fitted up**. Elizabeth, after slightly surveying it, went to a window to enjoy its prospect. The hill, **crowned** with wood, from which they had **descended**, receiving increased abruptness from the distance, was a beautiful object.[10] Every disposition of the ground was good; and she looked on the whole scene—the river, the trees scattered on its banks, and the winding of the valley, as far as she could **trace** it[11]—with delight. As they passed into other rooms, these objects were taking different positions; but from every window there were beauties to be seen. The rooms were **lofty** and handsome, and their furniture suitable to the fortune of their proprietor; but Elizabeth saw, with admiration of his taste, that it was neither **gaudy** nor uselessly fine, with less of **splendor**, and more real **elegance**, than the furniture of Rosings[12].

respectable[rɪ'spektəbl]：*adj.* 可敬的；品行端正的

elderly['eldəli]：*adj.* 上了年纪的

fine[faɪn]：*adj.* 纤细的

civil['sɪvl]：*adj.* 有礼貌的

notion['nəʊʃn]：*n.* 观念；见解

parlour['pɑːlə(r)]：*n.* 客厅；会客室

well-proportioned[ˌwelprə'pɔːʃənd]：*adj.* 比例恰当的

fit up：装备；装饰

crown[kraʊn]：*v.*（尤指通过增添成就等）使圆满；为……加冕

descend[dɪˈsend]：*v.* 下来

trace[treɪs]：*v.* 追踪；探索

lofty[ˈlɒfti]：*adj.* 高耸的；巍峨的

gaudy[ˈgɔːdi]：*adj.* 俗气的

splendor[ˈsplendə(r)]：*n.* 华丽；显赫

elegance[ˈelɪgəns]：*n.* 高雅

"And of this place," thought she, "I might have been mistress![13] With these rooms I might now have been familiarly acquainted! Instead of viewing them as a stranger, I might have **rejoiced in** them as my own, and welcomed to them as visitors my uncle and aunt.[14]—But no, '—**recollecting herself**, —' that could never be: my uncle and aunt would have been lost to me: I should not have been allowed to invite them[15]."

rejoice in：因……感到喜悦、高兴

recollect oneself：想起一时忘记的事

[选自：Jane Austen. *Pride and Prejudice*. London：Oxford University Press, 2008.]

Notes

①Pemberley Woods：彭伯里庄园的树林。彭伯里庄园是男主人公达西的祖传产业。

②"too…for…"，意为"太……而不能"。整句可译为：伊丽莎白满怀感触，无心说话，可是看到了每一处、每一角的美景，她都叹赏不已。

③…found themselves at the top of a considerable eminence：意为"最后来到了一个相当高的山坡上"。

④…the eye was instantly caught by Pemberley House：意为"彭伯里大厦马上映入眼帘"。

⑤…situated on the opposite side of a valley, into which the road, with some abruptness, wound：which 指代前文中的 a valley。with some abruptness 作插入语，放在定语从句中间。整句可译为：房子在山谷那边，有一条相当陡斜的路曲曲折折地通到谷中。

⑥…and in front, a stream of some natural importance was swelled into greater, but without any artificial appearance：of some natural importance 作定语，修饰 a stream，指"一泓颇有天然情趣的溪流"。整句可译为：屋前一泓颇有天然情趣的溪流正在涨潮，没有一丝一毫的人工痕迹。

⑦…a place for which nature had done more, or where natural beauty had been so little counteracted by an awkward taste：此句可译为“一个比这里更富有自然情趣的地方，也没有见过任何地方的自然之美能像这儿的一样不受到庸俗的玷污”。

⑧They were all of them warm in their admiration：可译为“大家都热烈地赞赏不已”。

⑨than she had any notion of finding her：意为“超出她的想象”。

⑩ The hill，crowned with wood，from which they had descended，receiving increased abruptness from the distance，was a beautiful object：这句话的中心结构为：“The hill was a beautiful object.”“crowned…”“from which…”“receiving…”分别为过去分词短语、定语从句和现在分词短语作后置定语，修饰主语 the hill。整句可译为：他们望着刚才下来的那座小山，只见丛林密布，从远处望去益发显得陡峭，真是个美丽的地方。

⑪…she looked on the whole scene—the river，the trees scattered on its banks，and the winding of the valley，as far as she could trace it：此句可译为“她纵目四望，只见一弯河道，林木夹岸，山谷蜿蜒曲折”。

⑫…but Elizabeth saw，with admiration of his taste，that it was neither gaudy nor uselessly fine；with less of splendor，and more real elegance，than the furniture of Rosings：在这句话中，with admiration of his taste 是插入语。此句可译为：既不俗气，又不过分侈丽，比起罗新斯来，可以说是豪华不足，风雅有余。伊丽莎白看了，很佩服主人的情趣。Rosings：罗新斯庄园，是达西先生姨母的庄园。伊丽莎白曾受邀在那儿做客，并受到达西先生的求婚。

⑬“I might have been mistress!”：作者用虚拟语气结构(might have been…)描写女主人公伊丽莎白的心理活动。此句可译为：“我差一点就做了这儿的主妇呢!”

⑭Instead of viewing them as a stranger，I might have rejoiced in them as my own，and welcomed to them as visitors my uncle and aunt：整句可译为“我非但不必以一个陌生人的身份来参观，而且还可以把这儿当作自己的住宅来受用，把舅父母当作贵客欢迎”。

⑮…that could never be：my uncle and aunt would have been lost to me：I should not have been allowed to invite them：这里连续使用虚拟语气，表示伊丽莎白设想如果答应了达西的求婚，那么就会见不到舅父母了，因为之前达西在求婚时非常不齿伊丽莎白低俗不入流的亲戚和出身，所以伊丽莎白觉得达西绝不会允许自己的舅父母被邀请过来。

Remarks

《傲慢与偏见》原名《第一印象》，是奥斯汀最为人津津乐道的一部小说，也是她最成功的一部作品。女主人公的偏见和男主人公的傲慢使这对青年男女在第一次见面时产生了误会。随着误会的逐渐消失，两人互生情愫，坠入爱河。

参考译文

傲慢与偏见(片段)

他们坐着车子一直向前去。彭伯里的树林一出现在眼前，伊丽莎白就有些心慌；等到走进了庄园，她更加心神不定。

花园很大，只见里边高阜低洼，气象万千。他们拣一个最低的地方走进去，在一片深邃辽阔的美丽的树林里坐着车子走了好久。

伊丽莎白满怀感触，无心说话，可是看到了每一处、每一角的美景，她都叹赏不已。他们沿着上坡路慢慢走了半英里光景，最后来到了一个相当高的山坡上，这也就是树林尽头的地方，彭伯里大厦马上映入眼帘。房子在山谷那边，有一条相当陡斜的路曲曲折折地通到谷中。这是一幢很大很漂亮的石头建筑物，屹立在高垅上，屋子后面枕着一连片树林茂密的高高的小山冈；屋前一泓颇有天然情趣的溪流正在涨潮，没有一丝一毫的人工痕迹。两岸的点缀既不呆板，也不做作。伊丽莎白高兴极了。她从来不曾看到过一个比这里更富有自然情趣的地方，也没有见过任何地方的自然之美能像这儿的一样不受到庸俗的玷污。大家都热烈地赞赏不已，伊丽莎白顿时不禁觉得：在彭伯里当个主妇也还不错吧。

管家奶奶来了，是一个态度端庄的老妇人，远不如她们想象中那么有丰姿，可是礼貌的周到倒超出她的想象。他们跟着她走进了餐室。那是一间宽敞舒适的大屋子，布置得很精致。伊丽莎白稍许看了一下，便走到窗口欣赏风景。他们望着刚才下来的那座小山，只见丛林密布，从远处望去益发显得陡峭，真是个美丽的地方。处处都收拾得很美观。她纵目四望，只见一弯河道，林木夹岸，山谷蜿蜒曲折，真看得她心旷神怡。他们再走到别的房间里去看，每换一个房间，景致总会两样，可是不管你走到哪个窗口，都自有秀色可餐。一个个房间都高大美观，家具陈设也和主人的身份颇为相称，既不俗气，又不过分侈丽，比起罗新斯来，可以说是豪华不足，风雅有余。伊丽莎白看了，很佩服主人的情趣。

她心里想："我差一点就做了这儿的主妇呢！这些房间也许早就让我走熟了！我非但不必以一个陌生人的身份来参观，而且还可以把这儿当作自己的住宅来受用，把舅父母当作贵客欢迎。可是不行，"她忽然想了起来，"这是万万办不到的事：那时候我就见不到舅父母了，他绝不会允许我邀请他们来。”

［选自：简·奥斯汀．傲慢与偏见．樊庆兰，译．上海：上海三联书店，2010.］

(3) Mansfield Park (Excerpt)

题注：《曼斯菲尔德庄园》是简·奥斯汀的另一部长篇小说。小说的女主人公范妮由于家中困顿，从小就被收养在姨父、姨妈的曼斯菲尔德庄园中。新入住的牧师夫人的姐弟来到庄园，他们带来了与这片乐土格格不入的伦敦之奢靡、自私、浅薄之风，严重影响了这座庄园的年轻人。只有范妮在这些新潮观念的冲击之下守住了自己的内心，最后与心爱的二表哥艾德蒙结成夫妇，永远居住在曼斯菲尔德庄园这片乐土之上。

前情提要：范妮内心不满克劳福特兄妹肤浅而浮夸的行事作风，回到自己的家乡朴次茅斯小住。没想到在此期间大表哥和两个表姐在赴伦敦之后均做出了有辱名声之事，让姨父、姨妈伤痛不已。二表哥艾德蒙接回范妮，一路上心事沉重。范妮在离开几个月后回到曼斯菲尔德庄园时内心充满想念和喜悦，但是转念想到家中各位手足的不幸及姨父、姨妈的伤痛，又难免潸然。

Fanny had been everywhere awake to the difference of the country since February①; but when they entered the Park her **perceptions** and her pleasures were of the **keenest** sort②. It was three months, full three months, since her quitting it, and the change was from winter to summer. Her eye fell everywhere on lawns and **plantations** of the freshest green③ and the trees, though not fully clothed, were in that delightful state when farther beauty is known to be **at hand**, and when, while much is actually given to the sight, more yet remains for the imagination④. Her enjoyment, however, was for herself alone. Edmund could not share it. She looked at him, but he was **leaning back**, sunk in a deeper **gloom** than ever, and with eyes closed, as if the view of cheerfulness **oppressed** him, and the lovely scenes of home must be **shut out**.

perception[pəˈsepʃn]：*n.* 感觉

keen[kiːn]：*adj.* 强烈的

plantation[plɑːnˈteɪʃn]：*n.* 种植园

at hand：即将来临

lean back：仰靠着；向后靠

gloom[gluːm]：*n.* 忧郁

oppress[ə'pres]：*v.* 使意气消沉；使无精神；压迫

shut out：把……关在外面

It made her melancholy again; and the knowledge of what must be enduring there, **invested** even the house, modern, **airy**, and well situated as it was, **with** a melancholy aspect.

invest ... with ...：赋予……某种性质

airy['eəri]：*adj.* 通风的；空气流通的

[选自：Jane Austen. *Mansfield Park*. London: Oxford University Press, 2008.]

Notes

①Fanny had been everywhere awake to the difference of the country since February：此句可译为"范妮一路上所看到的乡下景色已与2月份离开时大不相同"。

②"were of the keenest sort"意为"尤为强烈"。

③Her eye fell everywhere on lawns and plantations of the freshest green：此句可译为"她的目光落在各处翠绿的草地上和种植园中"。

④... and the trees, though not fully clothed, were in that delightful state when farther beauty is known to be at hand, and when, while much is actually given to the sight, more yet remains for the imagination：此句中的though not fully clothed作插入语；while作连词，表示"虽然"的意思。此句可译为：林木虽然尚未浓叶蔽枝，但却秀色可餐，更加绮丽的姿容指日可待。景色纵然悦目，却也更加赏心。

Remarks

简·奥斯汀是第一个描绘日常生活中的平凡人物的小说家。她的作品展示了当时英国中产阶级的生活，显示了"家庭文学"的可能性。她多次探索青年女主角从恋爱到结婚后自我发现的过程。这种着力分析人物性格以及女主角和社会之间紧张关系的做法，使她的小说摆脱了18世纪的传统而接近现代生活。正是这种现代性，加上她的机智和风趣、她的现实主义和同情心、她的优雅的散文风格和巧妙的故事结构，使她的小说能长期吸引读者。

参考译文

曼斯菲尔德庄园(片段)

范妮一路上所看到的乡下景色已与2月份离开时大不相同。但是，进入庄园之后，她的感觉尤为深刻，她的喜悦之情也尤为强烈。她离开庄园已经三个月了，足足三个月了，时节由冬天变成了夏天，触目皆是翠绿的草地和种植园，林木虽然尚未浓叶蔽枝，但却秀色可餐，更加绮丽的姿容指日可待。景色纵然悦目，却也更加赏心。不过，她只是自得其乐，埃德蒙不能与她共赏。她望着他，可他靠在座位上，比先前更加郁郁寡欢。他双眼紧闭，好像不堪这明媚的景色，他要把家乡的美景关在眼睑之外似的。

范妮心情又沉重起来。一想到家中的人们在忍受什么样的痛苦，就连这座时髦的、通风的、环境优美的大宅本身，也蒙上一层阴影。

［选自：简·奥斯汀．曼斯菲尔德庄园．孙致礼，译．南京：译林出版社，2011.］

Questions for discussion

Find your favorite part describing a park or a house in Jane Austen's works and discuss the beauty of the park or the house.

After-class reading

Read the novel *Emma* by Jane Austen.

Part B

(1) A Protest Against Bullfights

PAMPLONA, Spain (**Reuters**)—**Dressed in masks** and **holding up banners**, **dozens of** animal rights activists **staged** a protest against bullfights in Pamplona on Thursday, **ahead of** the northern Spanish city's **famed San Fermin Festival.**

Pamplona：(地名)潘普洛纳

Reuters：(英国)路透社

dress in：穿着……衣服

mask[mɑːsk]：*n*. 面具

hold up：举起

banner[ˈbænə(r)]：*n*. 横幅

dozens of：数十个；几十个

stage[steɪdʒ]：*v*. 举行

ahead of：在……之前

famed[feɪmd]：*adj*. 著名的

San Fermin Festival：圣佛明节；圣佛明奔牛节；奔牛节

The event's daily running of the bulls **draws** tourists from around the world to see runners leading the animals through the city's streets. Bullfights are held in the evening.

draw[drɔː]：*v.* 吸引

Standing outside Pamplona's city hall, **demonstrators** held up "Stop bullfights" signs and shouted **slogans** such as"**Fiestas** without blood" during the protest, organized by animal rights organizations **AnimaNaturalis** and **PETA**.

demonstrator[ˈdemənstreɪtə(r)]：*n.* 游行示威者

slogan[ˈsləʊgən]：*n.* 标语；口号

fiesta[fiˈestə]：*n.*（尤指西班牙和南美的）宗教狂欢节日

AnimaNaturalis：自然生命

PETA：(abbr. People for the Ethical Treatment of Animals)善待动物组织

"We want to let everyone know… that all the bulls that run in the morning in the bull runs are then driven to the **bull rings** in the evening," AnimaNaturalis director Aida Gascon said, describing bullfighting as "**torture**" for the animals.

bull rings：斗牛场

torture[ˈtɔːtʃə(r)]：*n.*（精神上或肉体上的）折磨

Protests are held each year ahead of the **weeklong** festival, which begins on Friday.

weeklong[ˈwiːklɒŋ]：*adj.* 为期一周的

Organizers have not commented directly on welfare **issues cited** by activists.

issue[ˈɪsjuː]：*n.* 问题

cite[saɪt]：*v.* 引证

Pamplona's mayor Joseba Asiron said in a recent interview he could not imagine the festival without bulls, but suggested the actual fight might disappear in future.

Others in Pamplona also said they could not imagine the fiesta without the animals.

"Pamplona does not **exist** without bull runs and the bull runs don't exist without the bullfights," Pamplona bull **enthusiast** Antonio Imizcoz said.

exist[ɪgˈzɪst]：*v.* 存在

enthusiast[ɪnˈθjuːziæst]：*n.* 狂热者

参考译文

一场针对斗牛的抗议

(路透社)在西班牙潘普洛纳，几十个动物权利保护激进分子头戴面具，高举横幅，于南西班牙城著名的圣佛明奔牛节前的周四举行了一场抗议斗牛活动的斗争。

节日中每天的公牛奔跑吸引了来自世界各地的观光客前来观看，奔跑者引领着动物们穿过城市的各条街道。斗牛大多在晚上举行。

示威者站在潘普洛纳城市大厅外，在由动物权利机构“自然生命”和“善待动物组织”组织的抗议中高举“停止斗牛”的标语并高喊出“节日不要流血”的口号。

“我们想让每个人都知道……所有上午在跑道上奔跑的公牛之后都会在晚上被拖回斗牛场，”自然生命协会主管阿伊达·嘎斯肯说。他把斗牛描述成对动物们的折磨。

抗议会在每年长达一周的奔牛节之前进行，也就是从周五开始。

组织者尚未直接评论激进分子引证的福利问题。

潘普洛纳市长约塞巴·阿斯铁在最近一次采访中说，他无法想象没有公牛的奔牛节，但暗示今后真实的斗牛可能会消失。

潘普洛纳的其他市民也说，他们也无法想象没有动物的狂欢节。

“没有公牛奔跑，潘普洛纳就不会存在，而没有斗牛，牛市也不会存在。”潘普洛纳公牛狂热者安东尼奥·伊米兹寇兹说。

(2)A Panda Wanders Around the Village

A giant panda made a surprise visit to Wenchuan county in southwest China's Sichuan Province on Thursday, wandering around the village.

China's state **broadcaster** CCTV showed the panda **roaming** through the village and exploring a vegetable garden before finding its way into the woods.

broadcaster[ˈbrɔːdkɑːstə(r)]: *n.* 广播公司

roam[rəʊm]: *v.* 漫游；漫步

Researchers at the China **Conservation** and Research Center for the Giant Panda told CCTV that the panda was 11-year-old female Zhenzhen, who was born in 2007 at the **San Diego Zoo** in the US and was returned to China in 2010.

conservation[ˌkɒnsəˈveɪʃn]: *n.* 保护

San Diego Zoo: 圣地亚哥动物园

She had been **raised** in **captivity** since then and was recently released into the wild on March 5 as part of a special **breeding** project.

raise[reɪz]：*v.* 养育

captivity[kæp'tɪvəti]：*n.* 囚禁

breed[briːd]：*v.* 产(后代)；交配；繁殖

Researchers hoped that Zhenzhen could **mate** with wild pandas—a major **mission** of the breeding project, according to the China Conservation and Research Center for the Giant Panda.

mate[meɪt]：*v.* (一对动物或鸟)交配

mission['mɪʃn]：*n.* 使命

After hours of **exploration** in the village, Zhenzhen was **captured** and taken back to the research center.

exploration[ˌeksplə'reɪʃn]：*n.* 探险

capture['kæptʃə(r)]：*v.* 捕获

参考译文

一只大熊猫漫步乡间

周四，一只大熊猫突然到访位于中国西南部的四川省汶川县，漫步在乡间。

中国中央电视台展示了大熊猫在乡间漫步并探索一座菜园的过程，直到它找到回森林的路。

中国大熊猫保护研究中心的研究员告诉中央电视台，这只熊猫是 11 岁的母熊猫珍珍，2007 年出生在美国圣地亚哥动物园，2010 年返回中国。

自从回国后她就一直被圈养，直到最近 3 月 5 日才被释放到野外，作为特殊繁殖项目的部分。

研究者希望珍珍能与野生大熊猫配对。据中国大熊猫保护研究中心说，这是此次繁殖项目的主要任务。

在村庄探险了数小时之后，珍珍被捕获，然后被带回了研究中心。

(3) For the Vaquita

As the sun **crept** above the horizon, CBS News' Don Dahler **headed out** in the **Gulf** of California with a **disparate** group of **volunteers**, **veterinarians** and marine **biologists** on a difficult—some would say impossible—mission to track the **rarest** of marine **mammals**: the vaquita, a species of **porpoise.** It's a mission two years in the making.

vaquita[və'kwɪtə]：*n.* 小头鼠海豚

creep[kriːp]：*v.* 缓慢地行进

head out：出发；启程

gulf[gʌlf]：*n.* 海湾

disparate[ˈdɪspərət]：*adj.* 完全不同的

volunteer[ˌvɒlənˈtɪə(r)]：*n.* 志愿者

veterinarian[ˌvetərɪˈneəriən]：*n.* 兽医

biologist[baɪˈɒlədʒɪst]：*n.* 生物学家

rare[reə(r)]：*adj.* 罕见的

mammal[ˈmæml]：*n.* 哺乳动物

porpoise[ˈpɔːpəs]：*n.* 鼠海豚

"This is bigger than vaquita. For conservation in general, for marine mammals, this is a big thing," said Lorenzo Rojas-Bracho who is directing the effort.

It's been an **uphill** battle against the **odds**, the cost—now in the $5 million range—and the elements. The challenge is **amplified** by the fact that there are so few of the **diminutive** porpoises left. Recent reports show the vaquita population has dropped from almost 600 in 1997 to just 30 today, found only in the Gulf of California.

uphill[ʌpˈhɪl]：*adj.* 费力的；辛苦的；艰难的

odds[ɒdz]：*n.* 逆境

amplify[ˈæmplɪfaɪ]：*v.* 放大；扩大

diminutive[dɪˈmɪnjətɪv]：*adj.* 小的；小型的

The vaquita's rapid decline is an unintended consequence of the increasing demand for tatoaba, a type of fish that can **fetch up to** $10000 each on the Chinese black market. Their **swim bladder** is believed to **boost fertility.**

fetch up to：达到……金额

swim bladder：鱼鳔

boost[buːst]：*v.* 促进

fertility[fəˈtɪləti]：*n.* 繁殖力

"Basically the **mesh** size is the same size of a vaquita head, so they easily get **entangled**," Rojas-Bracho explained.

mesh[meʃ]：*n.* 网孔；网眼

entangled[ɪnˈtæŋgld]：*adj.* 卷入的；被缠住的

Thus, the desperate **rush** to save some for **captive breeding** before they're all gone. The operation requires **delicate coordination. Spotter** boats search the water for **fins**. When one or more porpoise is **sighted**, **trained** U. S. Navy dolphins act as **herd dogs**, moving the porpoises into position for the capture boats to **net** them. They're then carefully **transferred** onto a transport boat.

rush[rʌʃ]：*n.* 繁忙的活动

captive breeding：人工养殖

delicate[ˈdelɪkət]：*adj.* 精妙的

coordination[kəʊˌɔːdɪˈneɪʃn]：*n.* 协调

spotter[ˈspɒtə(r)]：*n.* 观察机；检路器

fin[fɪn]：*n.* 鱼鳍

sight[saɪt]：*v.* 瞄准；发现

trained[treɪnd]：*adj.* 经过训练的

herd dog：牧羊犬

net[net]：*v.* 用网捕；捕获

transfer[trænsˈfɜː(r)]：*v.* 使转移

Their first stop was a **specially constructed marine hospital** for medical **assessment**. Then, a short trip to the vaquita's new home, a large **retrofitted** sea **pen** once used as a tourist **aquarium** that was **towed** there—nearly 2000 miles from the Pacific.

specially constructed marine hospital：专门建设的海洋医院

assessment[əˈsesmənt]：*n.* 评估；评价

retrofitted[ˈretrəʊfɪtɪd]：*adj.* 翻新的

pen[pen]：*n.* 围栏

aquarium[əˈkweəriəm]：*n.* 水族馆

tow[təʊ]：*v.* 牵引

The complicated plan worked, at first. On day two of the project, they captured one for the first time ever. But that six-month-old female was just too **stressed** from the experience. They had to let her go.

stressed[strest]：*adj.* 紧张的

The team took to the sea to try again, and again and again.

But all the effort and expense and frustration is also to bring the issue of **illegal gillnets** to the public's attention.

illegal[ɪˈliːgl]：*adj.* 违法的

gillnet[ˈgɪlnet]：*n.* 刺网

"If we can **absolutely ensure** that these **underwater** gillnets are not in a place where the **remaining** animals are, they would survive," one scientist explained.

"They just need a chance."

absolutely[ˈæbsəluːtli]：*adv.* 完全地

ensure[ɪnˈʃʊə(r)]：*v.* 确保

underwater[ˌʌndəˈwɔːtə(r)]：*adj.* 在水中的；在水面下的

remaining[rɪˈmeɪnɪŋ]：*adj.* 剩余的

参考译文

寻找小头鼠海豚

当太阳越过地平线，哥伦比亚广播公司新闻员唐·达勒带着一支与众不同的队伍从加利福尼亚湾出发了。这支队伍包括志愿者、兽医和海洋生物学家。他们的任务——去追踪最珍稀的海洋哺乳动物：小头鼠海豚——被很多人认为不可能完成。小头鼠海豚属鼠海豚的一种。这是一个为期两年的任务。

"这件事的意义远远不只是寻找小头鼠海豚。总的来说是为了保护它，而对于海洋哺乳动物来说，这是一件大事。"正在指导行动的洛伦佐·罗杰斯-布拉乔说。

这场艰难的战役一直在与逆境、经费——目前在500万美元以内——以及条件做斗争。挑战被扩大了，因为事实上几乎已经没有小头鼠海豚存在了。近期报道显示，小头鼠海豚的总量已经从1997年的600头降低到如今的30头，且仅在加利福尼亚湾有发现。

小头鼠海豚的迅速减少是tatoaba需求量上升而无意间导致的后果。tatoaba是一种鱼类，在中国黑市上每头售价高达1万美元。它们的鱼鳔据说能促进生育。

"基本上网孔和小头鼠海豚的大小相当，所以它们很容易被缠住。"罗杰斯-布拉乔解释说。

因此，这次希望渺茫的行动是为了赶在它们消失之前保留些许来进行人工养殖。这次的操作需要极精妙的协调。观测船在水面巡视寻找鱼鳍。当一个或几个小头鼠海豚被观测到时，训练有素的美国海军海豚就会像牧羊犬一样，把小头鼠海豚驱逐到某个位置以便于捕捞船捕获。被捕捞后，它们会被小心地转移到运输船上。

它们的第一站是一家为了医学评估而专门建设的海洋医院，然后是不远处的小头鼠海豚的新家——一个大型翻新过的海洋围栏，从大约两千英里外的太平洋牵引过来的一座曾经的游客水族馆。

首先，复杂的计划实施了。在项目的第二天，他们首次捕捉到一头小头鼠海豚。但是那头仅六个月大的母海豚在实验中紧张不堪。他们不得不放了她。

试验队去海上试了一次又一次。

但是所有的努力、花费和挫败只是换来了公众对非法刺网问题的关注。

“如果我们能完全确保这些水下刺网不出现在那些剩余动物们生活的地方，它们就会存活，”一位科学家解释道。“它们仅仅需要一个机会。”

Part C

The Grand Canyon①

The setting sun turns the western sky crimson red, lining higher clouds with golden borders. ② A dark shadow crawls slowly up the sides of the canyon ahead, first **blotting out** the tiny silver thread of the Colorado River 1500 meters below. ③ The red brown layers across the way shine as if they were fired to a glowing heat. ④ At times almost 29 kilometers across the great **chasm**, the North Rim is usually visible from the South Rim, which is more accessible for most tourists. As the silence of the desert night descends, one can only **marvel** at the **awesome** spectacle known as the Grand Canyon, America's most famous scenic wonder.

This is not a valley between two mountains; this is not a separation due to an earthquake. This is a gorge slowly carved away for nearly 6 million years by the waters of the Colorado River. The canyon is so deep that there are four distinct zones of climate from top to bottom, each with its own distinctive **flora** and **fauna**. When it is snowing on the upper rim, it is tropically hot and moist on the floor of the canyon.

blot out：遮住；挡住

chasm[ˈkæzəm]：*n.* 峡谷

marvel[ˈmɑːvl]：*v.* 感到惊奇；大为赞叹

awesome[ˈɔːsəm]：*adj.* 令人惊叹的

flora[ˈflɔːrə]：*n.* 植物群

fauna[ˈfɔːnə]：*n.* 动物群

Over 4 million people each year visit this place to see this spectacle of nature. Trails curve along the edge of the South Rim. And some trails lead down into the Canyon. Some tourists hike part of the way down, and slowly **trudge** back by evening. Others take a **mule caravan** either halfway down and back for the day, or else all the way to the river below to stay overnight and return the next day.

trudge[trʌdʒ]：*v.* 跋涉

mule['mjuːl]：*n.* 骡子

caravan['kærəvæn]：*n.* 大篷车

This scenic area is one of the US National Parks. The Park was established in 1908 by President "Teddy" Roosevelt⑤, and has continually incorporated more and more territory until, in 1975, the entire Grand Canyon, a total of 4930 square kilometers, is within the boundaries of the Grand Canyon National Park.

The Southwest

There are other national parks nearby. To the east, the Painted Desert National Park includes multicolored hills and small **uprisings** from the desert floor that glow in the daylight in colors of reddish-brown, yellow, orange, and even purple. Within this park is also the Petrified Forest, a field of fallen trees that have turned to stone by a process of **mineralization** known as **petrifaction**. The organic cells and tree rings can easily be seen in these ancient "rocks". To the south, the Sunset Crater Volcano National Park has the remains of a very early volcano explosion, much greater than the recent Mount St. Helen's eruption. ⑥

uprising['ʌpraɪzɪŋ]：*n.* 小山

mineralization[ˌmɪnərəlaɪ'zeɪʃn]：*n.* 矿化

petrifaction[ˌpetrɪ'fækʃn]：*n.* 石化

Moving north from the Grand Canyon National Park, one encounters many scenic areas that are not in parks. The desert areas of **Nevada** and the mountains and streams of southwestern Colorado are all quite beautiful. Many Native American **tribes** live in these areas as well, and visits to their villages hold much interest for the **inquisitive** traveler.

Nevada[nə'vɑːdə]：*n.* 内华达州

tribe[traɪb]：*n.* 部落

inquisitive[ɪn'kwɪzətɪv]：*adj.* 好问的；好奇的

The Northwest

To the far north, near the Canadian border is Yellowstone National Park⑦, named after for the river flowing through the area. Yellowstone was established in 1872, and is the oldest of the national parks and also one of the largest, being almost 8985 square kilometers in area. It is known for its **geysers** and hot springs, the most famous of the geysers being Old Faithful, which every hour or so sends an enormous plume of water and steam shooting high into the sky for 4 minutes. In addition to the several geysers, there are the hot springs and the pools of bubbling warm mud, all of which make this a very strange and **wondrous** place to visit.

geyser['giːzə(r)]：*n.* 间歇泉

wondrous['wʌndrəs]：*adj.* 奇妙的；令人惊奇的

Yellowstone National Park also contains beautiful **vistas** of waterfalls, rugged peaks, and **lush** valleys. The woodlands are home to many types of wildlife, especially rare species of birds. Many visitors take advantage of organized tours on horseback through the wilderness. Several days in the park is hardly enough time to see and do all the interesting things there. Incidentally, approach the park from the south, one will pass by **Grand Teton National Park**, which has immense scenic peaks and **glacier scoured** valleys. This park is not for the casual visitor but mountain climbers find it exhilarating.

vista['vɪstə]：*n.* 远景

lush[lʌʃ]：*adj.* 郁郁葱葱的

Grand Teton National Park：大蒂顿山国家公园

glacier['glæsiə(r)]：*n.* 冰川

scour['skaʊə(r)]：*v.* 冲刷

Not too far away is **Dinosaur** National Monument, the site of many **fossils** of **prehistoric** animal life. And nearby also is **Bryce Canyon National Park**, a small park with enormous sandstone **spires** and **pinnacles**, whose slopes are colored in red, white, pink and orange layers.

dinosaur['daɪnəsɔː(r)]：*n.* 恐龙

fossil['fɒsl]：*n.* 化石

prehistoric[ˌpriːhɪ'stɒrɪk]：*adj.* 史前的

Bryce Canyon National Park：布赖斯峡谷国家公园

spire['spaɪə(r)]：*n.* 螺旋

pinnacle['pɪnəkl]：*n.* 高峰

The Rocky Mountains

All of the places mentioned so far are to the west of the Rocky Mountains⑧, which are themselves worth touring. There is a national park covering the central Rockies, but there are also many state parks dotting the area from the Canadian border down to the southern part of the range in New

Mexico where one can picnic and hike and enjoy the landscape. The streams in the Rockies are a **trout** fisherman's paradise. Also, various old mining towns still retaining a certain 19th century charm provide entertaining sites to visit. During the winter months, travel along the roads is difficult because of the snow. Yet it is the snow that attracts many people to such towns, where skiing down mountain slopes is the major attraction.

trout[traʊt]: *n.* 鲑鱼

The Pacific Coast

To the west of the Rocky Mountains, towards the Pacific coast, there is in the south a stretch of desert area that suddenly becomes **verdant** in the Imperial Valley of California. In the north, after leaving Salt Lake City behind, until one reaches the coastline one encounters foothills and a few isolated mountains. In the very northern part of the Pacific coast region is the city of Seattle located on **Puget Sound** and neighbored by the Olympic Peninsula, on which is located Olympia National Park, the location of a completely fascinating temperate rain forest, and the Cascade Range, where Mt. Rainier stands. ⑨ Not too far away from the city is the site of the St. Helens Eruption, where visitors can observe the ecological recovery from that devastating explosion.

verdant[ˈvɜːdnt]: *adj.* 青翠的

Puget Sound: 普吉特湾

The coastline towards the south is quite rugged, with **precipitous** cliffs and **boulder-strewn** beaches. Only occasionally is there a sand beach suitable for picnicking and swimming. It is not until one reaches Los Angeles that one finds long stretches of sandy beaches occasionally interrupted by a sheer cliff now and then. ⑩

precipitous[prɪˈsɪpɪtəs]: *adj.* 陡峭的

boulder-strewn[ˈbəʊldə(r)-struːn]: *adj.* 铺满巨石的

Before then, the city of San Francisco remains an important center of urban sightseeing, with Berkeley and its University across the Bay, and Stanford University a short distance south of San Francisco. Farther south is Yosemite National Park⑪ with its spectacular scenery of valleys carved out by glaciers, and numerous magnificent waterfalls. And even farther south is **Monterey**, the scene of many **John Steinbeck** stories. The coast road continues south through Big Sur, a picturesque retreat for such authors as Henry Miller,

Jack Kerouac, and poet Robinson Jeffers. [12]

Monterey：（地名）蒙特雷

John Steinbeck：约翰·斯坦贝克（20 世纪美国作家）

There are few places of natural beauty in Southern California. Most of the interest lies in human creations such as Hollywood and Disneyland. Yet for **surfboard** riders, sunbathers, and ocean swimmers, there are few places in the United States that can match the beaches stretching from Los Angeles to San Diego. The weather is always temperate and there is little rain. People spend most of their leisure time outdoors.

surfboard[ˈsɜːfbɔːd]：*n.* 冲浪板

The Middle West

The Rocky Mountains slide down easterly towards the great-plains states, flat lands where grain fields extend for miles in either direction. In the northern part of this region, in the state of South Dakota, is the unusual artistic project at Mt. Rushmore, where enormous portraits of four famous US Presidents: George Washington, Thomas Jefferson, Abraham Lincoln, and Theodore Roosevelt, are **sculpted** on the face of the 1730-meter-high mountain. [13]

sculpt[skʌlpt]：*v.* 雕刻

To the south of this National Monument, flowing down to the Gulf of Mexico, is the mighty Mississippi River, whose shores are dotted with such famous American cities as the twin cities Minneapolis and St. Paul, St. Louis, Memphis, and finally in Louisiana, Baton Rouge and New Orleans. Each of these cities has its own distinctive charm and historic sites, yet surrounding the southern cities of Baton Rouge and New Orleans are **vestiges** of the old Southern plantations, where some old **mansions** can still be seen and even visited.

vestige[ˈvestɪdʒ]：*n.* 残留部分；遗迹

mansion[ˈmænʃn]：*n.* 宅第

Florida

The southernmost tip of the eastern United States is the state of Florida. Here the climate is mild all year. So when the weather is harsh and severe in the north, many people, especially older folks, visit Florida during the wintertime. The western side of Florida lies on the Gulf of Mexico, over which the sun sets to golden-red skies. There are several famous beaches along this coast, and fishermen have the choice of visiting fresh water streams and lakes inland, or casting their lines from the beach or a boat at sea in the saltwater Gulf.

Farther south is the Everglades, approximately 13000 square kilometers in size, where the Everglades National Park occupies about 6100 square kilometers. The Everglades is a **subtropical** wetlands, which one author has dubbed "The River of Grass". It contains a **motley** collection of wildlife including **reptiles** such as **alligators** and snakes. Plant life includes varieties of palm trees, **orchids**, and giant **ferns**. There are 400 species of birds native to Florida, including rare **herons**, **egrets**, **pelicans**, and different kinds of ducks.

subtropical[sʌbˈtrɒpɪkl]: *adj*. 亚热带的
motley[ˈmɒtli]: *adj*. 混杂的；各种各样的
reptile[ˈreptaɪl]: *n*. 爬行动物
alligator[ˈælɪgeɪtə(r)]: *n*. 短嘴鳄鱼
orchid[ˈɔːkɪd]: *n*. 兰花
fern[fɜːn]: *n*. 蕨类
heron[ˈherən]: *n*. 苍鹭
egret[ˈiːgrət]: *n*. 白鹭
pelican[ˈpelɪkən]: *n*. 鹈鹕

Stretching south of Miami towards Cuba is a chain of islands called the Florida Keys. These islands are connected by a series of bridges called the Overseas Highway reaching to the farthest island, Key West. Key West was a summer retreat for US President Harry S. Truman[14], and is also the site of the homes of novelist Ernest Hemingway.

The cities of Miami and Miami Beach are located at the southern tip of the peninsula on the Atlantic Ocean. From here northward to the Kennedy Space Center are located many small communities barely separated from each other, where many retired people live in the warm to moderate climate.[15] Inland is the city of Orlando, a favorite tourist stop because of the location of Disneyworld and Epcot Center[16].

The Southeast

North of Florida along the Atlantic Seaboard are the southern states of Georgia, South Carolina, North Carolina and Virginia. These states have the unusual property of having a coastline filled with beaches and fishing vessels to their east, and hills and mountains for hunting, camping, and freshwater fishing to heir west. Along the eastern coast are such historic cities as

Savannah, GA, with its stately mansions and 18th-century downtown area, and in South Carolina is the city of Charleston. Charleston is a rapidly modernizing city yet it still maintains many gardens famous for their **azaleas**, **magnolias**, and **camellias**. Visitors should not overlook Fort Sumter National Park, the site of the first battle of the American Civil War in April 1861.

azalea[əˈzeɪliə]: *n.* 杜鹃花

magnolia[mæɡˈnəʊliə]: *n.* 木兰花

camellia[kəˈmiːliə]: *n.* 山茶花

The Northeast

The Blue Ridge Mountains extend up through North Carolina to Virginia, but most visitors will stay along the Eastern seaboard to enjoy the Outer Banks, here deep-sea fishing is a major attraction. Kitty Hawk, where the Wright brothers[17] flew their first airplane, is also located in the Outer Banks. Along the coast from here to New York City are many beach communities where summer residents enjoy swimming in the moderate temperatures of the Atlantic and indulge in beach activities from lazy sunbathing to volleyball.

North of the island on which New York City is located, the beach communities continue northward to **Cape Cod**, the enormous peninsula shaped like a **flexed** arm that juts out into the Atlantic Ocean. The entire Cape is ringed with swimming beaches and docks for fishing boats and pleasure craft. Inland there are forests and fresh water ponds ideal for swimming and boating. The Cape is dotted with little towns that try to maintain a **quaint**, fishing village atmosphere. During the summer it is quite crowded with families fleeing the hot and stuffy cities, but in the spring and fall there are few tourists, and days on the Cape are very relaxing: Here the colorful sky, the reds and golds of a sun just below the horizon, are to be found in the east at dawn, a time for quiet walks on the beach, or calm half hour of casting a fishing line into the surf.

Cape Cod: 科德角

flexed[flekst]: *adj.* 弯曲的

quaint[kweɪnt]: *adj.* 古香古色的

The Green Mountains, one range of the **Appalachian** chain of mountains, run from central Massachusetts through Vermont to Canada. Few roads or pathways lead to the tops of mountains here. Between the sharply rising peaks are deep gorges, where public roads weave around the towering hills. Yet there is a wonderful and challenging footpath stretching for 3450 kilometers from Maine all the way back down to Georgia called the Appalachian Trail. (The full name is: The Appalachian National Scenic Trail.) Hikers, or just robust walkers, may join this trail at any point and proceed as far as desired.

Appalachian[ˌæpəˈleɪtʃiən]: *adj.* 阿巴拉契亚山脉的

New York State

The Adirondack Mountains, located mainly in the state of New York, contain some of the oldest rocks in the world. Mount Marcy, at 1629 meters, is the tallest peak, but Whiteface Mountain is more accessible. The peaks in this chain are separated by forests and woodlands that contain many famous lakes and unusual chasms and gorges. Lake Placid, the site of a Winter Olympics and a training area for winter sports competitors, is well known. Another one, Schroon Lake, was the **model** for Theodore Dreiser's **Loon** Lake in his novel *An American Tragedy*. Because of the moderate temperatures of this region, before home air-conditioning became available, many wealthy families constructed elaborate summer camps here, some of which are now open to the public.

model[ˈmɒdl]: *n.* 原型

loon[luːn]: *n.* 潜鸟

The western part of New York State contains a natural wonder comparable to the Grand Canyon. While the Canyon is a calm and static display of the slow effects of powerful natural forces, **Niagara Falls** is an awe inspiring, dynamic display of a torrent of water freely falling over a **precipice** for a distance of 55 meters. The spray created by the falling water, visible from miles away, and the roaring sound of water striking the rocks or river below never fail to impress spectators with the wonders of natural forces. ⑱

Niagara Falls: 尼亚加拉大瀑布

precipice[ˈpresəpɪs]: *n.* 悬崖；峭壁

Hawaii

Hawaii is unique in many ways: lying in the central Pacific Ocean, it is the only state that is not on the North American continent; it is entirely an **archipelago**; it does not have a straight line in its state boundary as other states; and over 40% of its population is American Asian. Indeed, it is where the east meets the west.

archipelago[ˌɑːkɪˈpeləgəʊ]: *n.* 群岛

Hawaii is made up of a chain of islands—124 **islets** and 8 main islands stretching 1523 miles in the Pacific. In total, the islands spread across an area of 6459 square miles. Each of the islands is the top of a submerged volcanic mountain. The Big Island of Hawaii, formed by five volcanoes, is the most recently created island of the Hawaiian island chain and two of its volcanoes are still active.

islet[ˈaɪlət]: *n.* 小岛

Mauna Kea is the tallest mountain in Hawaii at 13796 feet or 4205 meters. If measured from its base on the ocean floor Mauna Kea is the tallest mountain in the world. [19] Several areas of Hawaii are under protection. There are two national parks and three national historical parks. Another area under the control of the National Park Service[20] is the USS Arizona Memorial[21] at Pearl Harbor. At the northwest Hawaiian island chain, a National Marine **Monument** was declared by President Bush in 2006. The monument covers roughly 140000 square miles (360000 square kilometers) of **reefs**, **atolls** and shallow and deep sea out to 50 miles (80 kilometers) offshore in the Pacific Ocean, larger than all of America's National Parks combined.

Mauna Kea: 莫纳克亚(毛纳基)山

monument[ˈmɒnjumənt]: *n.* 纪念馆；历史遗迹

reef[riːf]: *n.* 礁

atoll[ˈætɒl]: *n.* 环状珊瑚岛

Because the islands are so far from other land habitats, life before human activity is said to have arrived by the "3 W's": wind(carried through the air), waves (brought by ocean currents), and wings (birds, insects, and whatever they brought with them). This isolation, a wide range of environments and the tropical climate produced a vast **array** of **endemic** flora and fauna. The temperature is mild, and cane sugar, pineapple, and flowers and **nursery** produce are the chief products. Hawaii also grows coffee beans, bananas, and **macadamia nuts**. The tourist business is Hawaii's largest source of outside income. Indeed, Hawaii's breathtaking natural beauty, warm tropical climate, inviting waters and waves, and active volcanoes, make it a popular destination for tourists, surfers, biologists, and volcanologists alike.

array[əˈreɪ]: *n.* 一批

endemic[enˈdemɪk]: *adj.* 地方性的

nursery[ˈnɜːsəri]: *n.* 苗圃；养殖场

macadamia nuts：澳大利亚坚果

Alaska

After enjoying warm and mild weather, white sand beaches and tropical flowers, etc. , people may want to see something different. Then they should come to Alaska, vast expanses of land covered with ice and snow. Half of the world's glaciers are found here. With global warming, most of glaciers in the world are gradually melting. Perhaps that is why Alaska is becoming a popular tourist attraction today. Tours are available for those who want to explore this "last great land" by land, sea or air.

Alaska is the largest state of the United States by area; it is situated in the northwest extremity of the North American continent. Alaska is bordered on the north by **the Arctic Ocean**, on the south by the Gulf of Alaska, and on the west by **the Bering Sea**. On the east, Alaska is bordered by Canada. The land area of Alaska is 1518800 square kilometers but less than 1% of that is inhabited by humans. About 27% of Alaska's land lies above **the Arctic Circle**. Marshlands and wetland **permafrost** cover large areas of land mostly in northern, western and southwest flatlands. Glacier ice covers some 41440 square kilometers of land. Many active volcanoes are found in the **Aleutian Islands chain** extending west from the southern tip of the Alaska Peninsula. Alaska has more volcanoes than any other state.

the Arctic Ocean：北冰洋

the Bering Sea：白令海

the Arctic Circle：北极圈

permafrost['pɜːməfrɒst]：*n.* 永久冻土

Aleutian Islands chain：阿留申群岛

What do visitors expect to see in Alaska? Well, lots of interesting and exciting things. For instance, they can see the famous **Northern Polar Light**. Fairbanks, Alaska, is known as one of the best places in the world to observe this fantastic light. It usually appears in the sky as light green, light yellow, and pink in constantly changing forms that seem to be dancing, waving and vibrating. There are many places where people can see glaciers in Alaska. They can view miles of glaciers from the air. However, if they want to get close to a glacier, perhaps the best way is to take a helicopter glacier trip. The helicopter will land tourists on a remote spot on a glacier where they set off for a guided glacier **trek** for two or three hours, walking on solid ice hundreds of feet thick. In Alaska, lucky tourists can encounter brown bears, **grizzly bears**, wolves, foxes, **caribou**, **moose**, golden eagles and **killer whales**.

Northern Polar Light：北极光

trek[trek]：*n*. 长途跋涉；徒步穿越

grizzly bear：*n*. 灰熊

caribou[ˈkærɪbuː]：*n*. 北美驯鹿

moose[muːs]：*n*. 驼鹿

killer whale：虎鲸

Alaska is called the "last great place" because many great places on our planet have been over-exploited by humans for economic gains. Alaska is also faced with the conflict between economic development and nature conservation. A case in point is the ongoing debate over oil drilling in **Arctic National Wildlife Refuge** (ANWR). This area on the north Alaskan coast is rich in oil resource. A debate has been going on over the question of drilling oil or not in ANWR since 1977. Some people support drilling to meet America's need for oil. Others oppose drilling for the protection of a national wildlife refuge. Shall we humans recklessly exploit nature to satisfy our growing needs or shall we do our best to preserve nature to save our planet from further damage? This controversy provides much food for thought.

Arctic National Wildlife Refuge：北极国家野生动物禁猎区

Notes

①The Grand Canyon：大峡谷。美国亚利桑那州西北部科罗拉多河的峡谷，由一系列错综复杂的、幽深的峡谷组成，岩壁陡峭，断层清晰可见。整个地貌十分奇特壮观，为世界罕见的自然奇观，其中最为壮观的一段于1908年被规划为"大峡谷国家公园"。

②The setting sun turns the western sky crimson red, lining higher clouds with golden borders：落日将西边的天空染成猩红色，给高处的云彩镶上金边。

③A dark shadow crawls slowly up the sides of the canyon ahead…1500 meters below：一片黑影慢慢爬上前面峡谷的两侧，先是盖住了位于1500米以下细细的银色科罗拉多河。The Colorado River：科罗拉多河，北美主要河流之一，发源于科罗拉多州北部的落基山脉，流向西南，注入加利福尼亚湾。站在大峡谷边缘观看1500米下面的科罗拉多河，那条大河就像一条细细的银线。

④The red brown layers across the way shine as if they were fired to a glowing heat：峡谷侧面的红褐色断层(在落日下)闪闪发光，犹如被点燃的火。

⑤"Teddy" Roosevelt：西奥多·罗斯福，美国第26任总统，人们对其昵称为Teddy。

⑥To the south，the Sunset Crater Volcano National Park…the recent Mount St. Helen's eruption：南面是落日火山口国家公园，它位于亚利桑那州中北部，内有早期火山爆发遗留下来的火山锥，比近期爆发的圣海轮斯火山大许多。圣海轮斯山峰位于华盛顿州西南部，曾于1980年喷发。

⑦Yellowstone National Park：黄石国家公园，美国最大、最著名、建立最早的国家公园，以流经其中的黄石河命名，内有森林、瀑布、山谷幽潭、间歇泉等各种景色，其中最著名的间歇泉是课文中提到的"老忠实泉"，因其有规律的喷发而得此名。

⑧the Rocky Mountains：落基山脉，南北贯穿北美中西部，南起新墨西哥州中部，北至阿拉斯加州北部，全长三千多千米。

⑨In the very northern part of the Pacific coast region is the city…where Mt. Rainier stands：太平洋海岸地区北部有西雅图市。它位于普吉特湾，毗邻奥林匹克半岛。半岛上有奥林匹克国家公园，里面有着令人着迷的温带雨林以及喀斯喀特山脉，其中矗立着最高的雷尼尔山峰。

⑩It is not until one reaches Los Angeles that one finds…by a sheer cliff now and then：到了洛杉矶人们才看到连绵的沙滩，偶尔被一些陡峭的石崖切断。

⑪Yosemite National Park：约塞米蒂国家公园，美国加州中部山地风景区，面积3064平方千米，其中的峭壁峡谷和高悬的瀑布最为壮观，闻名世界。

⑫The coast road continues south through Big Sur，a picturesque retreat for such authors as Henry Miller，Jack Kerouac，and poet Robinson Jeffers：海的公路向南继续，通过大瑟尔风景区，那里是许多作家的隐居所。这些作家包括亨利·米勒(1891—1980)、杰克·凯鲁亚克(1922—1969)，以及诗人罗宾逊·杰弗斯(1887—1962)。

⑬In the northern part of this region，in the state of South Dakota…1730-meter-high mountain：在这一地区的北部，南达科他州的拉什莫尔山上有一项独特的工程——四位著名美国总统的巨大头像被雕刻在1730米高的山坡上。这四位总统是乔治·华盛顿、托马斯·杰斐逊、亚伯位罕·林肯和西奥多·罗斯福。他们在美国历史上都有特殊的地位，分别代表着美国业绩的四大象征——创建国家、政治哲学、捍卫国家统一、扩张和保守。这组雕像成为国家纪念碑。

⑭ Harry S. Truman：哈里·S. 杜鲁门（1884—1972），美国第33任总统（1945—1953）。

⑮From here northward to the Kennedy Space Center ... in the warm to moderate climate：从这里到肯尼迪宇航中心以北有许多几乎连成一片的小社区。在那里，许多退休的人们生活在温暖的气候中。

⑯Disneyworld and Epcot Center：迪斯尼世界和埃普科特中心。迪斯尼世界是世界上最大的娱乐公园，在加利福尼亚州也有一个同样的公园，叫Disneyland。埃普科特中心是佛罗里达州的迪斯尼世界的一部分，包括“未来世界”和“世界陈列馆”。

⑰the Wright brothers：莱特兄弟。威尔伯·莱特(Wilbur Wright)和奥维尔·莱特(Orville Wright)是美国的飞机发明者、航空先驱者。1903年，他们制造的第一架可操纵的动力飞机试飞成功。

⑱The spray created by the falling water, visible from miles away ... natural forces：瀑布喷射出的水从几英里外就可以看到，水拍打石头和下面河流时发出雷鸣般的响声。这些无不使观光者对大自然的威力感叹不止。

⑲If measured from its base on the ocean floor Mauna Kea is the tallest mountain in the world：如果从海底测量，包括山体在海中的高度，那么莫纳克亚山将是世界上最高的山。

⑳National Park Service：美国国家公园管理局，于1916年8月25日根据美国国会的相关法案成立，隶属于美国内政部，主要负责美国境内的国家公园、国家历史遗迹、历史公园等自然及历史遗产保护。

㉑USS Arizona Memorial：亚利桑那号纪念馆，位于檀香山飞机场西2英里的珍珠港，被建在1941年12月7日被日军偷袭珍珠港时击沉的美国亚利桑那号的残舰上。当时战舰上的1177名官兵和战舰一起沉没。

Questions

1. Which of the places mentioned in the text do you want to visit most? Why?

2. What is the controversy over oil drilling in Arctic National Wildlife Refuge in Alaska? What is your view on this issue?

3. List what you consider to be ten most interesting places to visit in China. Give reasons for your selection.

Part D

Pre-reading activities

1. Could you make a brief description of Cuicui?

2. What are the main characters in *Border Town*? Could you make a brief introduction to them?

边城(片段 2)

管理这渡船的，就是住在塔下的那个老人。活了七十年，从二十岁起便守在这小溪边，五十年来不知把船来去渡了若干人。年纪虽那么老了，本来应当休息了，但天不许他休息，他仿佛便不能够同这一份生活离开。他从不思索自己的职务对于本人的意义，只是静静地很忠实地在那里活下去。代替了天，使他在日头升起时，感到生活的力量，当日头落下时，又不至于思量与日头同时死去的，是那个伴在他身旁的女孩子。他唯一的朋友为一只渡船与一只黄狗，唯一的亲人便只那个女孩子。

翠翠在风日里长养着，把皮肤变得黑黑的，触目为青山绿水，一对眸子清明如水晶。自然既长养她且教育她，为人天真活泼，处处俨然如一只小兽物。人又那么乖，如山头黄麂一样，从不想到残忍事情，从不发愁，从不动气。平时在渡船上遇陌生人对她有所注意时，便把光光的眼睛瞅着那陌生人，作成随时皆可举步逃入深山的神气，但明白了人无坏心后，就又从从容容地在水边玩耍了。

参考译文

The Border Town (Excerpt 2)

This **ferryman** is the old fellow who lives just below the **pagoda**. Seventy now, he has stayed since the age of twenty beside this stream, ferrying countless passengers in fifty years. It is high time the **sturdy** old man retired, but evidently fate will otherwise: no throwing in his hand for him. Without reflecting what this job means, he carries on quietly and faithfully. Fate, in his case, is the girl at his side who makes him feel the lure of life at sunrise and stops him from **brooding** about death at sunset. His sole companions are the ferryboat and Brownie, the dog; his sole relation this girl.

ferryman['ferimən]: *n.* 摆渡者；渡船夫

pagoda[pə'gəʊdə]: *n.* 塔

sturdy['stɜːdi]：*adj*. 强壮的；精力充沛的

brood[bruːd]：*v*. 沉思

Wind and sun have **tanned** the growing girl's skin，her eyes resting on green hills are as clear as **crystal**. Nature is her mother and teacher，making her innocent，lively and **untamed** as some small wild creature. She has the gentleness of a **fawn** and seems not to know the meaning of **cruelty**，anxiety or anger. Should a stranger on the ferry stare at her，she fixes her brilliant eyes on him as if ready to fly any instant to the mountains；but once she knows no harm is meant，she finishes her task calmly.

tan[tæn]：*v*.（使）晒成棕褐色

crystal['krɪstl]：*n*. 水晶

untamed[ʌn'teɪmd]：*adj*. 未驯服的

fawn[fɔːn]：*n*.（未满一岁的）幼鹿；小动物

cruelty['kruːəlti]：*n*. 残忍；残酷行为

[选自：沈从文．边城(英汉双语对照)．杨宪益，戴乃迭，译．南京：译林出版社，2013．]

After-reading activities

1. Describe the appearance of your grandfather or grandmother within 150-180 words.

2. Make a brief comment on Cuicui.